LENIN ON THE AGRARIAN QUESTION

LENIN on the Agrarian Question

Anna Rochester

AAKAR

Lenin on the Agrarian Question
Anna Rochester

First Published in India 2018

ISBN 978-93-5002-570-3

Published with the permission from International Publishers, New York for publication and sale only in South Asia.

Published by
AAKAR BOOKS
28 E Pocket IV, Mayur Vihar Phase I
Delhi 110 091, India
aakarbooks@gmail.com
www.aakarbooks.com

Printed at
Sapra Brothers, Noida

CONTENTS

FOREWORD

ONE ASPECT of V. I. Lenin's work which can have great value for us in the United States is his richly creative thinking on the problems of those who live by their toil on the land. True to the Marxist principles on which he built, Lenin's economic study was always related to his conviction that the time was approaching when the people would organise the productive capacities of human society in a genuinely social manner. Therefore his economic thinking was intertwined with analysis of class relationships resulting from the basic system of production.

How are those who work on the land exploited by those who own the land? Are their problems solved if the peasant becomes an independent farmer? Can the working class solve its problems without the aid of the rural poor? What is the most fruitful relation between workers in industry and toilers on the land who live on their individual farms and are isolated from industrial struggles?

For thirty years Lenin was thinking and writing on such questions as these. He saw the capitalist world as a whole, with certain common underlying principles veiled by wide variations in historical background and degree of capitalist development. He analysed the economic structure and class relations in many countries and took part vigorously in discussion within the international labour movement. In Russia he laid the basis of the agrarian policy under which peasants were won to support of the socialist revolution and which—after Lenin's death—guided Stalin's leadership in achieving mass collectivisation of agriculture throughout the Soviet Union.

As we study Lenin's thinking on agrarian questions and see it developing against the background of special periods and situations with which he was concerned, we realise how deeply his work was rooted in principles of social development common to the entire capitalist world.

Many of Lenin's writings on agriculture and the relation between industrial workers and those who live on the land are now available in English translations well supplied with historical notes. But these writings are voluminous and they grew out of issues and crises unfamiliar to many American readers. So the richness and clarity of Lenin's thought escape many who have little time for extended study.

The present volume sketches briefly the background of Lenin's agrarian work and traces chronologically, from his own writings, the course of Lenin's thinking on such questions. Many excerpts from Lenin's writings are included—some of them not yet otherwise available in English—but these should merely open the way to further reading of his works.

As this book is completed, a world-wide war is being waged. It is a war of democratic powers, the United States, Great Britain, the Soviet Union, China, and others of the United Nations, against the fascist powers—a war which directly concerns the most basic rights and the future of the American people. To assure victory in this just war against fascist tyranny, workers and farmers of the United States are urgently called upon to use their great creative powers in the united war effort of the entire American people.

For this difficult and most crucial period of world history the masses of people have a valuable heritage in Lenin's profound understanding of the interplay of class forces in the process of social change. This book will fail in its purpose if it does not stimulate a wider study of Lenin's writings.

A. R.

Spring, 1942.

CHAPTER I

Russia Before 1905

RUSSIA of the 1890's, when Lenin began his active life as a Marxist, was an industrially backward country. Peasants on the land outnumbered industrial workers. Tsarist feudal autocracy was notorious for its brutally reactionary methods. Such large factories as did exist used imported equipment, and industrial development had been largely dependent upon foreign capital. Even as late as 1913, French, German, and British concerns had important holdings in eleven Russian banks which had more than three-fourths of the total banking assets in Russia.[1] Luxuries enjoyed by the wealthy were also brought in from England and western Europe, while Russia exported little beyond lumber, furs, leather, and wheat.

Intertwined with this economic and political backwardness was a widespread growth of young native Russian capitalism. Because much of this was still in the early stages which England had outgrown nearly a hundred years before, the roots of the home-grown capitalism and even its basic trends were overlooked by most of Russia's nineteenth century revolutionary movements. The early Marxists focussed their thinking chiefly on the expanding industrial proletariat. The non-Marxist groups thought primarily of the semi-serf oppression of the peasants (which had continued in spite of "emancipation" from serfdom in 1861) and looked to the village commune for salvation.

Lenin was the first to uncover the native roots of capitalism within the village commune itself. He revealed the tangled network of capitalist trends interwoven with serf survivals in which the peasant masses were entangled.

Serf Survivals and Capitalist Trends

Peasants had supposedly been released from serfdom by the Great Reform of 1861. The world was given to understand that serfs were freed and provided with land on which they could produce without obligation to, and dependence upon, the landowner. Actually, they had paid a heavy price for a very restricted "freedom."

Part of the land on which the serfs had raised their own means of subsistence was retained by the landlord. As Lenin put it, they "were 'emancipated' from the pastures and water so necessary for their farms." [2] These pieces "cut off" from the peasant holdings—*otrezki,* as the Russians called them—often included land better than that which the peasants were allowed to retain. They were a grievance never forgotten by the peasant households.

The rest of the land that peasants had always used was sold (not given) to the peasants. Not only were they compelled to buy back their immemorial heritage, but the sums fixed for redemption of the land retained by the peasants were clearly and outrageously higher than any fair market valuation.[3] Peasants were allowed forty years to complete their payments, but even so these made an intolerable burden, for most of the peasants were extremely poor, with total incomes way below 200 rubles (that is, less than $100) a year. Before the Revolution of 1905, the total payments by peasants for land "given" to them in 1861 had amounted to some two billion rubles.[4]

Title to the land was not given to the individual peasants but to the village commune, the ancient Russian *mir,* supposedly restored to its pre-feudal independence. The peasants of each village were made jointly responsible for distribution of land among themselves, for the land redemption payments, and for the heavy taxes assessed against the individual peasants. A peasant could not legally abandon his allotment. He might rent it to another peasant, but he could not leave the village for work elsewhere without a police permit.

Peasants had many continuing grievances against the landlords. "The peasants' lands were wedged in between lands belonging to the landlords in order to provide the latter with an assured—and noble—revenue from fines for trespass, etc." [5] When peasants tried to rent additional pasture or to obtain access to the landlord's watering place, only the richer peasants could do this on a money basis. The most common rental payment by the "middle" peasant was labour for the landlord. This involved the peasant in continued personal subjection.

"The peasant, 'emancipated' from serf labour, emerged from the hands of the reformers a crushed, plundered, degraded man, tied to his plot of land, so much so that nothing was left for him to do except 'voluntarily' accept serf labour. And the peasant began to cultivate the land of his former master by 'renting' from him the very land that had been 'clipped' from his own allotment, and by hiring himself in the winter for work in the summer, in repayment of the loan of grain which he had borrowed from the landlord to feed his hungry family."[6]

Capitalism, mingled with these semi-serf survivals, had come to the Russian village by two distinct paths. The first originated in the growth of the market for wheat and the resulting increase in commercial output. Early in the nineteenth century, as Russian wheat began to move toward England and western Europe, some landlords began to think of their estates as business concerns and to reckon the income from commercial grain as of primary importance. This brought, on the one hand, pressure for more continuous labour by the serfs and resulting waves of peasant unrest. And, at the same time, it showed a minority of "progressive" landlords certain advantages to be gained by shaking off responsibility for serf tenants and reorganising their own methods of production. Increasing wheat exports thus played a role in the "emancipation" of the serfs in 1861.[7]

Emancipation brought the peasants themselves much closer to the world market. Russian villages became dependent not only on the size of the harvest but on the world price of wheat. And the peasant masses found themselves trapped in a new kind of oppression, even while they were not yet fully released from the old serf bondage. Less than ten years after they were thrown by emancipation into the turmoil of commercial production and money obligations, the world price of wheat began a long, slow, relentless decline while the landlords were jacking up, notch by notch, the rent they demanded from peasants who tried to obtain supplementary land beyond their village allotments.

This situation created new differences among the peasants themselves. The position of the old-type peasant—the "middle" peasant who was primarily a subsistence farmer—was undermined. Those who could not produce a sufficient surplus for the market fell into increasing debt. If they tried to earn by wage-labour in order to clear the debt, they had to neglect their farms and then they slipped down into the ranks of the new "poor" peasants, tied to an allotment but actually and permanently dependent upon selling their labour power.[8] Those who prospered and increased their commercial production tended to become petty capitalists, producing chiefly for the market and exploiting their poor-peasant neighbours.

The other path by which capitalism had come into the Russian village was the handicraft shop which developed first within the peasant household, as the peasant family began to sell its products and brought in additional workers to increase its market output. This old process, familiar to all students of economic history, began later in Russia than elsewhere. It leads, of course, to the quest for wider markets and subjection to merchant capital, which grows in turn to "manufacture" with minute division of hand labour. This prepares for machine production and the development of "big industry."

During his years in prison and exile (from December, 1895, to February, 1900) Lenin analysed a mass of documents and studies smuggled to him by his comrades and wrote his monumental book on *The Development of Capitalism in Russia.* He showed that all stages of this development still existed side by side throughout the Russia of that period. And he traced the roots of certain very large factories to these village workshops which were themselves essentially capitalist in nature.

Contrasts Within Old Russia

Contrasts were glaring between the great landowners and the peasants, but no less important were the new contrasts which had grown up among the peasants themselves. The data on both these points are important to any understanding of the class forces in pre-revolution Russia.

The 12,300,000 peasant households had allotments averaging only 30 acres, and half of them had considerably less than 22 acres.

The 753,000 private landowners had average holdings of more than 300 acres. These included 699 private landlords owning more than 27,000 acres apiece and averaging more than 80,000 acres apiece. Tsar Nicholas Romanov personally owned 110 to 115 million acres. His relatives owned, among them, more than 20 million acres. Lands held by the church for the support of the clergy amounted to about 5.5 million acres.[9]

LAND HOLDINGS IN EUROPEAN RUSSIA (1905)[10]

	Number of properties	*Total area in acres*
INDIVIDUAL PRIVATE OWNERS		
By size of property:		
Over 27,000 acres	699	56,155,961
1,350 to 27,000 acres	27,134	111,220,606
Under 1,350 acres	725,048	64,375,430
All individual owners	752,881	231,751,997
PEASANT ALLOTMENTS		
By size of allotment:		
Over 81 acres	617,715	88,277,877
40.5 to 81 acres	1,551,904	84,434,189
21.6 to 40.5 acres	3,932,485	113,893,892
Under 21.6 acres	6,175,251	82,989,584
All peasant allotments	12,277,355	369,595,542

The more than six million peasants with the smallest allotments averaging barely 13½ acres had in all only as much land as the 27,833 private landlords who owned more than 1,350 acres apiece and averaged about 6,000 acres.

Peasant holdings were usually larger in the Baltic provinces and in the recently settled regions of the south and southeast than in the older provinces of Russia. Notably the Cossacks had holdings that averaged more than 140 acres.[11] Cossacks were descended from peasants who had escaped from serfdom in the seventeenth century and settled on the plains along the River Don. Their independent status set them apart from the peasants and made them a peculiarly "useful" section of the army when poor peasants started disturbances.

Within each village community, also, allotments were unevenly distributed. Starting with some inequality, due to old gradations among the serfs, differences among the peasants had become very marked. The upper group who had developed into genuine petty-capitalist farmers had been able to buy and lease additional land and were the chief commercial producers among the peasants. They commonly had other sources of income as money-lenders, or merchants, or the owners of handicraft shops in which, as on the farm, family labour was supplemented by wage labour. "The moneyed peasants are sometimes even better at bullying and fleecing their fellow peasants than the landlords."[12] Dominating the village community and pressing heavily on their poorer neighbours, they won the name of "kulak" which literally means "fist."

At the other extreme, and making up at least half the total peasant households in European Russia, were the very poor who were unable even to produce their own subsistence on the land and depended almost wholly on working for wages. Although still classified as peasants because an allotment was registered in their names, many of these poor peasants leased their allotment to a neighbouring kulak and left the village in search of work. Others remained on their allotments but lived chiefly by doing wage work for a kulak or the landlord.

So the agricultural population in Russia before 1905 included four quite distinct and different groups.

1. At the top were those landlords who carried on large-scale commercial farming, with tenant labour and, increasingly, with up-to-date machinery and wage workers.

2. The well-to-do peasants (including kulaks) who made up about one-fifth of the peasant households but had nearly half of the peasant crop land and livestock.[13]

3. The middle peasants who with their own tools and livestock did tenant labour for the landlord in return for pasture and water privileges. These barely made a living from their allotments and had only a small marketable surplus of grain.

4. The poor peasants who lived chiefly by selling their labour power.

Autocracy and the Peasants

All peasants, from top to bottom, were allowed almost no part in political life. The tsar was supreme, the wealthiest and most powerful in the class of nobles and responsible to no one for his decisions. With the development of commerce and modern national life, administrative power had fallen into the hands of paid officials, completely subject to the tsar. Against this bureaucracy, drawn chiefly from the rising bourgeois class,[14] and notorious for its corruption and brutality, the peasant class was helpless.

"In no country is there such a multitude of officials as in Russia. The officials tower above the voiceless people like a dense forest—a mere workingman can never make his way through this forest, can never obtain justice. No complaint against the bribery, the robbery or the violence of the officials is ever brought to light; every complaint is smothered in official red tape. The voice of an isolated man can never reach the people, it is lost in the dense thickets, it is stifled in the police torture chamber. An army of officials, who were never elected by the people and who are not responsible to the people, has woven a thick web, and men and women are struggling in this web like flies." [15]

Rural district administrations known as "zemstvos" were set up in 1864 to look after such matters as roads and bridges and the barest minimum of education and public health. These marked the only approach to representative government. But when the zemstvo assembly met for its brief yearly sessions to instruct its administrative officials it was heavily weighted with nobles and merchants. Peasant communities had only slight and very indirect representation and their few delegates were mostly kulaks. Peasants carried the tax load for the zemstvo budgets.[16] In the extreme reaction that marked the 1890's and the years between 1906 and 1917 the mildly progressive activities of the zemstvo administrations were checked and continually subject to arbitrary interference by the appointed governors and other representatives of the tsar's bureaucracy.

The masses of old Russia, both peasants and workers, were "serfs of the officials." [17] Most obvious to non-Russian observers was the arbitrary and secret administration of "justice" and the complete censorship which left no freedom of meeting, writing, or speaking. But it was also important that the population was divided formally and legally into several "orders" or "estates," including the nobles, the merchants, the "citizens" in towns, the clergy, the peasants, and so on. Each order or "estate" was subject to separate laws giving special privileges to the nobles and the clergy and hemming in other classes with outgrown restrictions.

Peasants' freedom was peculiarly limited since they were tied to their allotments. Millions of these were too small to provide a living to the peasant family, but a peasant could not legally abandon his allotment and evade taxation and redemption payments. He might lease it, but he could not sell it. And even then he could not legally leave the village, even for seasonal wage labour, without permission of a police official who considered it his primary function to satisfy the landowners. Passports for travel were given only to those not wanted for service on the landowner's estate. As Lenin puts it in his masterly pamphlet *To the Rural Poor:* "Is this not serfdom, I ask you? Is it not an insult to the people when every tinpot profligate nobleman is allowed to order grown-up farmers about?" [18]

Differing Approaches to the Peasant Question

To Russian revolutionists and liberals of every shade, the peasant "question" had always been an important problem. Famines were a frequent scourge in the dry Russian plains, for the peasant masses were too poor to accumulate reserves and their methods were too primitive to prevent loss of crops in a season of drought. In 1891-92 misery among the peasants was made worse by a famine that was even more terrible than usual. Then in the course of three years the world price of wheat fell by some 40 per cent. This cut into the income of landlords and kulaks and greatly increased their pressure on the poor peasants. So when Lenin went to St. Petersburg in 1893 and shortly became (at the age of twenty-three) the recognised leader in a Marxist group, the finding of a correct approach to the peasant question was one of the primary tasks of the moment.*

The Emancipation of Labour Group under the leadership of George Plekhanov, the first outstanding Russian Marxist, had demanded in its program of 1885 "the radical revision of agrarian relationships (the conditions of redemption payments [for land—*A.R.*] and allotments of land to the peasants)." Later, in 1892, a Marxist pamphlet had discussed "The Tasks of the Socialists in Combating Famine in Russia." [19] But the subject had not been fully explored. And one of Lenin's first contributions to the revolutionary movement was his brilliant work in bringing a clear perspective on the relation of the peasant question to the class-conscious revolutionary movement of the wage workers.

In numbers and influence the Marxists in 1893 were quite overshadowed by the Narodniks, or Populists, who called themselves "Friends of the People." The Populists scarcely considered the problems of the industrial workers and wrote almost entirely about the Russian village. They dreamed of a socialism to be achieved by a few devoted leaders who would draw the unthinking masses toward a better life. They deplored the growth of industry and had no con-

* By 1900 the tsarist police were saying: "There is nobody bigger than Ulyanov [Lenin] in the revolution today." (*History of the Communist Party of the Soviet Union*, p. 24.)

ception of the revolutionary role of the industrial proletariat. All their hopes were centred in the peasants.

The Populists glossed over the sharp divisions among the peasants and idealised the village commune as a natural basis for socialism. They looked to an expansion of what they called "people's production." But Lenin made it very clear that the household peasant industries, idealised by the Populists, were expanding by drawing in poor peasants as wage workers. They represented the early stages of a genuinely *capitalist* development.

Throughout the 1890's Lenin was puncturing with hard facts the utopian dream bubbles of the Populists. And from every angle he exposed the peasant problem as part of the broader problem of development from feudalism to capitalism and beyond capitalism to socialism.

The pattern of this development was peculiarly confused in Russia. Survivals of landlord-tenant feudal agriculture were intertwined with increasing large-scale landlord farming with wage labour. In the village the class cleavage between petty-capitalist kulaks and destitute peasants was blurred by the fact that no peasant, whether kulak or wage-worker, was politically free. They belonged, all of them, to a rigid "order" or "estate," the lowest estate in a sharply graded society.

Where the Populists, and later the kindred group of Socialist Revolutionaries, saw in the village "commune" something rare and peculiar to the Russian people, Lenin saw only survivals of an earlier period, which confined and hindered the normal growth of productive forces. The Populists were traditionally against capitalism but they denied its importance in Russia and dreamed of socialism growing from the village commune. Lenin hated capitalism more deeply and consistently than the Populists hated it, but he saw that capitalism was already deeply rooted in Russian life, a native growth that must be reckoned with and utilised in the work of preparing for socialism. When his work on *The Development of Capitalism in Russia* was published in 1899, under the pen-name of V. Ilyin, its refutation of the Populist analysis of Russian economic life greatly increased the influence of Marxist thought among Russian intellectuals.

By way of conclusion in this basic volume, Lenin summed up "the question which in literature has come to be known as the 'mission' of capitalism, *i.e.*, of its historical role in the economic development of Russia. To admit that this role is a progressive one," Lenin wrote, "is quite compatible (as we have tried to show in detail at every stage in our exposition of the facts) with the fullest admission of the negative and gloomy sides of capitalism, with the fullest admission of the inevitable, profound and all-sided social antagonisms which are a feature of capitalism and which reveal the historically transitional character of this economic system." [20]

For us who live in the midst of a capitalism in sharp decline and general crisis, with mass unemployment, bitter class conflict and almost world-wide war, it is easy to overlook the constructive historic role which made capitalism more progressive than the forms of production that preceded it. Lenin demonstrated this phase of capitalism from two angles: (1) the increase in productive forces under capitalism which gave for the first time the material possibilities of abundance for all, and (2) the socialisation of labour. Note some of the points made by Lenin on this second aspect.

In 1894, writing against the Populists, Lenin had said:

"Fractionalised, individual, petty exploitation binds the toilers to a particular place, disunites them, prevents them from appreciating their class solidarity, prevents them from uniting and from understanding that the cause of their exploitation is not any particular individual, but the whole economic system. Large-scale capitalism, on the contrary, inevitably severs all the workers' ties with the old society, with a particular locality and with a particular exploiter; it unites them, compels them to think and puts them in conditions which enable them to commence an organised struggle." [21]

This idea was greatly expanded in *The Development of Capitalism in Russia.*

"Working for oneself is transformed into working for the whole of society, and the more capitalism is developed the greater is the contradiction between the collective character of production and the individualist character of the appropriation of the results of production. ... Compared with the labour of a dependent or bonded peasant, the labour of a free labourer is a progressive phenomenon in all branches of national economy." Capitalism "creates mobility among the population which was not required in previous systems of social economy and was impossible on any large scale under those systems." It increases "the need for union, for association, and gives these associations a special character compared with associations in previous times. While breaking down the narrow, local estate associations of mediaeval society and creating fierce competition, capitalism at the same time divides society into large groups of persons who occupy different positions in production, and gives a tremendous impetus to the organisation of the persons within each of these groups." [22]

Such changes "cannot but bring about a profound change in the very character of the producers." But capitalism in Russia was developing too slowly, "for there is not a single capitalist country in the world in which ancient institutions, which are incompatible with capitalism, which retard its development, which immeasurably worsen the conditions of the producers who 'suffer from capitalism as well as from the insufficient development of capitalism,' have survived in such abundance as they have survived in Russia." [23]

So Lenin looked to a political revolution against the autocracy as releasing Russian capitalism for a fuller and more rapid development and hastening the struggle for socialism. He looked to the workers entirely divorced from the land as the most active and consistent fighters for democracy. In this fight they would have many allies, including the great mass of peasants.

At the same time, the class struggle of workers and poor peasants against the capitalists of every type would be maturing, and a vanguard of the working class would be developed for leadership in the next stage of the struggle when the workers who could live only by selling their labour power would be the chief force in bringing about the socialist revolution. Even in those early years Lenin understood the special role in the socialist revolution of the poor peasants "whose support is an essential condition for the victory of the working class." [24]

CHAPTER II

Lenin's First Programme

"BY an agrarian programme we mean the laying down of the guiding principles for a Social-Democratic * policy in the agrarian question, *i.e.*, in relation to agriculture and the various classes, strata, and groups of the rural population." [1]

Immediately after his arrest in December, 1895, Lenin wrote in prison the first draft of a programme to serve as the basis for a Marxist revolutionary party. This draft was circulated and developed in several years of discussion. Its principles were embodied in a longer programme published in June, 1902, in *Iskra (The Spark)* † of which Lenin was at that time the chief editor. With slight additional changes, this *Iskra* programme was adopted at the Second Congress of the Russian Social-Democratic Labour Party in 1903.[2]

To Lenin the party programme was a charting of the road to be followed toward the ultimate goal of socialist revolution. First, however, it must define that goal and analyse the role within the revolutionary movement of the various exploited classes. Wage workers

* The Russian Marxists working with Lenin were known after 1898 as the Russian Social-Democratic Labour Party. Conflicting trends developed within the R.S.-D.L.P. in the 1905 Revolution and the Leninist group became known as Bolsheviks (*i.e.*, members of the majority), but until 1917 this party's official name was Russian Social-Democratic Labour Party (Bolshevik). During the World War the R.S.-D.L.P.(B.) broke with the reformist elements dominating Social-Democratic parties in other countries. In 1918 the Russian Bolsheviks became the Communist Party, taking the name used by Marx and Engels in their earliest organisation of the working class.

† *Iskra* was the Marxist newspaper published under Lenin's leadership from 1900 to 1903, when the party was beginning to grow and no unifying programme had yet been adopted.

who can live only by selling their labour power are set apart as the one class whose economic situation lays the groundwork for socialist revolutionary action. All other classes of contemporary society have a stake, large or small, in preserving property rights peculiar to the capitalist order. But the position of small "independent" producers and traders is increasingly undermined as the development of capitalism pushes more of them into the ranks of the wage workers.

"In so far as all these contradictions peculiar to bourgeois society increase and develop, there increases also the discontent of the toiling and exploited masses with the existing order of things. The number and the solidarity of the proletarians grow and their struggle against the exploiters is intensified." [3]

The function of the revolutionary party is then defined.

"Setting itself the task of making the proletariat able to carry out its great historic mission, international Social-Democracy organises it in an independent political party, opposed to all bourgeois parties; guides all forms of its class struggle; reveals to it the irreconcilable conflict between the interests of the exploiters and the interests of the exploited; and clarifies the historical significance and the essential conditions of the social revolution which lies ahead. At the same time, Social-Democracy demonstrates to all other toiling and exploited masses the hopelessness of their situation in capitalist society and the necessity of the social revolution for their own liberation from the yoke of capital. Social-Democracy, the party of the working class, calls into its ranks all strata of the toiling and exploited population in so far as these go over to the viewpoint of the proletariat." [4]

Lying nearer than the ultimate goal but marking steps on the road toward socialism were issues toward which the immediate struggle of Russian Social-Democrats in those years must be directed as preparing the way for the socialist revolution. To Lenin such an immediate programme was in no sense limited to easy issues on which some quick success might be expected. It was rather a guide to major points for struggle within the framework of capitalism. Such points, for immediate struggle, made up more than half of the first Leninist programme of the Russian Social-Democrats.

Democracy as a Step Toward Socialism

Lenin at that time placed primary emphasis on overthrowing the autocracy and establishing the democratic rights necessary for the fullest and most rapid development of capitalism and its clear-cut class struggles. For all wage workers, including those on the land, such general political demands as civil liberties and the right of free association were supplemented with demands for fair standards of working conditions.[5] This section of the programme rounded out and further developed the issues on which Russian industrial workers had already carried on determined and widespread strikes.

Struggles for political democracy and standardised conditions of work would strengthen the ties already established between the Social-Democrats and the wage workers. Victories on these issues would bring the workers a truer sense of their own power. And the winning of political liberty, of shorter hours and better pay, with protection of health and compensation for industrial accidents, would widen the workers' possibilities of education and study and of closely knit organisation.

Having stated very clearly that socialism was the ultimate goal, the programme of 1903 raised no immediate demand for socialisation of industry. As Lenin put it in the discussion:

> "On behalf of the wage workers we demand such *reforms* as would 'preserve them from physical and moral degeneration and enhance their fighting capacity'; on behalf of the peasants, however, we are striving to realise only such *changes* as would facilitate the 'eradication of the survivals of the old serf system and the free development of the class struggle in the countryside.' "[6]

More rapid development of capitalist agriculture would shorten the road to socialism. It would raise the productivity of labour on the land. It would clear away the remnants of feudal oppression which blurred the underlying issues. And as the relation of employer and wage worker became the primary and general form of exploitation in the village, the ground would be prepared for a close alliance between the rural poor and the industrial proletariat.

Lenin drew a fundamental distinction between the section of the programme dealing with the working class and the section on peasant demands.

"In both sections we keep within the confines of present-day (*i.e.,* bourgeois) society.... But the radical difference between them is that the demands contained in the working class section are directed against the *bourgeoisie,* while those contained in the peasant section are directed against the *feudal landlords.* In the former section we have to confine ourselves to *partial* improvements of the existing bourgeois order. In the latter we must aim at the *complete* cleansing of the present order of all survivals of serfdom." [7]

Peasant demands were more revolutionary in their nature than the workers' demands, for they squarely attacked certain property rights of the great landlords. But as Lenin explained again and again in the discussion of the programme, these revolutionary peasant demands represented only the belated and unfinished struggle against serfdom and feudalism. They would not bring socialism in the village, but they would hasten the development of Russian agriculture along capitalist lines.

"The peasant must first of all obtain for himself all the rights possessed by the nobility and the merchants. The peasant must obtain the unrestricted right freely to dispose of his land. Peasant committees must be established for the abolition of the more despicable forms of bondage and for the restitution of the *otrezki.* We want not the unity of the *mir* [the village commune], but the unity of the rural poor in the rural communities all over Russia, the alliance of the rural proletarians with the urban proletarians." [8]

Historic grievances of the "emancipated" peasants would be satisfied by the demands. But Lenin emphasised that the demands of the Social-Democrats could not be simply a hodge-podge of everything the peasants desired. Their grievances must be analysed with Marxist understanding of social development toward the ultimate goal of socialism. So the programme stated that the special peasant demands were introduced "with the object of removing the survivals of serfdom, the burden of which lies heavily on the peasants, and in the interests of the free development of the class struggle in the countryside." [9]

On the relation of peasants and great landowners the programme demanded that all land redemption payments, quit-rents * and special peasant taxes must be abolished. Further, that the peasants must be repaid all the hundreds of millions of rubles which landlords had already received from the peasants as land redemption and rental payments under the "emancipation" charters. Funds for these repayments to the peasants should be obtained by confiscation of estates owned by churches and monasteries and by the imperial family; also special land tax should be placed on other great landowners.

Landowners must also return to the peasants without compensation all of the *otrezki* cut from the peasant holdings in 1861, which "serve in the hands of the landlords as a means of keeping the peasants in bondage." Where such *otrezki* had been bought by new owners since 1861 and did not serve to keep peasants in bondage, the owner might receive indemnity from the government at the expense of the big landowning nobility, but in no case should any "compensation" payment be exacted from the peasants.[10] Lenin was opposed to compensation and warned those who overruled him on this point against allowing such a provision to give a revolutionary measure "the specific flavour of a mawkishly well-intentioned and bourgeois measure." [11]

Lenin called the Great Reform of 1861 a "legalised robbery" of the peasants.[12] He would have the Social-Democrats lead a movement for free restitution of lands of which the peasants had been "robbed," not simply because a great historic wrong should be righted, but as a practical and truly revolutionary measure. For in Lenin's opinion it was primarily the *otrezki* which provided the economic basis for conditions closely resembling serfdom. Replying to those who questioned the importance of pressing for restitution of these peasant lands, Lenin said:

* Money rents paid by feudal tenants in lieu of labour service.

"Here is what the labour-rent system of economy means. It means that in actual fact, *i.e.,* not according to ownership but according to economic utilisation, the land of the landlords and peasants, together with its appurtenances, has not been divided up definitively but remains merged: part of the peasant land serves, for example, for the maintenance of the cattle which are necessary for the cultivation not of the peasant land but of the landlord's land; part of the landlord's land is absolutely indispensable for the neighbouring peasant farm under the given system (watering places, grazing grounds, etc.). And this actual interweaving of land utilisation *inevitably* engenders the same (or, to put it more accurately, perpetuates the thousand-year old) relationship between muzhik and lord that existed under serfdom. The muzhik remains a serf *de facto,* working with the same old tools of ancient days, on the same old three-field system, for the same old 'lord of the manor.' What can be clearer than the fact that the peasants everywhere themselves call this work *panschina* and *'barschina,'* * that the landlords themselves in describing their farms say: my land is worked by 'my former' (that is, not only former, but present as well!) 'peasants' with their own implements in exchange for the use of my pasture land?" [13]

Guiding the Peasant Struggles

For realisation of the peasant demands, Lenin looked to the struggles of the peasants themselves. In his pamphlet addressed *To the Rural Poor* (in 1903), he explained very simply and clearly the organised movement among wage workers with its revolutionary purpose. He spoke of the importance of close alliance between wage workers and poor peasants in a movement to destroy the autocratic power of the tsar and his officials and to win basic democratic rights. But also the pamphlet was a call to the peasants to move for their own liberation.

"It is clear that the rural poor can expect no help from anyone or from any quarter as long as they do not unite as a single class in order to wage a fierce and stubborn fight against the landlord class." [14]

* Russian terms for feudal labour service rendered by the serf to the lord of the manor.

Restitution of the *otrezki* must not be begged from officials and landlords. It must be won by the peasants and carried through by peasant committees. People's courts must also be created with power "to reduce unduly high land rents and to annul transactions of a bondage character." [15]

Russian peasants had a long tradition of struggle against the landowners. The "emancipation" which gave them the appearance of freedom in 1861 had followed a rising wave of peasant disturbances. In the course of twenty years (1835-55) some 144 landlords had been killed. A report of the Chief of the Corps of Gendarmes, in 1858, had stated that "Disturbances of entire villages demanding the personal intervention of the highest provincial authorities or the aid of military detachments... have taken place in the course of the year in twenty-five provinces." [16]

After the tsar's manifesto of March 3 (February 19 old style), 1861, as peasants realised that some of their land had been taken from them and they must pay the landlord in hard cash even for such land as they were allowed to retain, the villages seethed with rebellion. In the course of the two years immediately following "emancipation," troops were called out in 2,115 villages to force the peasants to sign the new charters. And at least one pitched battle was fought, with 51 deaths.[17]

"Without the help of the military, without tortures and shootings, the committees of the nobles would never have been able to rob the peasants in the brazen way they did at the time of the emancipation of the serfs. The peasants must always remember the way they were robbed and defrauded by these committees of the nobles and landlords, because now, as then, the tsarist government, whenever it appoints a committee to make new laws concerning the peasants, never appoints anyone but landlords and officials to sit on it.... The peasants must demand that they be allowed to settle their affairs *themselves,* that they *themselves* be allowed to draw up, to pass and to carry out new laws.... No one will free the peasants from the official bloodsuckers until they free themselves, until they unite and take their fate into their own hands." [18]

A fresh wave of peasant disturbances had begun at the end of the nineteenth century. Early in 1902 Lenin stated: "What can be called problematical is by no means the attraction of the peasant masses to the movement against the survivals of serfdom, but only perhaps the *degree* of that attraction."[19]

Vigorous spontaneous revolts broke out shortly afterwards.* As Lenin described these later, peasants "rose and marched against the landlords, broke into their barns, shared the contents among themselves, distributed to the starving the grain that had been sown and reaped by the peasants but appropriated by the landlords, and demanded a new repartition of the land."[20]

The uprisings were brutally suppressed, with floggings, shootings, and heavy fines. Lenin, in writing *To the Rural Poor,* explained to the peasants the reasons for their defeat, and summoned them to further struggle.

"The peasant insurrection was put down because it was the insurrection of an ignorant and unintelligent mass, an insurrection that advanced no *political* demands, *i.e.,* no demands for changes in the constitution of the *state*. The peasant insurrection was put down because no *preparations had been made* for it *beforehand*. The peasant insurrection was put down because the rural proletarians had not yet allied themselves with the urban proletarians."[21]

He stressed the importance of organised resistance in each village based on the special immediate grievances of the poor peasants in that village. Equally important was the development of many peasant leaders who understood the underlying cause of their grievances.

"To show how it can be done, let me give one or two instances. Let us suppose that a Social-Democratic worker has come on a visit to his village, or that any Social-Democratic worker has come to any village. The village, like a fly in a spider's web, is entirely in the power of the neighbouring landlord; it cannot rid itself of its bondage, cannot escape from this bondage. The worker must at once single out the

* The peasant struggles of 1902 followed great workers' strikes, first in St. Petersburg (now Leningrad), where May Day, 1901, saw a clash between striking munition workers and the police, and in the following March in Batum and Rostov.

most sensible, intelligent, and reliable peasants, who are keen on seeing justice done and who will not be frightened by the first police dog they encounter, and explain the causes of this endless bondage, tell them how the landlords cheated the peasants and robbed them with the aid of the committees of the nobles, tell them how powerful the rich are and how they are supported by the tsarist government. He must also tell them about the demands of the Social-Democratic workers.

"When the peasants have understood all this, the next thing they must do is to put their heads together and devise some way of resisting the landlord, some way of presenting their first and principal demands, in the same way as the urban workers present their demands to the manufacturers . . . reduction of rent, fair terms for labourers on winter hire, no brutal persecution of the peasant when his cattle trespass on the landlord's land, or other appropriate demands." [22]

Some Social-Democrats thought that they should not stimulate revolutionary struggle of peasants against feudal landlords because capitalist elements were already developing in Russian agriculture which would of themselves weaken and ultimately destroy the serf relationships in the village. To such arguments Lenin replied that the survivals of serfdom increased the oppression of the poor peasants and needlessly retarded the development of capitalism.

"In order to clear the road for the free development of the class struggle in the countryside, it is necessary to remove all the survivals of serfdom, which now *cover up* the embryoes of capitalist antagonisms among the rural population and keep them from developing. And we are making a *final* attempt to help the peasantry to whisk all these survivals out of existence with a single decisive sweep—'final' because developing Russian capitalism is itself spontaneously doing the very same work, making for the very same goal, but making for it along its own peculiar road of violence and oppression, ruin and starvation. The transition from feudal exploitation to capitalist exploitation is inevitable, and it would be a harmful and reactionary illusion to attempt to hold it back or to 'get around' it. But this transition is also conceivable in the form of the forcible overthrow of those successors of the feudal lords who rely on the tradition of the erstwhile power of the slaveowner rather than on the 'power of money' to drain the last drop of blood from the patriarchal peasantry. This patriarchal peasantry, which lives under a system of natural economy by the labour of its own hands, is destined to disappear, but it is by no means 'necessarily' destined by an 'immanent' law of social and economic evolution to endure the tortures of being 'scourged with taxes' and whips, to endure the torments of a long-drawn out, horribly protracted death by starvation.

"And so, without fostering any illusions about its being possible for the small producers to thrive or even to lead a tolerable existence in a capitalist society (such as Russia is becoming to a greater and greater extent), we demand the complete and unconditional revolutionary, and not reformist, abrogation and extermination of the survivals of serfdom." [23]

Lenin emphasised the importance of limiting immediate peasant demands to points directly related to the struggle against autocracy and serfdom. These must not be confused with such issues as small credits, co-operative creameries, loan and savings co-operatives, unions of small farmers, peasant banks and agricultural experts.[24]

The programme of this period decisively rejects "all reformers' plans which are bound up in any way with the extension or solidifying of the police-bureaucratic tutelage over the toiling classes." [25] And in the discussion Lenin emphasised that until the fight against autocracy and serfdom was won, the government might utilise such measures (which could benefit only a small number of peasants) to split the relatively well-to-do away from the masses and thus weaken the peasant forces in the immediate revolutionary struggle against serfdom.

"Feudal relationships in the countryside are singularly interwoven with bourgeois relationships; and as a class of bourgeois society the peasants (the small farmers) are far more of a conservative element than a revolutionary one (particularly in view of the fact that the bourgeois evolution of agricultural relationships is only just beginning in our country). For this reason, in a period of political reforms it will be far easier for the government to divide the peasants (than, for instance, the workers); far easier to weaken (or even, in the worst event, to paralyse) their revolutionary spirit by means of petty and unimportant concessions to the small owners, who are comparatively few in number."[26]

Even in the struggle against survivals of serfdom, Lenin looked to the poorer peasants to take the lead, since the burden of feudal restrictions and labour rent lay most heavily upon them. But most of the richer peasants would also, temporarily, play a revolutionary role. Later, in the struggle for socialism, class lines within the village would be sharpened. Masses of poor peasants dependent chiefly upon wages would become allies of the class-conscious industrial proletariat. But what of the other peasants? What did Lenin expect of the petty-capitalist kulaks? What of the small producers who were hard-working and greatly exploited but were quite untutored by working-class experience? What would be their relation to the ultimate struggle for socialism?

CHAPTER III

Small Producers and Socialism

WHAT happens to small independent producers on the land has always been a subject of sharp disagreement between Marxists and capitalist social reformers of various kinds. Marxists emphasise the increasing separation of society into two opposing classes, capitalists and wage workers, while small "independent" producers are pushed down into deeper poverty, or squeezed out of their occupations entirely. From the ranks of destitute artisans, small traders, and small farmers, there are recruited the masses of workers who can live only by selling their labour power.

In every country this process has gone forward irregularly, and the pattern of two opposing classes has never come completely clear of survivals from an earlier form of production. So the anti-socialist reformers have been able to argue that the petty bourgeoisie, and especially the small producers on the land, are not inevitably doomed to increasing misery under capitalism.

Lenin considered a correct Marxist understanding of this question so important for the Social-Democrats in Russia that he used hard factual material from half a dozen countries to demonstrate the basic trends among peasants and farmers under more developed capitalist conditions. This was a constantly recurring subject in his writings from the 1890's right up to the stress of the revolutionary struggle in 1917.

Lenin showed that under the most varied conditions of different countries, production on the land was increasingly in the hands of large concerns and small employers, while the independent "family" producers were pushed out from a share in the market and existed only in the greatest poverty. Small farms offered no hope of meeting the needs of the rising generations. More and more small farmers and their children had to seek a living by wage work. And those who remained on the land could attempt to compete with their larger neighbours only at the cost of terrific exertion and a declining standard of living.

Relation of Small Farmers and Wage Workers

Only the Marxists accepted the idea that agriculture was already developing and would further develop along capitalist lines. To Lenin this idea was clearly demonstrated by actual facts and gave the true "line" for political analysis and revolutionary effort among the peasants. He saw that the majority of the peasants would be increasingly the victims of capitalist development but he insisted on a sharp distinction between these exploited toilers and the proletariat. As a class, workers having no property in the means of production were prepared by their experience to lead in the struggle for socialism. They had, truly, "nothing to lose but their chains and a world to gain." But the peasants who existed from their patches of land tended to cling to their miserable properties.

"Both logic and history teach us that the petty-bourgeois class outlook may be more or less narrow and more or less progressive, just because of the dual status of the petty bourgeois. And far from dropping our hands in despair because of this narrowness ('stupidity') of the muzhik or because he is governed by 'prejudice,' we must work steadily to widen his outlook and to help his judgment triumph over his prejudice."[1]

Only those peasants who could be convinced that the future under capitalism held nothing for them would be disentangled from these bonds of property and would throw themselves completely into the struggle for socialism.

Lenin summed up this difference between workers and peasants during the discussion on party programme in 1902. In a criticism of the draft programme offered by Plekhanov, Lenin said;

"Apart from the proletariat, the other sections of the 'toiling and exploited mass' (*i.e.,* mainly the small producers) are only *partly* revolutionary in their struggle against the bourgeoisie. To be precise, they are revolutionary 'only in view of their impending transfer into the proletariat . . . they desert their own standpoint to place themselves at that of the proletariat.' (*Communist Manifesto.*) . . . The 'aggravation of the struggle' of the small producers finds expression in anti-Semitism, and in Caesarism, and in peasant unions directed against the farm hands, and even in the struggle between the social Gironde and the Mountain.* The fact that the proletariat represents the whole of the toiling and exploited mass must find its expression in the programme in the fact that we *accuse* capitalism of being the cause of the poverty of the *masses* (and not of the working class alone) and the cause of the unemployment of 'ever more extensive strata of the toiling population' (and not only of the working class)."[2]

Peasant relationships, with increasing dependence upon commodity production, increasing burdens of debt, and increasing class divisions, expressed the early stages of capitalist development. The poverty of the village masses was no longer simply the poverty of feudal serfs but a poverty due to complex intertwining of several forms of exploitation which included semi-feudal remnants and various stages of capitalism.

A class of peasants was appearing who could exist only by doing wage labour for others. And Lenin saw that even in the village the struggle for socialism would be a class struggle between the rural proletariat (with such allies as it could win to its side from the ranks of middle peasants living by the land) and the capitalists (both landlords and peasant employers).

"This condition [the free development of the class struggle in the countryside] is the fundamental and central point of the theory of revolutionary Marxism in the sphere of the agrarian question. To recognise that the evolution of agriculture, despite all its confusedness

* In the French National Convention (1792-93) deputies from the Gironde led the conservative republican elements. The persistently uncompromising Jacobins sat on the topmost benches and were called "the Mountain."

and complexity, despite the multifariousness of its forms, is also capitalist evolution, that it also (like the evolution of industry) engenders the class struggle of the proletariat against the bourgeoisie, that it is *this* class struggle which must be our foremost and prime concern, which must be the touchstone to which we submit both questions of principle, and the political aims and methods of propaganda, agitation and organisation. To recognise this condition means to obligate oneself to take one's stand on an unswervingly class point of view in the particularly acute question of the participation of the small peasants in the Social-Democratic movement; it means never in any way to depart from the standpoint of the proletariat on behalf of the interests of the petty bourgeoisie, but, on the contrary, to demand that the small peasant, who is being oppressed and ruined by all modern capitalism, abandon *his* class standpoint and place himself at the standpoint of the proletariat.

"By setting this condition, we are resolutely and irrevocably fencing ourselves off not only from *our enemies* (*i.e.,* the direct or indirect, conscious or unconscious supporters of the bourgeoisie, who are our temporary and partial allies in the struggle against the survivals of serfdom), but we are at the same time fencing ourselves off from those *unreliable friends* who because of their irresolute presentation of the agrarian question are apt to bring (and actually do bring) much harm to the revolutionary movement of the proletariat." [3]

Abolition of serfdom and autocracy would encourage independent peasant farming and would bring some immediate relief to millions of peasants. But more important in the long run, it would clear the way for more rapid capitalist development in the village and thus bring those who were exploited in the village closer to the workers' struggle for socialism.

"The demand for the establishment of peasant committees for the restriction of bondage and for the restitution of the *otrezki* * is not a barrier. It is a *door*.... Until the peasants pass through this door they will remain in ignorance and bondage, without full rights, without

* Cut-off lands. See Chapter I, p. 12.

complete, real freedom; they will not even be able to decide among themselves who is the friend of the workingman and who his enemy." [4]

Small Property: Progress or Reaction?

To Lenin the possibilities of revolutionary change were tied in, at all times, with the immediate objective situation. The struggle against the survivals of serfdom was an essential preliminary to the struggle for socialism. But many Social-Democrats could not—or would not—understand this historical perspective. They objected that Lenin in throwing such emphasis on release from the remnants of serfdom was encouraging small property. And small property, Lenin himself had stated, was a reactionary rather than a progressive force. In answering such arguments Lenin pointed out again and again the peculiar factors in the Russian situation which justified temporary strengthening of the petty bourgeoisie in the village.

"Speaking generally, it is not the business of the Social-Democrats to develop, encourage, fortify, still less multiply small-scale farming or small property. But the point is that we are not faced with a 'general' but with an *exceptional* case of small-scale farming. . . . Speaking *generally,* the encouragement of small property is reactionary, *because* it is directed against large-scale *capitalist* economy and, consequently, retards the social revolution, and obscures and glosses over the class struggle. But in this case we want to support small property not against capitalism, but against feudalism; in this case, by supporting the small peasantry, we give a tremendous impetus to the development of the class struggle." [5]

In relation to feudalism small property marks an advance. But when the struggle against feudalism has been won, small property blurs the clear-cut alignment of class forces and the struggle on which further progress depends.

"In the West the peasant property owner has already played his part in the democratic movement, and he now defends his privileged position as compared with the proletariat. [Written in 1902.—*A.R.*]

In Russia the peasant property owner is still on the eve of a determined democratic movement of the whole people, with which he cannot but sympathise. He still looks forward rather than backward. He is still much more a fighter against 'estate' and feudal privileges, which are still so strong in Russia, than a defender of his own privileged position. In a historic moment *like the present* it is our duty to support the peasants and to try to guide their vague and blind discontent against their real enemy....

"Under capitalist economy, small property retards the development of productive forces by binding the worker to a small plot of land, by sanctifying routine in technique, by preventing the land from being drawn into the channels of commerce. Where the *otrabotki* * system predominates, small landed property by ridding itself of *otrabotki* stimulates the development of productive forces, releases the peasant from the bondage that binds him to one spot, relieves the landlord of 'unpaid' servants, deprives him of the possibility of substituting the unlimited aggravation of 'patriarchal' exploitation for technical improvements, and facilitates the drawing of the land into the channels of commerce. In a word, the contradictory position of the small peasantry on the borderline between serfdom and capitalist economy entirely justifies the exceptional and temporary support of small holdings by the Social-Democrats." [6]

And elsewhere Lenin replied to those who asked "where then is our proletarian distinctiveness and our proletarian independence?"

"The proletariat is distinguished from all other classes oppressed by the bourgeoisie and opposing it precisely in that it does not place its hopes in a retardation of bourgeois development, nor in the blunting or toning down of the class struggle, but, on the contrary, in the fullest development of the class struggle and in the acceleration of bourgeois progress. [Note by Lenin:] It is understood that not all measures accelerating bourgeois progress are *supported* by the proletariat, but only those that bear *directly* on enhancing the capacity of the working

* *Otrabotki* is, literally, "working-off." It is used for a tenancy under which rent is paid not in money but in labour. More broadly it means any relation under which the peasant is bound to work off a considerable debt unavoidably incurred.

class to struggle for its emancipation. And labour rent and debt bondage affect the section of the peasantry that is propertyless and close to the proletariat much more severely than they do the well-to-do section of the peasantry."[7]

When Lenin turned to the rural poor and not to the more well-to-do to take the initiative in the fight against remnants of serfdom he was turning to those who were most oppressed by these remnants. But he was also looking beyond this immediate struggle to the later sharpening of class differences that already existed within the village. In his pamphlet *To the Rural Poor,* Lenin did not hesitate to state clearly this apparent contradiction between the immediate struggle of *all* peasants against the landlords and the later struggle in which the poor peasants would rise against the capitalists, including the kulaks, the petty capitalists of the village.

"The sooner and the more completely we succeed in abolishing peasant bondage, the more real freedom will the peasants succeed in obtaining for themselves, the sooner will the rural poor unite among themselves and the sooner will the rich peasants unite with the rest of the bourgeoisie. Let them unite: we are not afraid of their uniting, although we know perfectly well that this alliance will make the rich peasants more powerful. But we too shall unite, and *our alliance,* the alliance between the rural poor and the urban workers, will be immeasurably wider; it will be an alliance of tens of millions against an alliance of hundreds of thousands....

"*...the rural poor will not have to march side by side with the rich against the landlords very long.* Only the first step will have to be taken in their company, after that their ways will part."[8]

Lenin's emphasis throughout the discussion of the 1903 programme was on revolutionary action by the peasants themselves. He saw that seizure of land by the peasants would not only give temporary relief to great numbers of the smaller peasants but would rouse their spirit of struggle and prepare them for further action.

"A revolutionary measure like the restitution of the *otrezki* would render a great service precisely by substituting the 'method' of open revolutionary transformation for the 'method' of gradual and imperceptible transformation of feudal dependence into bourgeois dependence: this *could not possibly* happen without *exercising the profoundest influence* on the spirit of protest and of independent struggle of all the rural toiling population." [9]

Importance of Small Producers' Problems

It would be the job of the Social-Democrats to channel the "spirit of protest and of independent struggle" aroused among the rural poor in the fight against serfdom and autocracy into the broader, more difficult struggle against capitalism. Socialism, which was always the ultimate goal in Lenin's thinking, could not be won unless the poor peasants and many of the middle peasants lined up *with* the class-conscious proletariat and not against them.

"We Russian Social-Democrats must try to avail ourselves of the experience of Europe, and must begin to attract the 'country people' to the socialist labour movement at a much earlier stage and much more zealously than our Western comrades were able to do." In the agrarian sphere "we may evolve something new. And in order to make the transition to socialism easier for our rural labourers and semi-labourers, it is highly important that the Socialist Party *at once* begin to 'intercede' on behalf of the small peasants and to do 'all it can' for them; it must never refuse a hand in solving the very urgent and very complicated problems of 'others' (other than proletarians), and it must teach all the toiling and exploited masses to regard it as their leader and their representative." [10]

Lenin appealed primarily to the very poor peasants who could not exist without selling their labour power, but he spoke to the middle peasants also as friends and not as enemies. He knew that a very small minority of them might develop into petty exploiters or kulaks, but most of them could maintain themselves from their plots of land only by endless drudgery which provided barely enough to keep them alive. In his pamphlet *To the Rural Poor* (1903) Lenin had already set the political "line" in relation to the middle peasant which was followed throughout the revolutionary struggle and the campaign for socialist collective farming.

He showed from every angle the ways in which the poverty of the middle peasants was bound up not only with survivals of serfdom but also with the development of capitalism in agricultural production. He wrote of this in its simplest terms for the peasants themselves, many of whom were still totally illiterate. And at the same time, as we have noted, he carried on scholarly controversy with Russian liberals and non-Marxist revolutionists to demonstrate the inevitableness with which capitalism develops in agriculture and destroys the small producer on the land.

Solution of the middle peasants' problems must come, not from attempts to bolster up their small individual properties with special credits, special outlets, special subsidies, but only through genuine socialist reconstruction under the leadership of a revolutionary working class. He appealed to them to recognise the hopelessness of their position as small producers; and to see the various "measures for economic improvement (cheap ploughs, agricultural banks, the introduction of grass sowing, the cheap sale of livestock and fertilizers, and so on)" as devices for drawing "the middle and even the small peasant, even the semi-proletarian, away from an alliance with the workers." [11]

Not only the rich and their officials talk about these things but they carry along many well-meaning liberals.

"The champions of the bourgeoisie, who pretend to be the champions and friends of the small peasant, approve of these efforts and encourage them by every means. And many simple-minded people fail to see the wolf in sheep's clothing and believe that they are helping the poor and middle peasants when they repeat this bourgeois humbug." [12]

"...improved farming is an excellent thing. There is nothing wrong in buying ploughs more cheaply.... But when a poor or a middle peasant is told that improved farming and cheaper ploughs will help all of them to rid themselves of poverty and to stand on their feet, and that this can be done without touching the rich—*it is deceiving them.* All these improvements, lower prices and co-operatives (societies for the sale and purchase of goods) *will profit the rich to a much greater degree.*"[13]

Not bourgeois remedies but only socialism would solve the middle farmers' problems.

"Here and there a middle peasant may be able to become rich with the help of all these improvements and co-operative societies, but the people and the middle peasants as a whole will sink deeper and deeper into poverty. In order that all the middle peasants may become rich, the rich must be turned out, and the only way to turn them out is to form an alliance between the urban workers and the rural poor."[14]

To Lenin, the middle peasant stood literally in the middle between the basic opposing classes of capitalist society: those who live by the labour of others and those who work for others for wages. Their sympathies would waver in the struggle between workers and capitalists. As poor toilers they would share the wage workers' resentment against exploiters. As small producers with small independent possessions they would be wooed by the enemies of the workers, who would "spread all sorts of falsehoods about the Social-Democrats." So Lenin answered some of these lies and tried to assure the middle peasants that the Social-Democrats were friends who could be trusted.

"The Social-Democrats want to deprive only the big proprietors, *only those who live by the labour of others,* of their property. The Social-Democrats *will never take away the property of the small and middle farmers who do not employ labourers.* The Social-Democrats defend and champion the interests of all the toilers, not only the interests of the urban workers, who are more class conscious and more united than the others, but of the agricultural workers as well, and of the small artisans and of the peasants, in so far as these do not employ labour, do not try to imitate the rich and do not take the side of the bourgeoisie. *The Social-Democrats fight for all improvements in the conditions of the workers and peasants* which can be introduced immediately, even before we have destroyed the bourgeoisie, and which will help them in the fight against the bourgeoisie. But the Social-

Democrats do not want to mislead the peasant, they tell him *the whole truth,* they warn him straightforwardly that as long as the bourgeoisie is in power no improvements will rid the people of want and misery." [15]

As early as 1903, Lenin told the middle peasants and the poor peasants that after the socialist revolution they would be free to carry on large-scale co-operative farming with the aid of labour-saving machinery or to continue small individual production if they preferred. His outline given then of farming under socialism foreshadows the way agriculture has been developed in the Soviet Union.[16]

In the course of the Revolution, class differences among the peasants played an important part. All peasant classes participated in the struggle against autocracy. Even the kulaks were interested in overthrowing tsarist rule (March, 1917) and in the weakening of landlord power completed by the land decree of the new Soviet government (November 8, 1917). But in the struggle for socialism the kulaks were sharply hostile to the working class.

Among the poor and middle peasants Lenin tried from the beginning of his work to develop socialist understanding. He looked to the poor peasants as firm class allies in the workers' struggle. From the middle peasants as a class he expected, at most, a friendly neutrality so long as the outcome of the struggle against capitalism was still undecided. Only after the socialist power was established could the working class expect to win the mass of middle peasants also to a close working alliance in the building of socialist economy.

CHAPTER IV

The Revolution of 1905

WITH the Russo-Japanese war of 1904-1905, unrest increased throughout the vast area of the Russian empire. Economic crisis which had preceded the war had brought wage cuts and mass unemployment.[1] Within a year after the war began the Russian army was decisively defeated at Mukden (February, 1905), and two months later the Russian fleet was destroyed in the straits of Tsushima. Loss of life was unprecedented.

In December, 1904, began a series of widespread strikes. Workers in the Baku oilfields won the first general collective agreement in Russian labour history.[2] In Petersburg a strike at the Putilov metal works spread to other large concerns. Some 150,000 Petersburg workers were out on strike when Father Gapon, a police agent who was trying to mislead the organised workers, conceived the idea of a mass demonstration bringing a petition to the tsar. It begged the "little father" to relieve their distress. Under pressure from Social-Democratic workers, Gapon had been compelled to include also a demand for basic rights and the calling of a Constituent Assembly. As the unarmed masses approached the tsar's palace, many of them carrying icons and crosses, Nicholas II ordered soldiers to fire on the crowd.[3]

More than a thousand men, women, and children died under the palace windows, and other thousands were brutally injured by gunfire and by the hoofs and swords of the cavalry. The tsar had signed his own death warrant with the blood of the people. Its execution was delayed some thirteen years, but from that "Bloody Sunday," January 22, 1905, the end of the Russian autocracy was clearly foreshadowed.

For "Bloody Sunday" destroyed the illusion among the masses that the tsar was a kindly man, quite different from his bureaucrats and the heartless exploiters. This unprovoked attack on unarmed workers and their families raised the unrest among workers and peasants to a new stage of development.

Industrial workers were in the forefront of the struggle but all classes were involved. Bourgeois liberals who had been reduced to inert despair by the tsar's curt refusal to consider any discussion of the mildest kind of constitution awoke again to political activity. Peasants from Poland to eastern Siberia renewed their attacks on the landlords. And in the strikes which spread to all the chief industrial areas political demands were increasingly interwoven with the economic demands.

Unrest appeared in the armed forces.[4] In the badly managed war both soldiers and sailors learned more than they had known before of the incompetence, corruption, and brutality of those who lorded it over them, and the survivors came home in a rebellious mood. Many regiments proved "unreliable" for suppressing disorders. Historic mutinies occurred on the cruiser *Potemkin* near Odessa (June, 1905), among sailors and soldiers at Kronstadt near Petersburg (October, 1905), among naval forces at Sebastopol (November, 1905), and (in the following July) at Sveaborg and again at Kronstadt.

Mass struggles were increasingly serious, involving armed resistance to attacks on strikers and the burning of over eleven hundred landlords' mansions.[5] October, 1905, saw a general political strike in all industrial centres and December armed insurrection in Moscow, followed by uprisings in Sormovo, Rostov-on-Don, the Donets Basin, Kharkov and other cities.[6] For a few weeks in the autumn of 1905 the workers' forces were so strong that illegal revolutionary leaflets and papers were openly published without interference by the tsarist censor.[7] And while the tsar's advisers were hesitating to allow an elected parliament, workers in Ivanovo-Voznesensk, St. Petersburg, and other cities were setting up enlarged strike committees or councils (Soviets) of their own as "a fighting organisation for the achievement of definite aims." [8]

"In several cities in Russia, these *Soviets of Workers' Deputies* began more and more to play the role of a provisional revolutionary government, the role of organs and leaders of rebellion."[9]

"Revolutionary power, not of intellectuals, not of a group of conspirators, but of workers and peasants has already taken place in Russia, has already been actually realised in the course of our revolution."[10]

Let us go behind these briefly sketched facts and see how Lenin analysed the alignment of forces in 1905-07 and the role and development of the peasant movement. What was the outcome of the Revolution? How did the events of those years affect Lenin's conception of his party's agrarian programme?

Nature of 1905 Revolution

The Revolution of 1905 was not a socialist revolution. It was an attack on autocracy and the survivals of landlord feudal power over the peasants. It was a fight for political democracy and the free development of capitalism. But this Russian revolution differed from the earlier bourgeois-democratic revolutions in England and western Europe in the fact that in Russia this political struggle grew out of industrial conflict, and the working class played, for the first time, the leading role in a revolutionary attack on feudal aristocracy.

"The peculiar feature of the Russian Revolution is that in its social content it was a *bourgeois-democratic* revolution but in its methods of struggle it was a *proletarian* revolution. It was a bourgeois-democratic revolution since the aim toward which it strove directly and which it could reach directly with the aid of its own forces was a democratic republic, an eight-hour day and the confiscation of the immense estates of the nobility....

"At the same time the Russian Revolution was also a proletarian revolution, not only in the sense that the proletariat was the leading force, the vanguard of the movement, but also in the sense that the specifically proletarian means of struggle—namely, the strike—was the principal instrument employed for rousing the masses and the most characteristic phenomenon in the wave-like rise of decisive events."[11]

In the course of the struggle, the peasants also developed a new political consciousness. For many years Russia had seen outbursts of peasant anger, with attacks on individual landlords. And revolutionists of one or another group had tried to focus the peasants' *feelings* of revolt on a political purpose. But none of the earlier movements of terrorists and intellectuals had been able to call forth a people's revolution. Now the peasants' pent-up resentment and hatred against the landlords, the bureaucrats, and the police were released as a mass revolutionary force.

"This was achieved only by the revolutionary struggle of the proletariat. Only the waves of mass strikes that swept over the whole country, coupled with the severe lessons of the imperialist Russo-Japanese War, roused the broad masses of peasants from their lethargic slumber. The word 'striker' acquired an entirely new meaning among the peasants: it signified a rebel, a revolutionary, a term previously expressed by the word 'student.' As, however, the 'student' belonged to the middle class, to the 'learned,' to the 'gentry,' he was alien to the people. On the other hand, a 'striker' was of the people; he belonged to the exploited class; when deported from St. Petersburg, he often returned to the village where he told his fellow-villagers of the conflagration which had broken out in the cities and which was to destroy the capitalists and nobility. *A new type appeared in the Russian village —the class conscious, young peasant.* [My italics.—*A.R.*] He associated with 'strikers,' he read newspapers, he told the peasants about events in the cities, explained to his fellow-villagers the meaning of political demands, and called upon them to fight against the big landlords, the priests, and the government officials." [12]

Peasants from twenty-two provinces created in 1905 the All-Russsian Peasant Union as a mass organisation opposed to the reactionary nobility.[13] The peasants demanded civil liberty, a Constituent Assembly, and abolition of private property in land. For several months the Union was a definite force but its influence declined as the peasants turned to the revolutionary parties of Social-Democrats and Trudoviks.* In the Dumas † of 1906 and 1907, peasant delegates stood consistently for "Land to the peasants!" and the setting up of peasant committees elected by secret ballot to administer the distribution of land.

To Lenin the political leadership assumed by the workers and the awakening of political consciousness among the peasants were the most important aspects of the 1905 Revolution. For he looked upon the fight against autocracy and the survivals of serfdom as preliminary to the struggle against capitalism. The more genuine the democracy achieved under capitalism, the greater is the workers' freedom to defend their class interests and move toward socialism.

Industrial workers were already showing a class-conscious solidarity which was finding organized expression and would be prepared to participate effectively in a democratic government. No other class except the peasants could be expected to move relentlessly against the great landlords whose estates were the economic bulwark of autocracy. Some liberal landlords, the industrial capitalists, the zemstvo officials, social reformers, and all other groups of the Russian intelligentsia opposed the autocracy, but Lenin emphasised repeatedly that none of these classes could be trusted to destroy the property rights and the political power of the landlords. Their political hopes would be satisfied by a limited "democracy" which placed the centre of power in their own hands and gave limited representation to the masses.

Revolutionary Role of Workers and Peasants

Workers and peasants must not let themselves be drawn along as subordinate to the propertied classes and their liberal spokesmen. They must struggle, by every means, to take power. And as the vast

* From the word *trud*, meaning toil. Peasant representatives in the Duma, imbued with Populist and Socialist-Revolutionary ideas.

† Frightened by the revolutionary uprising in December, 1905, the tsar convoked a Duma (parliament) intended to draw the revolutionary forces into a "safe" channel. Less than half the population was allowed to vote, and then only as the first step in indirect election of Duma members. Voters were so grouped in four curias (landlords, bourgeoisie, peasants, workers), that the delegates representing millions of workers and peasants were a tiny minority in the Duma.

majority of the population, they must place their will above the will of the propertied classes.

This power, of workers and peasants, could be maintained only if the peasants succeeded in their deepest desire and obtained through revolutionary struggle free possession of the landlords' land.

"The question of the method of applying the agrarian reform is of immense importance, for the method of application decides the character of the reform, concretely and actually how far it shall go. In this question too (as well as in many others), the Narodniks [Populists] taught that we should devote our attention mainly to the economic gain, ignoring or underestimating the political aspect of the matter. This point of view, natural for a petty bourgeois, logical in an 'independent farmer,' is absolutely out of place in a Social-Democrat. From the point of view of a Social-Democrat, shifts within the classes and categories of independent farmers and proprietors are of no consequence unless they are accompanied by a political gain that facilitates the class struggle of the proletariat.... The Social-Democrats will never forget that the ruling classes always and everywhere try to divide and corrupt the toilers with economic sops. In the sphere of agrarian reform this policy is particularly easy for them, and particularly skilfully applied by them.

"Therefore, we must insist all the more definitely and categorically on the *basic* demand of our agrarian programme: the establishment of revolutionary peasant committees that will themselves bring about really radical (and not 'radical' in the landlords' sense) agrarian reforms." [14]

Expropriation would completely undermine the power of the feudal nobility, and it would open the way to a much wider and more rapid development of independent farming. The forces of capitalism would be released from the hindering restriction of feudal survivals, and this would of itself be a definite historical advance. Wide extension of independent small farming, among peasants who had obtained their land through asserting their revolutionary will, would provide a relatively secure defence of genuine political democracy during the brief period that would precede the socialist revolution. Instead of riveting on the new bourgeois-democratic state the domination of the old large landowners, the economic basis for such reactionary political power would be destroyed. The new petty bourgeoisie in the village would be *temporarily* a mass bulwark against revival of the old reaction.

Of course this would mean rapid expansion of petty-bourgeois capitalism on the land. Lenin had none of the illusions constantly propagated by the Populists and their successor groups that any "fair" distribution of land could give a permanent equality among farmers producing commodities for capitalist markets. As capitalist farming developed, a sharper class struggle within the village would inescapably follow.

But already in 1905, Lenin was convinced that a successful bourgeois-democratic revolution dominated by workers and peasants could move rapidly forward to the struggle for socialism. In this the working class would take the lead. And most of the small peasants could be drawn into the socialist revolution as allies of the working class. Middle peasants, independent small producers who had not been able to expand as commercial farmers exploiting wage workers, must be won to a friendly neutrality in the struggle and, ultimately, to active participation in the building of socialism.

If the working class failed now to support to the limit the peasants' attacks on feudal landlordism, the workers would find it infinitely more difficult to win the support of the small and middle peasants in the later stages of the Revolution.

"The peasants should know that the Red Banner, which has been raised in the cities, is the banner of struggle for the immediate and urgent demands not only of the industrial and agricultural workers, but also of millions and tens of millions of small farmers." [15]

Results of 1905

The Revolution of 1905 was defeated. Peasant actions were too scattered and too unorganised. Military unrest was too limited. Among the workers, the gap was too great between the advanced sections of the working class and the less industrialised areas; the vanguard was weakened before the others rallied to the struggle. And workers were confused and held back by the vacillating policies of the Mensheviks (Minority) whose disagreements with the Leninist Bolshevik (Majority) group made a division within the Social-Democratic Party.[16]

The autocratic power of the tsar was temporarily shaken and was compelled to grant some concessions. But no Constituent Assembly was elected or convoked. The Duma (parliament) created by tsarist decree was granted limited legislative power, subject to veto by the tsar's appointed council of ministers. It was arbitrarily dissolved at the will of the tsar. Its members were elected by class groupings which gave preponderant voice to the landlords and capitalists and very meagre representation to peasants and workers. Delegates supposedly enjoyed the right of free public discussion, but those who voiced revolutionary ideas were arrested and punished.

"The people are convinced *by experience,* that a popular representative body is *naught* if it is not vested with full power, if it is convoked by the old regime, if the old regime remains intact side by side with it. The objective course of events is now bringing into the forefront, not the question of how the laws or the constitution are to be worded, but the question of *power,* of real power. Laws and deputies are naught if they possess no power. That is what the Cadet * Duma has *taught* the people." [17]

Tsarist gestures of "democracy" were accompanied by other measures of extreme repression. To divide the masses, the tsar set up patriotic organisations—popularly known as "Black Hundreds"—which utilised the police and hired gunmen to carry out mob violence against Jews and active revolutionists. "It is calculated that in 100 cities at that time 4,000 were killed and 10,000 were mutilated." [18] As the mass revolutionary force gradually declined from its high point in December, 1905, its leaders were hunted down and subjected to brutal punishment. So many were executed that the hangman's noose was nicknamed "Stolypin's necktie" for the tsar's new Minister of the In-

* Cadets (Constitutional-Democratic Party), the party of the liberal bourgeoisie, opposed tsarist autocracy and stood for parliamentary government.

terior brought in to specialise in combining liberal gestures with brutal repression.

To divide and pacify the peasants, Stolypin handed them (August to November, 1906), a series of agrarian reforms which looked well to the unthinking. A peasant could now legally withdraw from the village commune and acquire full title to his allotment. Part of the state lands and of the lands belonging to the imperial family were transferred to the state-owned Peasants' Bank for *sale* to peasants. And credit for buying land was made available by this government bank. As Lenin wrote in 1907:

"The forcible breaking up of the commune by the laws of November 22 (9), 1906, etc., the setting up and subsidising of homesteads are not a chimera, as frivolous, prattling, democratic journalists sometimes declare them to be; they are the realities of economic progress *based upon the preservation of the power and the interests of the landlords.* It is an incredibly slow and incredibly painful method for the wide masses of the peasantry and for the proletariat, but it is the only possible way for capitalist Russia if the peasant agrarian revolution is not victorious." (My italics.—*A.R.*) [19]

Actually the Stolypin reforms *gave* nothing. They merely served to separate the poorest peasants from their land and to increase the holdings of the kulaks whose loyalty to the old regime was thus assured. This hastened the process of capitalist development in agriculture with no interval of temporary relief to the poorer peasants. Instead their misery was definitely increased.

With the defeat of the Revolution of 1905, the liberal and revolutionary forces were more than ever sharply divided from one another. The stalwart compact group of Bolsheviks lost many faint-hearted friends. But Lenin's faith in the strength of the masses and the development of greater struggles and ultimate victory never wavered. Looking back ten years later upon this first revolution, Lenin summed up the permanent gains won even in defeat:

"Only the struggle educates the exploited class. Only the struggle discloses to it the magnitude of its own power, widens its horizon, enhances its abilities, clarifies its mind, forges its will; and, therefore, even reactionaries had to admit that the year 1905, the year of struggle, the 'mad year,' definitely buried patriarchal Russia."[20]

And during the darkest period of reaction (in February, 1909) Lenin gave memorable expression to his faith in the future:

"Let the liberals and terrified intellectuals lose heart after the first genuinely mass battle for freedom, let them repeat like cowards: don't go where you have been beaten before, don't tread that fatal path again. The class conscious proletariat will answer them: the great wars in history, the great revolutionary problems were solved only by the advanced classes returning to the attack again and again; and they achieved victory after having learned the lessons of defeat. Defeated armies learn well. The revolutionary classes of Russia have been defeated in their first campaign, but the revolutionary situation remains. In new forms and by other ways, sometimes much more slowly than we would wish, the revolutionary crisis is approaching once more, is maturing again. We must carry out the prolonged task of preparing larger masses for the revolutionary crisis; this preparation must be more serious, taking into consideration the higher and more concrete tasks; and the more successfully we fulfil this task, the more certain will be our victory in the new struggle.

"The Russian proletariat may be proud of the fact that in 1905, under its leadership, a nation of slaves for the first time transformed itself into a mighty host attacking tsarism, into an army of the revolution. And now the same proletariat will know how to carry out persistently, staunchly, and patiently the work of educating and training new cadres of a mightier revolutionary force."[21]

CHAPTER V

The Land Question in 1905-1907

"EVASION or lack of principle in theoretical questions precisely in a revolutionary period is equivalent to complete ideological bankruptcy, for especially necessary now [1905] is a well-thought out and firm world-view, in order that the socialist may control events instead of events controlling him."[1]

The rise of the peasant movement in the Revolution of 1905 made it essential for the Social-Democratic Party to clarify its position on the land hunger of the peasants. In demanding return to the peasants of lands cut from their holdings in 1861, was the programme of 1903 setting a limit to the revolutionary land measures which the party should support in the struggle against autocracy? Or would the party back the peasants (now, in a bourgeois-democratic revolution) even up to confiscation of all the great landowners' properties?

In the discussion preceding the Third Congress of the party (held in London, in the spring of 1905), Lenin emphasised that the party should support the peasants up to general confiscation of land.

But how the land thus taken over by the revolutionary people should be disposed of was a separate question. Should it be divided among the more than ten million peasant households as owners, in what the Narodniks (Populists) had called a "Black Redistribution"? * Or should all private property in land be abolished, even under capitalism, leaving the peasants free to lease what they wanted from the state?

* A section of the Populists had advocated confiscation of large landed property and such free distribution of it among peasant owners as would (temporarily) equalise the peasant holdings.

On these questions Lenin believed that no programmatic statement should be attempted until the trend of the revolution and the balance of political power were made clearer by the actual course of events. For the moment it was far more important to develop revolutionary organs of power—in this case, peasant committees—than to set in advance an exact economic programme.

Revolutionary Peasant Committees

Lenin proposed that the Third Congress of the party should amend its programme, reaffirming the principles set forth in 1903 and making clear that the demand for return of the *otrezki* was not intended as a limiting maximum but as a first step against the landlords. His statement published shortly before the Congress is so illuminating that we quote it at length:

"I doubt if anyone will deny that it is not our business to dabble in schemes of land reforms, or that we must strengthen the ties with the proletariat and *support* the peasant movement, without losing sight of the property-owning tendencies of the peasant proprietor—tendencies whose antagonism to the proletariat will be revealed the more rapidly and pronouncedly the quicker the advance of the revolution.

"On the other hand, it is plain that the present revolutionary moment calls for a perfectly clear-cut and concrete slogan. The formation of *revolutionary peasant* committees must become such a slogan, and our party's agrarian programme quite rightly advanced it. The peasant movement is simply ridden by ignorance and prejudice, and it would be most dangerous to foster any illusions on that score. The ignorance of the peasant finds expression, first of all, in his failure to understand the *political* aspect of the movement—his failure to understand, for instance, that without radical democratic changes in the *whole* political structure of the *entire state* it is absolutely impossible to make any lasting progress in the direction of wider ownership of the land. The peasant needs land, and his revolutionary feeling, his instinctive, primitive sense of democracy *cannot* find expression in any other way than by laying hands on the landed estates. No one will try to deny this, of course.... The Social-Democrats can, of course, have no objection if the rebellious muzhik 'strikes the landlord the final blow' and takes away *all* his land, but they cannot lapse into adventurism in a proletarian programme, they cannot let the class struggle against the property owners be obscured by the rosy prospects of such changes in the structure of land ownership (even though these changes may be democratic) as would merely reshuffle the classes or categories of property owners....

"The fact that I do not point out any concrete methods for expropriating the land may appear to be a defect in my formulation. But is it, properly speaking, a defect?

"Social-Democrats who have written on the agrarian question have pointed out repeatedly how inappropriate it would be for us to indulge in flights of the imagination on this score, since the chief measure of an agrarian reform—the nationalisation of the land—would *in a police-ruled state* necessarily be perverted and serve only to obscure the class nature of the movement. Yet all other measures for recasting agrarian relations will, under a capitalist system, be only an approach to nationalisation; they will be only partial measures, only a few of the possible measures, *i.e.*, measures to which the Social-Democratic Party has no intention whatever of *confining itself*. At the present time the Social-Democrats are opposed to nationalisation, and even the Socialist-Revolutionaries, under the influence of our criticism, have become much more cautious on the subject (compare their draft programme with their former 'dash and daring').

"But the point is that the revolutionary movement leads us toward a democratic republic, which, like the abolition of the standing army, etc., constitutes one of our immediate demands.

"Under a democratic republic, with the people armed and other measures of a like republican character already carried out, the Social-Democrats cannot foreswear the nationalisation of the land and tie their own hands on this question. And so, the defect in the formulation I propose is only an apparent one. In reality, however, this formulation provides a consistent class slogan for the present moment—and an absolutely concrete slogan at that—leaving at the same time ample scope for those 'revolutionary-democratic' measures which may prove necessary or desirable in the event of a favourable development of our revolution. At the present time and also in the future, pending the complete victory of the peasant uprising, a revolutionary slogan must necessarily take into account the antagonism between *the peasant and the landlord;* and the point on the *otrezki* quite rightly emphasised this circumstance. On the other hand, every kind of 'nationalisation,' 'transfer of rents,' 'socialisation,' etc., ignores and obscures this characteristic antagonism, and therein lies their chief defect.

"At the same time the formulation I propose enlarges the aims of the revolutionary peasant committees to include 'recasting all rural relationships in general along democratic lines.' The formation of peasant committees is made a slogan in our programme, which correctly describes them as *peasant committees, i.e.,* as representing a social estate, for oppression by a social estate can be destroyed only by the whole of the lower, oppressed estate.... If we could succeed, even in only a few instances, in linking up the effective revolutionary measures taken by the peasantry to ameliorate their position (confiscation of grain, livestock, *land*) with the formation and activity of *peasant committees* and with the full endorsement of these committees by the revolutionary parties (or, under especially favourable conditions, by a Provisional Revolutionary Government), then we could consider that the fight to gain the support of the peasants for a democratic republic was won. Unless the peasantry is thus won over, all their revolutionary steps will be very insecure, and all their gains will easily be wrested from them by the social classes in power." [2]

At the Third Congress these ideas were briefly stated in a resolution which did not formally revise the party's programme but set up new tasks in relation to the peasants. It committed the party to support all revolutionary actions which the peasants might take against the landlords, including demonstrations, mass political strikes (against taxes and military service), and direct confiscation of land. Party organisations were advised to organise peasant committees and, even then, to encourage independent organisation of the rural proletariat, with the city workers, in close relation with party members.[3]

Differences Within Lenin's Party

This Third Congress of the Russian Social-Democratic Labour Party was boycotted by the anti-Leninist Minority (Mensheviks). But the Mensheviks at a conference of their own also voted support of the peasant movement even up to confiscation of all landlords' land.[4] The differences between the two sections of the party in the spring of 1905 did not include serious disagreement on the immediate agrarian programme.

As the revolutionary events of 1905 developed, the extreme importance of trying to restore unity within the party was recognised by both groups and a "Unity Congress" was arranged which met in Stockholm in the spring of 1906. Meantime, it had also become imperative to define the party position more exactly both as to confiscation of land and the decisions that would necessarily follow. Four different viewpoints set forth by the Social-Democrats during 1905 were analysed by Lenin before the "Unity Congress" began.

A few members opposed confiscation. They argued that breaking up of large estates would be a reactionary measure. They wanted to retain the old demand for return to the peasants of the *otrezki*. But Lenin believed that events demanded explicit support of general confiscation of landlords' estates.

"We are told that large estates are of a progressive capitalist type. To confiscate them and divide them is a reactionary measure, a step backward to small economy....

"Such a view seems to us incorrect.

"We must take cognizance of the general and ultimate result of the contemporary peasant movement, and not dissolve it piece by piece. In general and on the whole the present landlord economy in Russia rests more on serf bondage than on a capitalist system of economy. He who denies this cannot explain the current broad and deep revolutionary peasant movement in Russia. Our mistake in setting forth the demand for return of the *otrezki* [cut-off lands] consisted in underestimation of the breadth and depth of the democratic, really bourgeois-democratic movement among the peasantry. It is stupid to persist in this mistake now when the revolution has taught us much. For the development of capitalism, confiscation of all landlords' land will give an incomparably greater plus than that minus which would come from breaking up of large capitalist agriculture. The breaking up will not destroy capitalism and will not hold it back but will, to a tremendous degree, cleanse, make general, expand, and strengthen the basis for its (capitalism's) new development. We have always said that to limit the sweep of the peasant movement is in no sense the business of the Social-Democrats, and at the present time refusal of the demand for confiscation of all landlords' land would be a clear limiting of the sweep of a crystallised social movement."[5]

Other groups within the party accepted the demand for confiscation but were divided on the disposition to be made of land taken from the landlords. Some stood for a "Black Redistribution," to enlarge and roughly equalise the private holdings of the peasants. Others stood for nationalisation of all land. A third group, which included leading Mensheviks, proposed to combine private property in land for peasants and other small owners with the transfer of confiscated estates to public ownership by the *zemstvo* authorities.

This third proposal won general support among the Mensheviks and drew the sharpest criticism from Lenin. In his opinion, "Black Redistribution" and nationalisation were both reasonable, clear-cut measures, on which decision would be shaped by the development of the peasant movement and the balance of political forces as the revolution progressed. But this so-called "municipalisation" he considered a useless hybrid. In riddling the arguments offered by its supporters, Lenin showed up the proposal as an unrealistic compromise.

Peasants aroused to the point of confiscating the great estates would not relish any setting apart of this land as a separate category from their own. And why the local government instead of the national? Such revolutionary action against the landlords could not succeed unless the old autocratic state had been destroyed. Confiscation must presuppose a genuine political revolution. To argue that the *zemstvo* governments would be more democratic than the national government meant, in Lenin's opinion, a failure to understand the essence of the conflict.

If the national government could not be trusted to express the will of the revolutionary workers and peasants, the estates would certainly be restored to their former owners and all talk of *any* disposal of them, either by redistribution or public ownership, would be merely idle chatter.[6]

This programme of "municipalisation" was, however, adopted at the Fourth ("Unity") Congress of the party in the spring of 1906. For at this Congress, the Menshevik (Minority) group mustered a slight majority among the delegates. Many Bolsheviks had been seized after the December uprising. The Mensheviks had swelled their ranks during 1905 with new recruits from among the intellectuals, totally undeveloped in revolutionary understanding.[7] Later events supported the contention of the Bolsheviks that the balance of delegates at this Congress of 1906 did not fairly represent the relative strength of the two groups.

Lenin's criticism of "municipalisation" continued, but at the Fifth Congress of the party (May, 1907) this section of the programme was not revised, although the Bolshevik group then carried a clear majority of the votes. In Russia, the crest of the revolutionary wave had passed and the mass forces of revolution were in retreat. Problems of policy in a victorious revolution were less pressing than those concerned with fruitful activity in a period of extreme reaction. So the land question was not acted upon by the Congress.

Which Kind of Capitalist Development?

Throughout this period, when socialist revolution was not yet on the order of the day, Lenin approached the land question with certain basic principles in mind. Russian agriculture was still on the borderline between feudal-serf methods and capitalist methods of production and exploitation. Looking forward to socialism as the ultimate goal for popular struggle, he saw that more rapid development of capitalist farming would raise the level of production and extend and clarify the class struggle through which the socialist revolution could be accomplished. But this development of capitalist farming might follow either one of two paths. Semi-feudal landlord farming might be transformed to large-scale capitalist farming as the exploitation of semi-serf peasants yielded gradually to the exploitation of wage workers. Or peasant agriculture might have free development as small-scale independent farming, with a great expansion of the rural petty bourgeoisie. Either way, the peasant commune was doomed. Either way, a sharper division between very poor peasants and petty-capitalist peasants would result.

"The struggle is being waged principally around the feudal latifundia [great estates] which are the most outstanding embodiment and the strongest mainstay of the survivals of serfdom in Russia. The development of commodity production and capitalism will inevitably put an end to these survivals. In this respect, Russia has only one path before her, that of bourgeois development.

"Yet there may be two forms of this development. The survivals of serfdom may fall away either as a result of the transformation of the landlord estates or as a result of the abolition of the landlord latifundia, *i.e.*, either by reform or by revolution. Bourgeois development may pursue its course having at its head big landlord economy, which will gradually become more and more bourgeois and gradually substitute bourgeois methods of exploitation for feudal methods. It may also pursue its course having at its head small peasant economy which, in a revolutionary way, will remove the 'abscess' of feudal latifundia from the social organism and then freely develop without them along the road of capitalist economy.

"These two paths of objectively possible bourgeois development may be described as the Prussian path and the American path, respectively. In the first case, feudal landlordism gradually evolves into bourgeois, *Junker* landlordism, which dooms the peasants to decades of most painful expropriation and bondage, while at the same time a small minority of *Grossbauern* (big peasants) arises. In the second case there is no landlordism, or else it is broken up by the revolution, as a result of which the feudal estates are confiscated and divided into small farms. In this case the peasant predominates, becomes the exclusive agent of agriculture and evolves into the capitalist farmer. In the first case the outstanding content of the evolution is the transformation of serfdom into usury and capitalist exploitation on the land of the feudal lords—the landlords—the *Junkers*. In the second case the main background is the transformation of the patriarchal peasant into a bourgeois farmer."[8]

For the peasants themselves and for the road toward socialist revolution the choice between these two paths was immensely important. Landlord capitalism would mean increasing misery for the rural masses. Free expansion of small-scale independent farming would mean a widespread improvement in the peasants' standard of living. Landlord capitalism would find adequate political expression in mild reform, a strictly limited "democracy." Free development of independent peasant agriculture would be impossible without a revolutionary change, carried through by the masses themselves and placing the workers and peasants in control of the state.

Revolutionary forces in 1905 were battling for capitalist development without landlords. Definitely opposed to peasant capitalism were Stolypin's agrarian reforms. These served to clear the path for landlord capitalism, separating poor peasants from the land and strengthening the small class of kulaks as a buttress supporting the landlords' power. Writing of the Stolypin programme, Lenin said:

"There can be no doubt that this follows the line of capitalist evolution, facilitates and pushes forward this evolution, hastens the expropriation of the peasantry, the break-up of the commune and the creation of a peasant bourgeoisie. Without a doubt, this legislation is progressive in the scientific economic sense.

"But does this mean that Social-Democrats should 'support' this legislation? Not at all. Such might be the reasoning only of vulgar Marxism. . . . No; in order to facilitate the development of the productive forces (the highest criterion of social progress) we must give our support not to bourgeois evolution of the landlord type, but to bourgeois evolution of the peasant type. The former implies the utmost preservation of bondage and serfdom (remodeled in a bourgeois fashion), the least rapid development of the productive forces and the retarded development of capitalism; it implies infinitely greater misery and suffering, exploitation and oppression for the large masses of the peasantry and, consequently, also for the proletariat. The second type implies the most rapid development of the productive forces and the best conditions of existence for the mass of the peasantry possible under the commodity system of production."[9]

If landlord power were destroyed by the revolutionary struggle of peasants and workers, and agriculture was to develop in the "American" way of small-scale independent farming, nationalisation of land would give a sounder, broader base for this development than any "Black Redistribution" of private property in land. Lenin's firm conviction on this point carried forward the reasoning of Marx and was tied in with his analysis of rent. But its economic correctness could not, in practical development, be separated from political issues which were of paramount importance in working toward socialist revolution.

Conditions for Nationalisation of Land

Already in 1902, Lenin had referred to nationalisation of land "in the bourgeois and not in the socialist sense" and stated that "in principle we fully endorse it. It goes without saying that at a definite stage of the revolution we shall not fail to advance it."

"However, to advance the demand for land nationalisation under the autocracy, or even under a semi-constitutional monarchy, would be fundamentally wrong. For as long as we lack firmly established and deep-rooted democratic institutions, such a demand would be more likely to turn our minds towards absurd experiments in state socialism, than to give a stimulus 'to the free development of the class struggle in the countryside.' "[10]

Even in September, 1905, Lenin thought that a demand for nationalisation would distract attention from the political revolution which must precede such a measure.

"Indeed, unlike the petty-bourgeois Socialist-Revolutionaries, we lay the main emphasis *at the present time* on the revolutionary-democratic aspect of the peasant uprising and the special organisation of the rural proletariat into a class party. The crux of the question now is not the projects of 'Black Redistribution,' or nationalisation, but to make the peasants conscious of the necessity of securing the *revolutionary* break-up of the old order and of their breaking it up." [11]

Six months later, in the discussion that preceded the so-called "Unity Congress" of the party, Lenin agreed that distribution of land to peasants as private owners would be a generally progressive measure, but he held that the political situation now justified a conditional endorsement of nationalisation.

"We wholly and unconditionally agree that a division of landowners' lands would be at the present time, in general and on the whole, a definitely progressive measure both in the economic and in the political sense. We also agree, further, that in a bourgeois society the class of small owners is, *under certain conditions,* 'a more solid bulwark of democracy than a class of tenants dependent upon a state which (even though constitutional) represents the police power of a class.'

"But we believe that to *limit ourselves* to these considerations at the present moment of democratic revolution in Russia, to limit ourselves to maintaining the old position of 1902, would be completely to leave out of the reckoning the essentially changed social-class and political situation. *Zarya* [a Bolshevik journal] pointed out in August, 1902 (article by Plekhanov), that here *Moscow Vedomosti* [a monarchist-landlord newspaper] was defending nationalisation and carried through the unquestionably correct idea that demand for nationalisation of land is far from being always and everywhere revolutionary....

"Unquestionable that now the situation of affairs is essentially changed as compared with 1902. Revolution rose high in 1905 and is now preparing forces for a new advance. Of defense of nationalisation of land (in any serious sense) there can be no discussion by *Moscow Vedomosti.* On the contrary, defense of the inviolability of private property in land has become the basic motif in the speeches of Nicholas II and the outcries of Gringmut [editor of *Vedomosti*] and Co....

"This movement, like every deep popular movement, has already called forth and continues to call forth tremendous revolutionary enthusiasm and revolutionary energy of the peasantry. In their struggle against landlord ownership of land, against landlord possession of land, peasants will inevitably move and have already moved, in the person of their most advanced representatives, to the demand for abolition of all private ownership of land in general.

"That the idea of ownership of land by the people as a whole is now circulating very widely among the peasantry cannot be doubted in the least. And it is certain also that, in spite of all the backwardness of the peasantry, in spite of all the reactionary-utopian elements in their longings, this idea, in general and on the whole, has a revolutionary-democratic character.

"Social-Democrats must cleanse this idea of its reactionary and petty-bourgeois socialist perversions—about this there is no dispute. But Social-Democrats would be committing a serious error if they threw overboard this whole demand, not having been able to single out its revolutionary-democratic aspects. We must with all sharpness and decisiveness tell the peasant that nationalisation of land is a bourgeois measure, that it is useful *only* under stated political conditions, but to come out with *bare* opposition to this measure in general would be for us Socialists a short-sighted policy in relation to the peasant mass. And not only a short-sighted policy but also a theoretical distortion of Marxism which has established with fullest precision that nationalisation of land is possible, is conceivable, even in a bourgeois society, that it will not hold back but will strengthen the development of capitalism, that it is the *maximum* bourgeois-democratic reform in the field of agrarian relationships."[12]

Lenin proposed a revision of the agrarian programme which was adopted by the majority of the agrarian commission of the party and recommended to the "Unity Congress." * This draft (except its closing paragraph) was rejected by the Congress, which adopted instead the Mensheviks' municipalisation programme previously described. The draft proposed by Lenin and the agrarian commission of the party included a demand for nationalisation of land, *provided* "a decisive victory of the present revolution in Russia fully assures sovereignty

* Text of Lenin's draft is given in Appendix A.

of the people, that is, creates a republic and a completely democratic state order."[13]

Lenin did not propose that the party's programme should define the difference between the "reactionary-utopian elements" in the peasants' idea of nationalisation and the Social-Democratic concept of it as the freest possible basis for petty-bourgeois farming and the development of capitalist agriculture. But this had been fully developed in his own writings and was clearly understood by the Bolshevik group.

In a socialist revolution, nationalisation of land gives the basis for socialised farming. In a bourgeois-democratic revolution, nationalisation of land eliminates the landlord and all private ownership of land but leaves undisturbed the farmer as an individual producer of commodities. The peasants desired nationalisation primarily because they recognised it as the only way to destroy the confusion of various kinds of tenure prevailing in most of European Russia. The poorer peasants had little or no genuine ownership to lose. The better-off peasants had assorted patches of land which held back efficient production.

"The land that is now cultivated by a more or less prosperous Russian peasant, *i.e.,* by one who is really capable of becoming transformed into a free farmer in the event of a favourable outcome of the revolution, consists partly of his own allotment, partly of an allotment he has rented from his communal peasant neighbour, partly, perhaps, of land rented on long-term lease from the state, of land leased annually from the landlord, of land purchased from the bank, and so forth. Capitalism demands that all these distinctions of categories be dropped, that all farming on the land be built up exclusively in accordance with the new conditions and requirements of the market, the requirements of agriculture. Land nationalisation fulfils this requirement by the revolutionary peasant method; at one stroke it completely relieves the people of the burden of the decayed lumber of mediæval forms of landownership. There must be neither landlordism nor peasant allotments, there must be only the new, free land holding—such is the slogan of the radical peasant."[14]

Land and the Peasant Problem

Lenin did not expect nationalisation of land to solve even temporarily the problems of the very poorest, "horseless" peasants who were, in 1905, about one-fourth of the total number in European Russia.[15] For the rest of the rural population, the "equality" the peasants expected from nationalisation of land would be only approximate and very temporary. Fair access to a larger and better acreage would, however, raise the level of production and the standard of living for all who owned any animals and other equipment. And the Populists with their slogan of "Black Redistribution," and their successors, the Socialist-Revolutionaries, who wanted nationalisation of land, had encouraged the peasants to look for the perpetuation of a petty bourgeois, small-producer paradise.

Building on the heritage of Marx, Lenin rejected such a paradise as a reactionary utopia.[16] He showed that such rough equality among peasants as might be achieved by the revolutionary overthrowing of landlordism would give place to a new inequality among free and independent farmers, pushed by commodity production toward a higher stage of capitalist development. Instead of acreage, capital for farm equipment would be the obviously decisive factor in expansion and prosperity or failure and poverty. The class struggle within the village would be clear-cut and sharp.

This development, which would help to prepare the way for the socialist revolution, would go forward most rapidly if the land were removed from any form of private ownership. As tenants of a genuinely democratic state the farmers would have secure possession of their land. They would not have to withhold capital from actual farming operations in order to buy title as owners. Rental payments would be lower than before as the element of absolute rent, based on the landlord's monopoly control of land, would disappear. Only a differential rent would be paid to the state. This would be related to the quality of land, advantages of location, etc., and would represent, in general, the difference between an average rate of profit and the returns on the more favourably situated farms.

"Nationalisation means abolition of absolute rent, lowering of prices for bread, guarantee of maximum freedom of competition and freedom of penetration of capital into agriculture." [17]

Private property in land has been everywhere a barrier to the fullest development of capitalism in agriculture. It has involved "mortgage and usury" which Lenin as a true Marxist characterises as "forms in which capital overcame the obstacles which private property in land creates for free penetration of capital into agriculture." [18] This point is so basic and at the same time so alien to much current thinking on farm problems that we quote at length from Lenin's statement on the nature of rent and the true significance of nationalisation of land in relation to capitalist development.

"Marx's theory distinguishes two forms of rent: differential rent and absolute rent. The first springs from the limited nature of land, its occupation by capitalist farms, irrespective of whether the land is owned, or of the form of ownership. Among the various farms there are inevitable differences arising out of differences in the fertility of the soil, in distance from markets, and in the productivity of additional investments of capital in the land. For the sake of brevity these differences may be summed up (without, however, forgetting that these differences spring from different sources) as the differences between better and worse soils. To proceed. The price of production of agricultural produce is determined by the conditions of production, not on the average soil, but on the worst soil, because the produce from the best soil alone is insufficient to meet the demand. The difference between the individual price of production and the highest price of production is differential rent. (We will remind the reader that by price of production Marx means the capital expended on the production of the product, plus average rate of profit on capital.)

"Differential rent inevitably arises in capitalist agriculture, even if the private ownership of land is completely abolished. Under the private ownership of land, rent is appropriated by the landowner; for the competition between capitals compels the tenant farmer to be satisfied with the average rate of profit on capital. When the private ownership of land is abolished, this rent is appropriated by the state.

This rent cannot be abolished as long as the capitalist mode of production exists.

"Absolute rent arises from the private ownership of the land. This rent contains an element of monopoly, an element of monopoly price.* Private ownership of land hinders free competition, hinders the equalisation of profit, the formation of average profit in agricultural and non-agricultural enterprises. And as technique in agriculture is on a lower level than in industry, the proportion of variable capital compared with constant capital is larger than in industry; the individual value of the agricultural product is above the average. Hence, by hindering the free leveling of profits in agricultural enterprises on a par with non-agricultural enterprises, the private ownership of land creates the possibility of selling agricultural produce, not at the highest price of production, but at the still higher individual value of the product (for the price of production is determined by average rate of profit on capital, while absolute rent prevents the formation of this 'average' by monopolistically fixing the individual value at a level higher than the average). †

"Thus, differential rent is an inevitable concomitant of any form of capitalist agriculture. Absolute rent is not the concomitant of any form of capitalist agriculture; it arises only under the private ownership of land, under the historically ‡ created backwardness of agriculture, a backwardness riveted by monopoly....

* [Note by Lenin.] "In Part 2 of Vol. II of *Theories of Surplus Value,* Marx reveals the 'essence of different theories of rent': the theory of the monopoly price of agricultural produce, and the theory of differential rent. He shows what is true in both these theories, in so far as absolute rent contains an element of monopoly. *Cf.* page 125 [first German edition] concerning Adam Smith's theory: 'It is quite true' that rent is monopoly price, in so far as the private ownership of land prevents the leveling of profit by keeping profit at a level higher than the average."

† To those familiar with the present-day action of monopoly processors and traders in depressing the prices of farm products, this may seem unreal. But the argument was developed in an earlier period and is a valuable and correct interpretation of the economic basis of absolute rent which still survives as a monopoly claim against the tenant, although the higher values produced in agriculture are seldom realised by the present-day farmer. (Note by *A.R.*)

‡ [Note by Lenin.] "*Cf. Theories of Surplus Value,* Vol. II, Part 1 (German [first] edition), p. 259: 'In agriculture hand labour still predominates, while the capitalist mode of production develops industry more quickly than agriculture. However, this is

"Thus, the question of the nationalisation of the land in capitalist society is divided into two materially different parts: the question of differential rent, and the question of absolute rent. Nationalisation changes the owner of the former, and undermines the very existence of the latter. Hence, on the one hand, nationalisation is a partial reform within the limits of capitalism (a change of owners of a part of surplus value), and on the other hand, it abolishes the monopoly which hinders the whole development of capitalism in general.

"Without distinguishing between these two sides, *i.e.*, the nationalisation of differential rent and of absolute rent, it is impossible to understand the economic significance of the question of nationalisation in Russia."[19]

In relation to land, the forces of the Russian bourgeois-democratic revolution had an opportunity, unprecedented in European history. In other countries, revolutions against feudal power had been dominated by the rising bourgeoisie. Even the peasants who played an active role in the great French Revolution could not look beyond the horizon of small private property in land. In the Russian Revolution of 1905, nationalisation of land was, for the first time, a political slogan backed by the peasants themselves and supported by the most far-seeing revolutionary leaders.

Lenin, true to the economic principles of Marx, understood the possibilities and advantages of nationalising land as a part of the bourgeois-democratic revolution. It would hasten the development of independent small-scale farming toward a higher stage of capitalist agriculture, even while it would destroy one important category of private property in the means of production. It would more quickly reveal the instability of the middle peasant. And the class of landowners (whether nobles or peasants) would no longer obscure in the village the clear-cut issue between workers and capitalists.

Actually, of course, the Revolution of 1905 was crushed by the forces of reaction. Nobles and capitalists retained their private ownership of land until November, 1917, when the Soviet government of workers and peasants took power in Russia.

---

a *historical* distinction which may disappear.' (See also Vol. II, Part 1, p. 275, and Vol. II, Part 2, p. 15.)"

CHAPTER VI

The Years of Reaction

IN the village such organisation as there had been was temporarily destroyed by the defeat of the 1905 Revolution and yet resentment against landlords and the tsarist government persisted and deepened. Outbursts of fires and hooliganism alarmed the landlords, although throughout this pre-war period there was no effective and organised activity by the peasants. Among the workers, also, there came a shorter lull in political activity. But by 1911 the city masses were stirring again. The shooting of strikers in the Lena gold-fields in April, 1912, brought a new stage of class consciousness throughout Russian industry. That same year saw revolutionary outbreaks in the armed forces. And the summer of 1914 saw barricades in the streets of St. Petersburg.

Lenin, looking as always below the surface, knew that the lull in activity which followed the defeat of the 1905 Revolution was not an unfruitful period. Writing at the end of 1908, he said:

"Millions of the population have acquired practical *experience* in the most diverse forms of struggle that is genuinely mass struggle and directly revolutionary, up to 'a general strike,' expulsion of landlords, burning of their manor-houses, open armed rebellion. He who was already before the revolution a revolutionary or a class-conscious worker cannot all at once picture to himself in all its tremendous significance this fact, which has brought a most radical change in a whole series of former conceptions on the course of the development of political crisis, on the tempo of this development, on the dialectics of the history actually created by the masses. Evaluation of this experience by the *masses* is an invisible, laborious, and slow process, playing a very much more important role than many appearances on the surface of the political life of the state, which lead astray the infants in politics, not only the young but sometimes even those of considerable maturity."[1]

"Our peasantry went into the revolution immeasurably less politically conscious than the liberal bourgeoisie on the one side and the socialist proletariat on the other. Therefore the peasants more than any others got from the revolution difficult but useful disillusionments, most bitter but salutary lessons. It is quite natural that they digest these lessons with particular difficulty and particularly slowly."[2]

Two years later, Lenin gave slightly different expression to this idea:

"The millions, suddenly awakened from their long sleep, and suddenly confronted with extremely important problems, could not remain on this level long, could not carry on without a respite, without a return to elementary questions, without a new training, which would help them to 'digest' lessons of unparalleled richness and enable incomparably broader masses again to march forward, but this time more firmly, more consciously, more confidently, and more persistently.

"The dialectics of historical development was such that in the first period [1905-07] it was the accomplishment of immediate changes in every sphere of the country's life that was on the order of the day, while on the order of the day in the second period [1908-10] was the study of the experience, its assimilation by wider strata, its penetration—if one may so express it—to the subsoil, to the backward ranks of the various classes."[3]

While the faint-hearted and wavering intellectuals were certain only that the revolutionary forces were impotent and all was lost, Lenin was vigorously setting forth the true basis of the increasingly reactionary government policy. The tsar's ministers and the parties of the Right were obviously fighting *one* enemy, revolution.

"This direct setting-up of *all* questions on the basis of *counter-revolution,* this subordinating of *all* considerations to one chief and basic consideration, the struggle against revolution, contains within itself a deep truth.... The unrestrained rage with which the Rights attack the revolution . . . shows better than any long deliberations that the defenders of the autocracy see before them a *living* enemy, that they do not consider as finished the fight against revolution, that revival of the revolution stands before them every moment as a most real and immediate threat. With a dead enemy they do not fight in this way. They do not hate thus one who is dead." [4]

Tsarist Government Woos Richer Peasants

Part and parcel of this drive against revolution was the Stolypin agrarian reform. Landed property was so genuinely threatened that peasant property in land must be aggressively encouraged. At whatever cost to the peasant masses, a minority of peasants must be drawn to solid support of this sacred principle. So the tsarist government abandoned its former policy of "supporting and strengthening the old commune" and turned sharply to "a policy of accelerated official breaking up and plundering of it." [5]

"This change is no accident, no wavering in the course of the ministers, no invention of the bureaucracy. No, this is a fundamental 'turn' towards *agrarian bonapartism,* towards liberal (in the economic sense of the word, *i.e.,* = bourgeois) policy in the field of peasant relations to the land. Bonapartism is a manœuvring of monarchy, which has lost its old, patriarchal or feudal, simple and permanent support—a monarchy, which is compelled to intrigue in order not to fall, to flirt in order to rule, to bribe in order to please, to fraternise with the dregs of society, with real thieves and crooks in order to be supported not by the bayonet alone. . . . And the agrarian bonapartism of Stolypin—who on this point is quite deliberately and very firmly supported by the Black-Hundred landlords and the Octobrist * bourgeoisie—could not even have been born, let alone endured already for two years, had not the village commune itself in Russia developed capitalistically, had not elements gradually arisen within the village communes with whom the autocracy could begin to flirt and to whom

* The Octobrists were the party of the most reactionary capitalist elements, including the big industrialists.

it could say: 'Enrich yourselves!' 'Plunder the village commune but support me!' Therefore any evaluation of the Stolypin agrarian policy would be unconditionally in error which did not take into account, on the one side its bonapartist methods, and on the other side, its bourgeois (= liberal) essence.

"For example, our liberals express their confused consciousness that the Stolypin agrarian policy is bonapartism, attacking its police character, idiotic bureaucratic interference in peasant life, etc., etc. But when the Cadets lament over violent breaking-up of the 'immemorial' foundations of our village life, they reveal themselves as *reactionary* whiners. Without violent, revolutionary breaking up of the foundations of the old Russian village there can be no development of Russia. The struggle goes on—although very, very many of the participants do not realise it—*only* over this: shall this violence be violence of the landlord monarchy against the peasants or of a peasant republic against the landlords." [6]

Poverty among peasants increased under the reforms initiated with the Stolypin decrees of 1906. For these attacked the communal restrictions, under which peasants had at least some security of possession in their allotments, without allowing any compensating increase of peasant land. When Lenin and the Social-Democratic Party had demanded the breaking down of communal restrictions, this was tied in with other revolutionary demands including a free, broad transfer of land from the great estates to the peasants. Stolypin's way of attacking the peasant commune was characterised by Lenin in 1907 as "mass violence against the peasantry" and a "clearing of estates for capitalism by the landlords." [7] By 1913 hard facts had filled in the picture of the disasters wrought by the Stolypin policy.

The attack on the peasant commune, which masqueraded as a "homestead" policy, was one of the trump cards in the Stolypin hand. And the more than a million new "homesteads" set up in the course of five or six years were hailed by the government as marking a tremendous advance. But the true facts about these "homesteads"—clear to all honest observers—were never officially admitted. Lenin said of them in 1913:

"One category of homestead peasants, an insignificant minority, are the well-to-do peasants, the kulaks, who even before the new land settlement schemes were introduced, lived very well. Such peasants, by leaving the village commune and buying up the allotments of the poor, are undoubtedly enriching themselves at other people's expense, still further ruining and enslaving the masses of the population. But, I repeat, there are *very few* homestead peasants of this type.

"Another category of homestead peasants predominates, and predominates to an overwhelming degree, *viz.*, the ruined destitute peasants, who went to the homesteads out of sheer need, for they had nowhere else to go.... Starving and toiling on their beggarly farms, they clutch at the last straw for the sake of the resettlement grant, for the sake of the settlement loan. On these farms they suffer untold hardships; they sell all their grain in order to pay their instalment to the bank; they are always in debt; in a state of dire distress, they live like beggars; they are *driven* from the homesteads for *non-payment of instalments* and they are finally transformed into homeless tramps....

"...the government does its utmost to conceal this truth about the homesteads. Independent, detached observers of peasant life are prosecuted and deported from the villages. Peasants writing to the newspapers come up against tyranny, oppression, and persecution by the authorities and the police, of a nature unparalleled even in Russia.

"...The 'new' agrarian policy of the Council of the United Nobility * did not affect the *old* serf-owners or mitigate the oppression exercised through their huge, thousand and ten thousand dessiatina † estates. The 'new' agrarian policy enriched the *old* landlords and a handful of the peasant bourgeoisie, and ruined the masses of the peasants to a still greater extent." [8]

The other "trump card" of the Stolypin reform was encouragement of voluntary migration from European Russia to Siberia. This was supposed to ease the pressure of crisis and in the five years from 1906 to 1910 inclusive it drew some 2,600,000 settlers away from the vil-

* An organisation of feudal landlords formed in May, 1906, to combat revolutionary activities. It backed the policies carried out by Stolypin.

† A measure of area. A dessiatina equals 2.7 acres.

lages of European Russia. But the scheme developed into "nothing but a long and nasty anecdote," according to an honest, conservative forestry official who resigned after twenty-seven years of government service in Siberia in order to expose the cruel fiasco he had witnessed there. This involved "thefts and embezzlement of government funds," "impenetrable stupidity" in administration, and "brutality and wastefulness" in the resettlement policy.[9]

Voluntary migration to Siberia reached its peak in 1908 and 1909, then rapidly lessened as news of failure to obtain land suitable for cultivation was brought by destitute migrants returning to their native villages. On these "ruined and destitute returned settlers," Lenin quotes the forestry official as follows:

"'*Many hundreds of thousands*... return as elements of a type,' writes the official, Komarov, 'such as in the future revolution, if such takes place, is destined to play a terrible role.... It is not those who have been farm labourers all their lives... who return... but men who only recently were property owners, men who could never conceive of their being divorced from the land, and these men, justly angry at the injury done them, because they have been reduced to ruin, because of the failure to settle them—these men are a menace to any political system.'"[10]

"Right" Peasants Demand Land

The peasants themselves had never accepted the Stolypin reforms as a final solution. In each of the Dumas, peasant deputies demanded access to more of the landlord's land. Even some of the conservative peasants in 1908 signed the "Bill of the Forty-two" demanding expropriation, administered by freely elected committees.

"The peasant deputies—even though they are sifted through several police sieves, selected by landlords, terrorised by the 'diehards' in the Duma—have revealed quite recently their true desires. A group of non-party peasants and a section of the *Right* peasants have come out, as is known from the newspapers, for forcible expropriation of land and for local land administrations to be elected by the *whole population!* Not without reason did a Cadet in the agrarian commission say that the Right peasant is more Left than the Cadets. Yes, on the agrarian question, 'Right' peasants in all three Dumas stand further left than the Cadets, proving by this that the monarchism of the peasants is a naïveté that is passing away—as distinguished from the monarchism of the liberal men of affairs who are monarchists for class reasons." [11]

A conservative peasant deputy who had not signed this "Bill of the Forty-two" opened his speech with a blessing on the tsar and wound up by saying:

"But if the tsar had said that there would be right and order, then, surely, if I have 3 dessiatinas of land and beside me there are 30,000 dessiatinas, that is not order and right." [12]

That the famine three years later was related to the extremely small holdings of the peasants was made explicitly clear by the conservative peasant deputies who all agreed in demanding that a definite limit be set for the size of a landlord's estate and all the land beyond such a limit be distributed among the peasants.

"The seeds of immeasurably more profound doubt as to the salutary effect of Stolypin's 'agrarian reform' have been planted by this year's famine in the minds of the Right peasants. The motion made by Andreychuk, a Right peasant, 'that the government shall, at an early date, introduce in the State Duma a bill to limit the amount of land in the hands of big landowners'—a motion supported by all the Right peasants and even by rural priests—shows more than anything else along what lines the peasants, even the Rights among them, think the 'struggle against the famine' should be conducted.

"This 'innermost' peasant demand provides additional proof (recall the statement of the Right and Left peasant deputies suggesting the compulsory alienation of landed estates in order to provide allotments for those who possess little land, recall the speeches of the peasant deputies in the debate on the ukase of November 9,* etc.) showing how deeply the need for an agrarian revolution is penetrating into

* The chief Stolypin land decree.

the minds even of the Right peasants, how far even they conceive of the struggle against famine as *inseparable from the struggle 'for land.'*

"A real struggle against famine is inconceivable without appeasing the peasants' land hunger, without relieving the pressure of taxes which crush them, without raising their cultural standard, without a decisive change in their legal status, without the confiscation of the landed estates—*without a revolution.*" [13]

That the peasants were drawing "dangerous" conclusions from the worsening of their condition and their helplessness in the famine of 1911-1912 was beginning to dawn on some of the landlords. A landlord deputy from Saratov, in the fourth Duma, spoke his doubts about the Stolypin policy:

"'As a result of the law of November 9 [Stolypin land decree, 1906] many newcomers have appeared in some provinces, including the province of Saratov, the land prices have risen and the condition of the poorest population has become extremely difficult.... A terrible hatred is welling up among the peasant population, we hear the curses of the village poor—and against this state of affairs some measures ought to be taken.... For the stake on the strong [slogan used by Stolypin] by no means implies that the poorer peasants ought to be hastened to their doom and left to perish in poverty,' and so on and so forth." [14]

Stolypin himself had admitted that his policy would benefit chiefly the small minority of well-to-do peasants. And in 1913 Lenin recalled Stolypin's words as "exceptionally truthful."

"'We put our stake on the strong,' exclaimed the late Stolypin in explanation and justification of his agrarian policy. These words are well worth noting and remembering as extraordinarily truthful, exceptionally truthful words for a minister. These peasants well understood and learned to their own cost the truthfulness of these words, which mean that the *new* laws and the *new* agrarian policy were laws for the *rich* and made by the *rich,* a policy for the *rich* and carried out by the *rich*. The peasants understood the 'simple game,' *viz.,* that the master class Duma makes laws for the master class—that the government is the instrument of the will and the instrument of the rule of the feudal landlords over Russia.

"If Stolypin wanted to teach *this* to the peasants by means of his 'famous' (infamous) dictum: 'We put our stake on the strong,' we are sure he has found and will find apt pupils among the masses of the ruined and embittered who, having learned *on whom* the government places its stake, will understand so much the better *on whom they themselves* should place their stake: on the working class and on its struggle for freedom." [15]

Semi-Serf Conditions Persist

In spite of the Stolypin reforms, great numbers of poor peasants continued in a semi-serf dependence upon the landowners. "Winter hiring" for summer work in return for winter advances from landowner to peasant was still a common arrangement.

"The peasant accepts the most severe conditions, at a price only one-half or one-third of the spring and summer pay for labor. Winter pay per dessiatina—three times to plough, to sow, to cut (with a scythe or a sickle), to bind and carry into the barn—is approximately what in summer is paid just for harvesting (cutting and binding)." [16]

In the spring of 1913 households "bound" under winter hiring were from 48 per cent to 56 per cent of all peasant households in three regions of European Russia, according to local studies.[17]

Share tenancy was another form of semi-serf dependence.

"Renting on halves, working of the land for half the harvest or getting in the hay for a third of the crop ('on thirds'), represent in themselves also a direct survival of serfdom. The quantity of land worked on halves by the peasants amounts to from 21 per cent to 68 per cent of the peasant's own lands in the various districts of Russia even according to the latest data. [Written in May, 1914.—*A.R.*] ... 'In some cases,' we read in a moderately liberal journal, 'in addition to paying for land with half the crop and two-thirds of the hay, the half-share tenant is obliged to give one to two weeks of *unpaid labour* on the owner's estate, oftener than not with a horse or a boy.' "[18]

Such facts were emphasised by Lenin in the discussions which continued throughout the years between the Stolypin decrees of 1906 and the Socialist Revolution of 1917. For the many differences between the Bolshevik group and the Mensheviks of various shadings included a marked disagreement as to the political role of the peasants in the revolution.

Lenin's opponents insisted that the Stolypin reforms had so cleared the way for capitalism that all revolutionary efforts must now be directed solely to the development of the working class. Lenin maintained that in spite of some further development of capitalist agriculture in Russia the conflicts between peasants and landowners due to survivals of pre-capitalist relationships were still of primary importance. Large-scale capitalist farming was advancing, but it had not yet taken possession. The struggle between the two possible types of capitalist development (a widespread petty-bourgeois peasant farming and fully developed landlord capitalism) had not reached a decisive outcome.[19] The three basic slogans set up by the Bolsheviks before the 1905 Revolution were still inscribed on their banners as they approached the 1917 Revolution: the eight-hour day for all wage workers; a genuinely democratic republic; confiscation of landlord estates.

As the revolutionary movement among the Russian workers rose to new levels before the World War so that the possibilities of socialist revolution loomed on the horizon, Lenin still emphasised again and again that for every reason the revolutionary desires of the peasants must be not only recognised but actively encouraged. Capitalist agriculture in Russia was still so closely interwoven with semi-serf conditions that expropriation of the landowners would be most genuinely progressive in an economic sense.[20] And success for the workers' movement demanded a truly popular government, which could be achieved only if the landowners' economic power was destroyed. For this the peasant movement was a great reservoir of revolutionary strength.

Throughout his work, Lenin had opposed the petty-bourgeois utopia of the Populists, their dream that equality of small peasant properties would assure economic stability and prosperity. But he had also recognised that underlying this dream—which might later develop into a reactionary force—there was a sound and essentially progressive struggle against the stranglehold of feudal landlord power. The historical importance of this underlying peasant struggle Lenin contrasted in 1912 with the futility of the liberals' utopia, which looked for progress without class struggle.

"The utopia of the Populists, perverting their *socialist* consciousness, is an accompaniment, a symptom, partly even an expression of their democratic upsurge.

"The dialectics of history is such that as an anti-capitalist remedy the Populists and Trudoviks offer and promote the most logically and decisively capitalist measure in relation to the agrarian question in Russia. 'Equality' of a new distribution of lands is a utopia, but a complete break with the whole old landownership—landlord, imperial, and 'crown'—is essential for a *new* distribution. This break is the most necessary, the most economically progressive (especially for such a state as Russia), the most pressing measure in a bourgeois-democratic direction." [21]

Lenin then quotes part of the following paragraph from Engels' preface to Marx's *Poverty of Philosophy:*

"But what formally may be economically incorrect, may all the same be correct from the point of view of world history. If the moral consciousness of the mass declares an economic fact to be unjust, as it has done in the cause of slavery or serf labour, that is a proof that the fact itself has been outlived, that other economic facts have made their appearance, owing to which the former has become unbearable and untenable. Therefore, a very true economic content may be concealed behind the formal economic incorrectness." [22]

Lenin continues:

"It is essential to remember this profound statement of Engels in evaluating the present Narodnik [Populist] or Trudovik utopia in Russia (perhaps not only in Russia but in a whole group of Asiatic states, going through in the twentieth century the bourgeois revolution).

"False in a formally economic sense, the Narodnik [Populist] *democratism* is true in a *historic* sense; false, as a socialist utopia, *this* democratism is *true* in that particular historically-conditioned democratic struggle of the peasant masses which constitutes an inseparable element of the bourgeois transformation and a condition for its complete victory." [23]

Lenin had no patience with the leftist idea that industrial workers were the only class which would benefit from the socialist revolution and that therefore a long struggle between proletariat and peasantry was inevitable.[24] He saw—and history has vindicated his wisdom—that in Russia the chief enemies of the working class were the great landowners, together with the industrial and financial bourgeoisie. To join with the peasants in destroying first the power of the landlords would greatly weaken the enemies of the working class. And in the course of this struggle, the workers would win the masses of poor peasants as staunch allies for the next stage of the revolution, the fight for socialism.

CHAPTER VII

Workers and Peasants Take Power

MOBILIZATION for the world imperialist war broke temporarily the wave of the workers' movement that was rising high in the summer of 1914, and all parties except the Bolsheviks shouted for support of the imperialist policies of the tsarist government. Lenin drove home repeatedly that in the Russia of 1914 the military forces were serving a predatory government and that workers and peasants had nothing to gain from a tsarist victory. Equally he denounced the German Socialists who supported the kaiser.

First to awaken from the delirium of war fever were industrial workers and the soldiers, most of whom were peasants. A new wave of strikes arose in the industrial centres in the spring of 1915. And even under the extreme repression of wartime ever greater numbers were drawn under the influence of the underground Bolshevik Party.[1] From the second year of the war occasional mutinies began to occur at the front.[2] Hardships of war were enormously increased both for the soldiers and for the masses at home by the corruption and mismanagement of the tsar's war machine and the relative backwardness of Russian industry as a whole.

When some 14,000,000 men had been sent into the armed forces,[3] the peasant families left in the villages were unable to maintain full production of grain. Not only high prices but actual shortage of bread roused the working-class sections of Petersburg and other cities to a deeply revolutionary feeling. Soldiers at the front were more and more badly equipped. Driven back by the advance of the German forces, the tsarist army was enduring hunger and cold, and suffering enormous losses. Both tsarist ministers and capitalists were alarmed over the rising discontent at the front and at home.

January 22, 1917, anniversary of Bloody Sunday, saw unprecedented mass demonstrations in many cities. A month later a great strike movement spread from the Putilov metal and armament works to other factories. March 10 (February 25—old style) brought a general strike in Petrograd and March 13 a general strike in Moscow. Political slogans swept through the masses along with their wage demands: "Down with the tsar!" "Down with the war!" "We want bread!" Strikers and demonstrators were repeatedly attacked by the police. As the demonstrations continued and drew in greater numbers of workers, soldiers were called out to shoot them down, but whole companies, and then whole regiments, joined the workers and turned their fire upon the police.

The Russian capitalists, meanwhile, who were all for the war and for Russian imperialist expansion, raged over the defeats of the Russian army and the corruption and inefficiency of the tsarist regime. Taking advantage of the rising revolutionary activity of the masses, the capitalist politicians engineered a palace revolt, deposing Nicholas II (who fled from the capital) and installing his brother Michael who seemed more friendly to the bourgeoisie. When Michael also fled, after one day on the throne, the executive committee of the Imperial Duma set up a Provisional Government in which not only the frankly capitalist parties but also the Socialist-Revolutionaries were represented.

Acting independently, the workers and soldiers had been creating their own representative bodies, Soviets (or councils) made up of delegates informally elected by the rank and file in factories and regiments.

"The Revolution of 1905 had shown that the Soviets were organs of armed uprising and at the same time the embryo of a new, revolutionary power. The idea of Soviets lived in the minds of the working-class masses, and they put it into effect as soon as tsardom was overthrown, with this difference, however, that in 1905 it was Soviets only of *Workers'* Deputies that were formed, whereas in February,

1917, on the initiative of the Bolsheviks, there arose Soviets of *Workers'* and *Soldiers'* Deputies."[4]

Furthermore, the whole revolutionary situation was far more developed than it had been twelve years earlier, and the Soviets functioned from the beginning on a much higher political level.

Thus began the months of "dual power" which marked the first stage of the 1917 Revolution. Tsarist autocracy had been overthrown by the Russian masses. Peasants in army uniform and workers had used their power in this initial act of revolution, but their Soviets did not then create a government of workers and peasants. They voluntarily accepted the Provisional Government of big capitalists and landlords, scarcely realising at first that this new government still represented classes opposed to the revolutionary masses. The Provisional Government promised a Constituent Assembly for the creation of a bourgeois democratic republic, but such an assembly had not yet been convoked when eight months later the Soviets of workers, soldiers, and peasants swept beyond this first stage of the revolution and set up a government of their own.

The situation did not exactly fit any of the previous theoretical patterns of revolution. But as Lenin said in his "Letters on Tactics" (April, 1917):[5] "Theory, my friend, is grey, but green is the eternal tree of life." * Control of government apparatus had passed from feudal autocracy to the capitalist class. In this sense it was a bourgeois revolution. But actual power rested with the broadest masses who had overthrown the tsar and had most of the armed forces behind them. Their Soviets were a flexible organ of power, directly expressing the will of the people. In this sense it was a democratic revolution, carried through by workers and peasants.

"The revolutionary-democratic dictatorship of the proletariat and peasantry has already been realised, but in an extremely original form, and with a number of highly important modifications....

"According to the old conception, the rule of the proletariat and

* Evidently a reference to Goethe's *Faust* (I, 4:515):

"Grau, theurer Freund, ist alle Theorie
Und grün des Lebens goldner Baum."

peasantry, their dictatorship, can and must come after the rule of the bourgeoisie.

"But in actual fact, it has already turned out differently: an extremely original, novel, and unprecedented *interlacing of the one with the other* has taken place. Side by side, existing together and simultaneously, we have both the rule of the bourgeoisie (the government of Lvov and Guchkov) and a revolutionary-democratic dictatorship of the proletariat and peasantry, the latter *voluntarily* ceding power to the bourgeoisie and voluntarily transforming itself into an appendage of the bourgeoisie.

"For it must not be forgotten that in Petrograd the power is actually in the hands of the workers and soldiers: the new government does not and cannot use violence against them, for there is no police, no army separate from the people, no officialdom standing omnipotently above the people....

"And actuality reveals the *fact*—that the freely elected soldiers' and peasants' deputies freely enter the second, the parallel government and freely supplement, develop, and complete it. And, just as freely, they *surrender* their power to the bourgeoisie; which phenomenon does not in the least 'undermine' the theory of Marxism, for, as we have always known and have repeatedly pointed out, the bourgeoisie maintains itself not only by virtue of force but also by virtue of the lack of class consciousness, the clinging to old habits, the timidity and lack of organisation of the masses." [6]

Revolutionary Desires of the Masses

From the beginning the Soviets and the masses they directly represented had underlying desires and purposes that were bound to clash with the desires and purposes of the Provisional Government. Early in April Lenin showed the beginnings of such conflict:

"This government has already begun to hinder the revolutionary initiative of mass action and the seizure of power by the people *from below,* which is the *sole* guarantee of any real success of the revolution ...and no support of that [new bourgeois] government by the proletariat is permissible." [7]

The masses wanted *peace* and they knew that the German soldiers wanted peace. One of the first acts of the Petrograd Soviet of Workers' and Soldiers' Deputies had been the issuance of a manifesto "To All the Peoples of the World," summoning them to struggle against the predatory aspirations of their governments. But within Russia these very Soviets supported the war because they thought they were thereby defending their own revolution. Once they realised that this first stage of the revolution was serving the big capitalists and had nothing to offer the workers and poor peasants, their "revolutionary defencism" for the support of the Provisional Government would evaporate.

At the first All-Russian Congress of Soviets of Workers' and Soldiers' Deputies (June, 1917), Lenin sharply analysed the "hopelessly entangled situation into which the workers and peasants have fallen" in their support of the war:

"For when you, Russian workers and peasants, appeal to the workers and peasants of Austria and Germany, where the governments and ruling classes are conducting the same cut-throat, predatory war as the Russian, British, and French capitalists and bankers; when you say, 'Refuse to serve as the instruments of your bankers,' while at the same time you admit your own bankers into the cabinet and seat them side by side with Socialist ministers, you are reducing all your manifestoes to naught and are in practice negating your whole policy. In practice it is as though you never had these excellent aspirations and wishes; for you are helping Russia carry on exactly the same sort of imperialist war, exactly the same sort of predatory war. You are contradicting the very masses whom you represent, for those masses will never accept the standpoint of the capitalists...."[8]

Earlier, Lenin had summed up the class background of the war at the Petrograd Conference of Bolsheviks.

"The objective class position of the capitalists is one thing. They fight for themselves. The soldiers are proletarians and peasants. This is another thing. Are they interested in seizing Constantinople? No, their class interests are against war! That is why they can be enlightened, their minds can be changed.... 'Down with war' does not mean to fling the bayonet away. It means the passing of power to another class. The thing on which all our present efforts must be concentrated is to explain that."[9]

And, more explicitly:

"The class conscious proletariat can consent to a revolutionary war, which would really justify revolutionary defencism, only on condition: (a) that the power of government pass to the proletariat and the poor sections of the peasantry bordering on the proletariat; (b) that all annexations be renounced in deed as well as in words; (c) that a complete and real break be made with all capitalist interests."[10]

The masses wanted *bread*. But the Provisional Government, caring chiefly for capitalist profits, could not solve the economic crisis which moved rapidly toward greater hunger and profound catastrophe. Nothing but a strict workers' control of production and distribution could provide bread for the city masses. Nothing but a revolutionary solution of the land problem could give bread to the poorer peasants.

"It cannot give bread because it is a bourgeois government. *At best,* it can give the people a 'brilliantly organised starvation,' as Germany did. But the people will not tolerate starvation. The people will learn, and probably very soon, that bread exists and can be obtained, *but only by methods that do not respect the sanctity of capital and landownership.*"[11]

The masses wanted *freedom*. But the freedom they achieved in the March Revolution was constantly threatened by the intrigues of the Provisional Government. These intrigues culminated in the outlawing of the Bolshevik Party in July and the attempt of General Kornilov in September to set up a military dictatorship. As Lenin had stated in his first analysis of the Provisional Government: "It cannot give freedom because it is a government of landlords and capitalists, and *fears* the people."[12]

Objectively, the situation was ripe for carrying the revolution rapidly toward full assumption of power by the workers and peasants. And the immediate duty of the Bolsheviks was a broad and intensive campaign of education, for the Russian masses, governed hitherto by ruthless force, were unprepared to resist the high-sounding phrases with which the Provisional Government was deceiving them.

"The bourgeoisie rules either by deception or by violence. At the present moment flattery and deception prevail, and this lulls the revolution to sleep. In matters of secondary importance they do make concessions. But in matters of prime importance (the agrarian revolution, for example), they do nothing." [18]

It would be fatal to the revolution to wait passively until events alone had unmasked the real purposes of the Provisional Government. Lenin had infinite faith in the revolutionary power of the workers, and he felt it of crucial importance that this power be aroused to positive action while the situation was still fluid and the capitalists had not yet consolidated their position.

Quite as decisive for the future would be the action of the peasant millions. They had fallen the most ready victims of the new government and its deceptions. As petty producers and holders of tiny properties, they naturally followed the lead of capitalists decked out in revolutionary garb. Particularly, since these new rulers had drawn in at the very start a prominent Socialist-Revolutionary (Kerensky) as Minister of Justice. But the Provisional Government, even after the formal coalition (set up in May) with Socialist-Revolutionaries and Mensheviks, was still dominated by the big bourgeoisie who were unwilling to attack the property rights of the feudal landlords. And the "revolutionists" in the government accepted meaningless promises and postponements. Lenin was hopeful that as this fact became clear to the peasants they would turn against the Provisional Government and support the Bolsheviks in carrying through an agrarian revolution.

History had, however, moved beyond the point where a common front of workers and *all* peasants against the feudal landlords was the primary task of the moment. Economic crisis within Russia, the setting up of a capitalist government enmeshed in imperialist intrigues and fearful of proletarian revolution, and the highly revolutionary mood of the masses on the land, as well as in the cities, had placed on the order of the day the creation of a positively, aggressively class-conscious government by the workers and their natural class allies, the poorest peasants.

"Had it not been for the war, Russia could have existed for years and even for decades without a revolution against the capitalists. With the war, it is a question of either ruin, or a revolution against the capitalists. Thus the question stands. Thus is it propounded by life itself.

"Instinctively, emotionally, temperamentally, the majority of Russia's population, . . . the workers and the poorest peasants, are in sympathy with a revolution against the capitalists. But so far there is no clear idea with regard to that, no determination. To develop these is our task." [14]

Lenin's Tactics

It was imperative that the poorer peasants, the semi-proletarians, and the rural wage workers be drawn away from any wavering to the Right. Once they understood that capitalists and their hangers-on had no solution for their problems, while the Bolsheviks had a positive programme toward which a government of workers and poor peasants could push rapidly forward, these impoverished petty bourgeoisie would become effective allies of the working class. Success or failure in winning the support of the poor peasants might well be the decisive factor in the outcome of the workers' revolution. As was stated in a resolution drafted by Lenin:

"It will depend on whether the urban proletariat succeeds in securing the following of the rural proletariat, together with the mass of rural semi-proletarians, or whether this mass follows the peasant bourgeoisie, which is inclining towards union with the . . . capitalists and landlords and the counter-revolution in general—as to how the fate and issue of the Russian revolution will be determined, if the incipient proletarian revolution in Europe does not exercise a direct and powerful influence on our country." [15]

Revolution in March had left untouched the economic power of the feudal landlords which a bourgeois revolution would be supposed to destroy. But the fact that the bourgeois-democratic revolution had in this important respect been incomplete, and that semi-serf relationships were still intertwined with a low stage of capitalist development in agriculture, must not be allowed to hold back the workers and poorer peasants from taking the road to power which lay open before them.

In making this analysis and winning an overwhelming majority of the Bolshevik Party to agreement with his position, Lenin never for a moment underestimated the serious difficulties. He knew that in April the Bolsheviks had support from only a small minority within the Soviets and from a somewhat larger minority among the workers in the chief industrial centres. For many workers were under the influence of the Mensheviks who held that Russian capitalism was not yet ripe for socialist development. And the Socialist-Revolutionaries, with their faith in the village commune and their talk of nationalising the land, had at first larger peasant support than the Bolsheviks. But Lenin trusted the deeply revolutionary desires and the intelligence of the masses. He knew that the workers would shortly lose patience with the hesitations of the Mensheviks, and the peasants would not wait indefinitely for Socialist-Revolutionaries in the Provisional Government to fulfil their promise of land. He had unshakable faith that coming events would underscore his own analysis, and that the workers and peasants would respond to the honest thinking of Bolshevik leadership.

Never for a moment did Lenin propose or approve seizure of power by a minority isolated from the masses. But he had confidence—fully justified by later developments of 1917—that within a few months the majority of the workers and great numbers of the poorer peasants would move whole-heartedly with the Bolsheviks.

"In order to obtain the power of state the class conscious workers must win the majority to their side. *As long as* no violence is used against the masses, there is no other road to power. We are not Blanquists,* we are not in favour of the seizure of power by a minority.

* Followers of Louis Auguste Blanqui (1805-81), a French Socialist who believed that a relatively small number of resolute, well-organised men could seize power *without mass support* and hold power until they had drawn the masses after them. (See Engels' Introduction to Marx, *Civil War in France*, Marxist Library, IX, 1940 ed., p. 19.)

We are Marxists, we stand for a proletarian class struggle against petty-bourgeois poison gas, against chauvinist defencism, phrases, and dependence on the bourgeoisie.

"Let us create a proletarian Communist Party. Its elements have already been created by the best adherents of Bolshevism; let us close our ranks and carry on proletarian class work; then from among the proletarians, from among the *poor* peasants ever greater numbers will come over to our side." [16]

Furthermore, Lenin had no illusions about the possibility of "introducing socialism" suddenly and immediately in a backward country. But he did propose that a government of workers and peasants should immediately nationalise the land and take over without compensation the entire banking apparatus and those industries which were already organised in large corporations. Such a government, with the aid of workers employed by those capitalists who were still allowed to function, would exercise a genuine control of production and profits in industries remaining in private ownership. They could not have at once a completely socialist economy, but under a government from which capitalist representation was entirely excluded they could enter a period of consciously directed transition toward socialism.[17]

"If the Soviets wish to assume power, it is only for such ends.... Either the Soviets develop, or they die an ignominious death, like the Paris Commune.* For a bourgeois republic we need no Soviets; Cadets [Constitutional-Democrats] will do." [18]

During the months between March and the taking of power by the Soviets in November, the masses on their own initiative began to carry out locally various measures that conflicted with property claims of capitalists and landlords. In September, Lenin wrote:

"The situation is falsely pictured as if somebody wished to 'introduce' socialism in Russia by one ukase [decree], with no attention either to the existing technical level, or to the abundance of small

* The working class government which held power in Paris from March 18 to May 28, 1871.

enterprises, or to the habits and the wishes of the majority of the population.

"All this is a fabric of lies. Nobody ever proposed anything of the kind. No party, no single individual was about to 'introduce socialism' by ukase. What we have been and are concerned with, are measures which, like the social duty established for the rich in Ekaterinburg, meet with the full approval of the mass of the poor, *i.e.,* of the majority of the population, measures that have perfectly matured, both technically and culturally, that give immediate relief to the poor and permit the mitigation of the burdens of the war and their more equitable distribution.

"Almost half a year of revolution has passed, and the S.-R. [Socialist-Revolutionary] and Menshevik leaders still obstruct all such measures, thus betraying the interests of the people in the interest of 'understandings' with the bourgeoisie." [19]

Agriculture was, of course, the most backward section of the whole economy: backward in the relative importance of small producers and backward in the prevailing technique of production. Rural wage workers and the poorest semi-proletarian peasants would from the beginning be represented in the workers' government, which would supervise production and profits of kulaks as of other capitalists. Every effort would be made to win over to the workers' revolution the middle peasants, the hard-working poor households which managed to subsist on the land and employed no wage labour.

"There will now develop in the village a struggle for the petty, and partly the middle, peasantry. The landowners, basing themselves on the well-to-do peasants, will lead them to submission to the bourgeoisie. We, basing ourselves on the hired agricultural workers and poor peasants, must lead them to the closest possible alliance with the proletariat of the cities." [20]

Later Lenin said that "it [the proletariat] must entirely destroy the influence of the bourgeoisie and the petty-bourgeois compromisers over the *majority* of the non-proletarian toiling masses by satisfying their economic needs *in a revolutionary way at the expense of the exploiters.*" [21]

Such ideas ran through all of Lenin's writings of early 1917. They were summed up in the so-called "April Theses" [22] which aroused a storm of discussion and set forth the line adopted by a large majority of the Bolsheviks, first at a Petrograd Conference, shortly afterward at an All-Russian Conference of the Bolshevik party.

Lenin's Agrarian Programme

Fundamental points of Lenin's agrarian programme included, first, nationalisation of *all* land.

"But the *disposal* of the land, the determination of the local regulations governing land tenure and use, must in no case be left in the hands of bureaucrats and officials, but must be vested exclusively in the local and regional *Soviets of Peasants' Deputies*." [23]

Second, the importance of large-scale production must be emphasised.

"In order to improve the technique of grain growing and to increase output, and in order to develop rational cultivation on a large scale under public control, we must endeavour through the Peasants' Committees to secure the transformation of every confiscated estate into a large model farm controlled by the *Soviets of Agricultural Labourers' Deputies.*

"In order to counteract the petty-bourgeois phrases and policy prevailing among the Socialist-Revolutionaries . . . the party of the proletariat must make it clear that small peasant farming under a commodity production system *offers no escape* for mankind from the poverty and oppression of the masses." [24]

Or, as Lenin put it in a *Pravda* article of this period:

"We cannot conceal from the peasants, least of all from the village proletarians and semi-proletarians, . . . that it is necessary to consider changing over to economic enterprise on a large scale and of a public nature, and to begin working for it now, by teaching the masses, and in turn learning from the masses the practical and feasible methods of bringing about such a change." [25]

Third, the Bolsheviks must encourage separate organisations of the rural wage workers and of poorest peasants.

"Without necessarily splitting the Soviets of Peasants' Deputies at once, the party of the proletariat must make clear the necessity of organising separate Soviets of Agricultural Labourers' Deputies and separate Soviets of deputies from the poor (semi-proletarian) peasants or, at least, of holding regular separate conferences of deputies *of this class position* in the shape of separate fractions or parties within the Soviets of Peasants' Deputies. Otherwise all the sugary petty-bourgeois talk of the Narodniks [Populists] regarding the peasants in general will but serve as a shield for the deceit played on the propertyless mass by the well-to-do peasants, who are but a variety of *capitalists*." [26]

Fourth, they should encourage the peasants to take organised local action immediately against the landlord estates.

"To counteract the bourgeois-liberal or purely bureaucratic sermons preached by many Socialist-Revolutionaries and Soviets of Workers' and Soldiers' Deputies, who advise the peasants not to seize the landlords' estates and not to start agrarian reform pending the convocation of the Constituent Assembly, the party of the proletariat must urge the peasants to set about putting agrarian reform into effect at once, on their own initiative, and to confiscate the landlords' estates immediately upon the decision of the local peasants' deputies." [27]

Fifth, the party must encourage mass action for increasing the food supply.

"At the same time, it is particularly important to insist on the necessity of increasing the production of foodstuffs for the soldiers at the front and for the towns, and on the absolute inadmissibility of any damage to livestock, tools, machinery, structures, etc." [28]

And two months later, in June:

"In view of the complete disorganisation of the whole financial and monetary systems, in view of the impossibility of restoring order while the war lasts, the aim of the state organisation should be to organise on a wide regional, and later on a national scale, the exchange of agricultural implements, clothes, shoes, and other products for bread and other agricultural products. City and village co-operatives should be drawn into a wide participation in this matter." [29]

Without guidance from the Bolsheviks, peasants had begun to take possession of landlords' property. This was what the revolution meant to them and local action rapidly outran the dilly-dallying tactics of the Provisional Government. Dominated by capitalists, the government was essentially unable to put through any revolutionary land measures. For the Russian banks, loaded with mortgages against all sorts of landed property, would collapse if land "values" were destroyed by expropriation of private owners. Mensheviks and Socialist-Revolutionaries who had talked boldly of expropriation *before* the revolution moved softly and followed the capitalists' lead when the living issue confronted them. The fact that, on the land question, all other parties fell back on promises and postponements was a primary factor in throwing peasant support to the Bolsheviks and preparing the second stage of the revolution in November.

From the beginning Lenin had emphasised the importance of land confiscation by the peasants themselves. As such action took place, his emphasis turned more and more to the need of *organised* action by the poorer peasants. He made it clear that chaotic *individual* seizures would solve nothing.

"This would, indeed, be the height of anarchism, the height of absurdity....

"Private estates must be confiscated *immediately, i.e.,* they must immediately be taken from the owners *without any compensation.*

"But how about possession of these lands? Who should forthwith take hold of them, cultivate them? The local peasants, in an organised way, *i.e.,* in accordance with the decision of the majority. This is what our party counsels. The local peasants are to have the immediate use of the land; the ownership, however, is to remain with the people as a whole. The final right of ownership will be settled by the Constituent Assembly (or by the All-Russian Soviet of Soviets, should the people turn the latter into a Constituent Assembly)." [30]

"What measures are possible and necessary to prevent the rich peasant from injuring the poor one?

"1. Majority rule (there are more poor peasants than rich ones). This is what we propose.

"2. A *separate* organisation of poor peasants, where they *themselves* can consider *their own* interests. This is what we propose.

"3. Collective cultivation of lands; the livestock and implements on the landowners' estates to be held in common; the management to be in the hands of Soviets of Agricultural Workers' Deputies. This is what we propose." [81]

"If the peasants do plant the fields poorly, then the peasants must be helped. And it is the poorest peasants that must be helped by means of collective cultivation of the large estates. There is no other way of helping the poorest peasants." [82]

When the All-Russia Peasant Congress opened in May and brought 1,115 peasant delegates from the front and from the provinces, Lenin, through the press, through the Bolshevik delegates, through a resolution presented to the Congress, and through a great speech in favour of the resolution, drove home the high points in the party's agrarian programme.

He also urged alliance between the poorest peasants and the city workers and explained what the peasants would gain from social ownership and workers' control of industry.

"Further, a close alliance between the urban proletariat and the poorest peasants (semi-proletarians) is necessary if the whole land is to be placed in the hands of the toilers. Without such an alliance it is impossible to defeat the capitalists, and unless they are defeated the transfer of the land into the hands of the people will not save the people from distress. The soil cannot be eaten, and it is impossible, without money, without means, to get hold of tools, cattle, and seed for the sowing. The peasants must not put their trust in the capitalists nor in the rich peasants (for they are capitalists too), but only in the urban proletariat. Only in alliance with the latter, can the poor peasants insist on the lands, the railways, the banks, and the factories being recognised as the property of all toilers; without such measures, the mere handing over of the land to the people will not remove misery and distress.

"In some districts of Russia the workers are introducing a kind of supervision (control) of the factories. This supervision on the part of the workers greatly benefits the peasants, for in this way production is increased and the goods become cheaper. The peasants, to the best of their ability, must support this action of the workers, and refuse to believe the calumnies spread by the capitalists concerning the workers." [38]

Preparing to Take Power

From the middle of July events moved rapidly toward the final clash and the overthrowing of capitalist class power on November 7. Conflict between the masses and the Provisional Government had been sharpened by the failure of the July 1 army offensive against Germany. This revealed to the blindest the breakdown of Russian military supplies and of Russian industry. Disintegration of army morale brought back to the villages thousands of soldiers who were completely disillusioned with the "revolution" of the capitalists and their "Kerensky" friends. Fresh demonstrations of armed workers together with soldiers and sailors bordered on armed uprising in Petrograd. "Loyal" counter-revolutionary troops were brought from the front by Kerensky and started violent disorders contrary to the will of the Petrograd Soviet.

These events marked a turning point. They showed the masses in conflict with the Provisional Government which could no longer hold power without appeal to force. But the masses were not yet aroused to the importance of taking government into their own hands.

Decision was still delayed by the unreadiness of the petty-bourgeois peasant masses to break away from the petty-bourgeois "revolutionists" and throw in their lot with the proletariat. Lenin analysed as follows the sharp crisis of the "July Days" and the lesser crises that had preceded it:

"In all three crises the movement took the form of a *demonstration*. ...But the fact of the matter is that it is not an ordinary demonstration; it is something considerably more than a demonstration and less than a revolution. It is an outburst of revolution and counter-revolution *together;* it is a rough, sometimes sudden 'washing out' of the middle elements, while the proletarian and bourgeois elements make a stormy appearance....

"The objective situation is this. A tremendous majority of the country's population is petty bourgeois by its living conditions and more so by its ideas. But big capital rules the country, primarily through banks and syndicates. There is in this country an urban proletariat strong enough to go its own way, but not yet able to draw at once to its side the majority of the semi-proletarians. Out of this fundamental class fact follows the inevitability of such crises as the three we are now examining, as well as their forms.

"... The S.R.'s [Socialist-Revolutionaries] have promised the peasants (1) to abolish private property in land; (2) to transfer the land to the toilers; (3) to confiscate the landowners' lands and transfer them to the peasants without compensation. These great reforms can never be realised without the most decisive revolutionary measures against the bourgeoisie, measures that can be undertaken *only* when the poorest peasantry joins the proletariat, *only* when the banks and syndicates are nationalised." [34]

Meantime petty-bourgeois "revolutionists" remained in the government which had turned against the masses, "leading the peasants by the nose for months and deceiving them by delays and procrastinations."

"So far has the government gone in brazenly defending the landowners, that it begins to put the peasants on trial for seizing land 'wilfully'....

"Let us wait with the land till we have the Constituent Assembly. Let us wait with the Constituent Assembly till the end of the war. Let us wait with ending the war till we have complete victory. This is what it comes to. The capitalists and the landowners, having their own majority in the government, are simply mocking the peasantry." [35]

When the Sixth Congress of the Russian Social-Democratic Labour Party (Bolshevik) * was held in August, 1917, Lenin was in hiding

* Early in 1918 the name of the party was changed to Communist Party.

in a village near Petrograd, but his ideas were conveyed to the congress in the chief political report presented by Joseph Stalin. This stressed the prime importance of immediate agitational work among the peasants and led to the drafting of practical instructions to the membership on this point. For it was clear that the counter-revolutionary bourgeoisie already held a power which would not yield peaceably to the workers and peasants. Further, this counter-revolutionary power might move actively *against* the revolutionary workers, while the majority of the peasants were still bound by illusions extremely dangerous not only to the workers' revolution but to the achievement of the very aims about which the peasants themselves cared most deeply.

The Congress warned sharply against premature attempts at the seizure of power.

"The proletariat must not permit itself to be provoked by the bourgeoisie, which is very anxious to provoke the proletariat at the present moment into a premature battle. It must direct its every effort towards the organisation and preparation of its forces for the moment when the general national crisis and a profound stirring of the masses will create favourable conditions for the *passing over* of the city and village poor to the side of the workers, against the bourgeoisie." [86]

Early in September the Kornilov revolt attempted to set up a military dictatorship, but this was defeated by the armed workers and revolutionary regiments. The reactionary forces behind Kornilov immediately started more serious preparations for a second attempt definitely to smash the revolution. With the defeat of Kornilov, September 12, Lenin began to urge definite preparations for the final showdown.

The many factors leading to this decision included a marked change in the temper of the peasants. Disorders increased and became a definite mass movement of peasants in at least six widely separated regions of European Russia. The peasants had passed beyond the moderate demands and acceptance of government promises which had marked the First Congress of Peasant Deputies (May 17 to June 15). They had always wanted to do away with private ownership of land. But the great majority had been willing to wait for the Constituent Assembly, provided all sale and purchase of land was immediately prohibited. Before such a compromise law was tardily enacted (under pressure from the Socialist-Revolutionaries), masses of peasants had turned to violent seizure of land owners' property, with rioting and destruction that spread from village to village.

November 7 and the Land Decree

November 7 (which was October 25 by the old Russian calendar) opened the socialist stage of the revolution, in which workers and peasants under Bolshevik leadership overthrew the Provisional Government and took the power of government into the hands of the Soviets of Workers', Soldiers', and Peasants' Deputies. In the Manifesto to the Citizens of Russia which Lenin drafted, announcing this second decisive stage of the 1917 Revolution, "the abolition of landed proprietorship" was guaranteed.

"The Provisional Government has been overthrown. The power of state has passed into the hands of the organ of the Petrograd Soviet of Workers' and Soldiers' Deputies—the Revolutionary Military Committee, which is leading the Petrograd proletariat and garrison.

"The cause for which the people have fought, namely, the immediate proposal of a democratic peace, the abolition of landed proprietorship, workers' control over production and the creation of a Soviet government—the success of that cause is guaranteed.

"Long live the revolution of the soldiers, workers, and peasants!" [37]

The following day, Lenin reported on the land question to the All-Russian Congress of Soviets and presented a decree which was forthwith adopted. In his report he directly blamed the Provisional Government for "pogroms and anarchy" in the villages.

"Where and when did pogroms and anarchy result from wise measures? If the government had acted wisely, and if their measures had met the needs of the peasant poor, would there have been unrest among the peasant masses?" [38]

The main points in the decree were the following: [39]

1. "Landed proprietorship is abolished forthwith without compensation."

2. All landed estates, "with all their live stock, implements, farm buildings and everything pertaining thereto," were placed temporarily under control of local Land Committees and Soviets of Peasants' Deputies.

3. "All damage to confiscated property, which henceforth belongs to the whole people, is declared to be a felony, punishable by the revolutionary courts. . . ."

4. As "a guide in carrying through the great land reforms" the decree includes much of the summary of peasant instructions on land, compiled by the Socialist-Revolutionaries from 242 local instructions to delegates at the first All-Russian Peasant Congress (May-June, 1917). These instructions (which had been practically ignored in the S-R policy) make a sharp distinction between "lands with *highly* developed forms of cultivation" (which were to be maintained intact and cultivated either by the state or by the communes) and the land and implements of peasants employing no wage labour (which were to remain in their possession for use, but not for sale or for renting). Each village would have complete freedom to decide on its form of land tenure: "household, farm, communal, or co-operative." Equality of holdings is to be the goal, with provision for distribution of confiscated lands, and possible resettlement of farmers in other regions.*

For several reasons, the new government did not propose immediate collectivisation. Most of the peasants did not yet desire it. And collective farming without a fair minimum of good technical equipment would give little real advantage. Russian industry was not equipped to produce great quantities of farm machinery, and in the midst of war devastation and extreme economic crisis it was totally impossible to dream of importing new machines. For rural wage workers and poor

* When the Constituent Assembly was dissolved (January 18, 1918), the Third Congress of Soviets adopted a "*Declaration of Rights* of the Toiling and Exploited People," which forms part of the Fundamental Law of the Soviet Republic. Article 2, paragraph 1, of this Declaration states that "Private property in land is hereby abolished." (Lenin, *Selected Works*, VII, 198-99.)

The Land Socialisation Act of February 19, 1918, confirmed the abolition of all private property in land and placed the land and *all private stock* at the disposal of the Soviet authorities *under the control of the federal Soviet Government*. Public property in land was re-affirmed in the Soviet Constitution of 1936.

peasants to make good use of the relatively few highly developed large farms was the one practical immediate step toward demonstrating the advantages of collective farming.

Lenin, as always, was confident that the masses who had been exploited on the land would learn "in the fire of experience." As he finished reading the decree on the land question, Lenin followed it with words whose wisdom will never grow stale.

"I hear voices stating that the decree itself and the Instructions were drawn up by the Socialist-Revolutionaries. Be it so. Does it matter who drew it up? As a democratic government, we cannot ignore the decision of the rank and file of the people, even though we may disagree with it; in the fire of experience, applying the decree in practice, and carrying it out locally, the peasants will themselves understand where the truth lies. And even if the peasants continue to follow the Socialist-Revolutionaries, even if they give this party a majority in the Constituent Assembly, we shall still say, be it so. Experience is the best teacher and it will show who is right. Let the peasant solve this problem from one end and us from the other. Experience will bring us closer in the general stream of revolutionary creation, in the elaboration of new state forms. We must follow experience; we must allow complete freedom for the creative faculties of the masses.

"The old government, which was swept away by armed insurrection, tried to settle the land question with the help of the old tsarist bureaucracy, which remained intact. But instead of solving the question the bureaucracy fought the peasants. The peasants have learned something during the eight months of revolution; they want themselves to settle all questions concerning the land. Therefore we declare ourselves opposed to all amendments to this draft law. We want no details in it, for we are writing a decree, not a program of action. Russia is great, and local conditions vary. We believe that the peasants will be able to solve the problem correctly, better than we could ourselves. Whether in our spirit, or in the spirit of the program of the Socialist-Revolutionaries is not the point. The point is that the peasants should be firmly assured that there are no more landlords in the countryside, that they must themselves arrange their own lives."[40]

CHAPTER VIII

Toward Socialism: The First Three Years

LENIN'S land decree of November 8, 1917, expressing the inmost immediate desires of the peasants, immensely strengthened the revolutionary forces of the Bolsheviks. As a frontal attack on the peasants' ancient enemies, the landlords, it increased the peasants' confidence in Lenin's leadership.

"Every peasant who hitherto had seen from government only oppression and robbery now sees in power a government of the poor, which is chosen by him, which has led him out of oppression and, in spite of all the unheard of obstacles and difficulties, knows how to lead him further." [1]

While nationalisation of land does not bring socialism in the village, the annulment of property rights in land was a sharply revolutionary measure against the banks and the capitalists, as well as the feudal landlords. And the socialist revolution was consciously directed first against capitalist banking and large-scale industry. These must be brought under control by the workers, and the building of socialist industry must be well under way before it would be possible to draw the peasant masses toward collective farming.

Politically, the workers needed the support of the peasant masses in consolidating their power. They could not risk coercion against the millions of very small rural producers. For without active support by the poor peasants and at least a friendly neutrality from most of the middle peasants, the workers could not win in their struggle against the capitalists and non-Bolshevik political parties. Also, more basically,

Lenin emphasised repeatedly that the peasant masses could be won for socialist agriculture only when they were convinced from their own experience that it would bring them definite advantages.

"While great difficulties were encountered in industry, where we had to traverse a path which to many seemed long, but which was actually brief, a path which led from workers' control to workers' management, in the more backward countryside far greater preparatory work had to be performed. . . . And here, comrades, when the Petrograd proletariat and the soldiers of the Petrograd garrison took over power, they fully realised that constructive work would encounter far greater difficulties in the countryside; that here one must proceed more gradually; that to attempt to establish social cultivation of the land by means of decrees and legislation would be the height of folly; that an insignificant number of enlightened peasants might agree to this, but that the vast majority of the peasants had no such object in view.

"We therefore confined ourselves to that which was absolutely essential in the interests of the development of the revolution, namely, in no case to endeavour to outrun the development of the masses, but to wait until, as a result of their own experience and their own struggles, a progressive movement grew up. In October [*i.e.*, November, 1917] we confined ourselves to sweeping away forthwith the ancient enemy of the peasants, the feudal landlord, the latifundist. That was the struggle of the peasantry as a whole. There was no division as yet within the peasantry as between proletariat, semi-proletariat, the poorest section of the peasantry, and bourgeoisie. We Socialists knew that socialism was impossible without that struggle. But we also knew that our knowledge in itself was not enough; that it was essential that that knowledge should reach the millions, and not by means of propaganda, but as a result of the experience gained by the millions themselves." [2]

The land decree had indicated that the confiscated lands should be so distributed as to equalise the peasant holdings, and it had formally outlawed the private employment of hired labour on the land. Shortly afterwards, also, the kulaks were made subject to a property tax.[3] Enforcement of these principles rested with local land committees and district soviets of peasant deputies which were dominated at first by the kulaks. In February, agitators were sent into the provinces to give counsel to the poor peasants and explain their rights under the new laws.[4] Then in the summer of 1918 the Bolsheviks carried on a mass campaign that roused the poor peasants to organised independent action against the kulaks.

"If the Bolshevik proletariat in the capitals and large industrial centres had not been able to rally the village poor to its side against the rich peasants, this would have proved that Russia was 'unripe' for the socialist revolution. The peasantry would then have remained an 'integral whole,' *i.e.*, it would have remained under the economic, political, and moral leadership of the kulaks, of the rich, of the bourgeoisie, and the revolution would not have passed beyond the limits of a bourgeois-democratic revolution....

"On the other hand, if in October-November, 1917, the Bolshevik proletariat, without waiting for the class differentiation in the rural districts, without being able to *prepare* for it and bring it about, had at once attempted to 'decree' a civil war or the 'introduction' of socialism in the rural districts, had attempted to do without the temporary *bloc* (alliance) with the peasants in general, without making a number of concessions to the middle peasants, etc., that attempt would have been a Blanquist distortion of Marxism, an attempt of the minority to impose its will upon the majority; it would have been a theoretical absurdity, it would have revealed a failure to understand that a general peasant revolution is *still* a bourgeois revolution, and that *without a series of transitions, transitional stages,* it cannot be transformed into a socialist revolution in a backward country."[5]

Workers and Peasants

At every stage of the revolution, Lenin had the most profound conviction that actual leadership in political life must remain with the industrial workers and not with the peasants.

"The overthrow of bourgeois rule can be accomplished only by the proletariat, as the particular class whose economic conditions of existence train it for this task and provide it with the opportunity and the power to perform it. While the bourgeoisie breaks up and disintegrates the peasantry and all the petty-bourgeois strata, it welds together, unites, and organises the proletariat. Only the proletariat—by virtue of the economic role it plays in large-scale production—is capable of acting as the leader of *all* the toiling and exploited masses, whom the bourgeoisie exploits, oppresses, and crushes not less, and often more, than it does the proletarians, but who are incapable of waging an *independent* struggle for their emancipation.

"... The overthrow of the bourgeoisie can be achieved only by the proletariat becoming transformed into the *ruling class,* capable of crushing the inevitable and desperate resistance of the bourgeoisie, and of organising *all* the toiling and exploited masses for the new economic order." [6]

To those who objected that the workers should have held back from taking power until they had formal assurance of majority support from the peasant masses, Lenin replied:

"There is absolutely no possibility of the petty-bourgeois or semi-petty-bourgeois masses of the toilers deciding in advance the complex political question of whether they should side with the working class or with the bourgeoisie. *Vacillation* on the part of the non-proletarian toiling strata is inevitable. It inevitably requires their own *practical* experience to enable them to *compare* the leadership of the bourgeoisie with the leadership of the proletariat." [7]

"The dictatorship of the proletariat is the class war of the proletariat fought with the weapon of the power of the state; it is a class war one of the aims of which is to demonstrate to the non-proletarian toiling strata by protracted experience and by a long series of practical examples that it is better for them to side with the dictatorship of the proletariat than to side with the dictatorship of the bourgeoisie, and that *no third course exists.*" [My emphasis.—*A.R.*] [8]

The first Soviet Constitution recognised "the privileged position of the proletariat over the peasantry and the disfranchisement of the exploiters." [9] * That this was a *temporary* necessity in the struggle for

* One delegate to All-Russian Congress of Soviets was allowed for every 25,000

socialism was set forth in the programme adopted in March, 1919, by the Eighth Congress of the Russian Communist Party. The programme stated:

"The leading role, in the whole revolution, of the city industrial proletariat, as the most concentrated, united, educated section of the labouring masses, the section most tempered in struggle, has appeared both in the very origin of the Soviets and in the whole course of their development into organs of power. Our Soviet Constitution reflected this, maintaining a certain privileged position for the industrial proletariat in comparison with the more scattered petty-bourgeois masses in the village.

"The Russian Communist Party, explaining the temporary character of this privileged position, historically bound up with the difficulties of socialist organisation of the village, must strive for consistent and systematic utilising of this situation of the industrial proletariat, so that as a counter-balance to the narrow craft and occupational interests which capitalism has cultivated among the workers there may be closer unity between the advanced workers and the more scattered masses of the village proletarians and semi-proletarians, and also of the middle peasantry."[10]

Lenin constantly stressed the fact that workers' power was, as it were, on trial before the peasant masses. The proletarian leaders would take the initiative in guiding the transition toward socialist agriculture, but they could not function properly if they tried to put over measures which the poorer peasants did not yet understand and desire, even if such measures seemed to express the underlying hopes and purposes of these peasants.

As a first step toward socialist agriculture, the Soviet power would sharpen the class lines in the village and undermine the power of the petty-capitalist kulaks by policies appealing to the poor and middle peasants and enforced by them.

Poor peasants who could not live without selling their labour power were the closest allies of the industrial workers. They had everything

electors in towns; one for every 125,000 inhabitants in rural districts. Equal suffrage for all is provided in the present Soviet Constitution adopted in 1936.

to gain from a revolution in the village. To them, primarily, the Bolsheviks appealed for carrying out a fairly equal distribution of land. On them also was laid the task of enforcing the collection of surplus grain to increase the city food supply. From the Committees of Poor Peasants set up in the mass campaign of 1918, there developed a reorganisation of the rural Soviets which gave the poor peasants instead of the kulaks a predominant voice.

"We had to save the non-agricultural population, which was suffering from hunger. That could be done only with the aid of Committees of Poor Peasants, as proletarian organisations. And it was only when the October Revolution in the countryside began and was accomplished in the summer of 1918 that we found our real proletarian base; it was only then that our revolution *became a proletarian revolution in fact,* and not merely by virtue of proclamations, promises, and declarations." [11]

Less stable was the relation with the middle peasants who hired no labour and lived without selling their own labour power. Here was a large, strategic group whose interests brought them into conflict with the kulaks and the big capitalists, but whose small property holdings made them wary of committing themselves and easily misled by anti-Bolshevik propaganda.

"Our task in the rural districts is to destroy the landlord and smash the resistance of the exploiter and the kulak profiteer. For this purpose we can safely rely *only* on the semi-proletarians, the 'poor peasants.' But the middle peasant is not our enemy. He vacillated, is vacillating, and will continue to vacillate. The task of influencing the vacillators *is not identical* with the task of overthrowing the exploiter and defeating the active enemy. The task at the present moment [November, 1918] is to come to an agreement with the middle peasant, while not for a moment renouncing the struggle against the kulak and at the same time relying solely on the poor peasant." [12]

As the revolution developed, the question of consolidating an alliance with the middle peasantry became increasingly important. At the

Eighth Congress of the Russian Communist Party (March, 1919), for example, when the counter-revolutionists were again trying to stir up peasant revolts, Lenin gave special emphasis to the question of the middle peasantry.

"The merciless war with the village bourgeoisie and the kulaks made of primary importance the task of organising the proletariat and semi-proletariat of the village. But as a further step, for the party which desires to create the firm basis of communist society, there arises the task of correctly deciding the question of our relation to the middle peasantry. This is a task of a much higher order. We could not set it forth in all its breadth until the basis of existence of the Soviet republic was assured. This task is much more complex. It requires the determining of our relation to a numerous and powerful stratum of the population. This relation cannot be defined with a simple reply: struggle or support....

"The Socialists, the best representatives of old-time socialism—when they still believed in revolution and served it theoretically and ideologically—talked of *neutralising the peasantry,* that is, to make of the middle peasantry a social stratum which if not actively aiding the proletarian revolution would, at the very least, not hinder it; a neutral social stratum not standing on the side of our enemies. This abstract, theoretical statement of the question is completely clear for us. But it is insufficient.

"We have arrived at such a stage of socialist construction that it is necessary to work out concretely, in detail, basic principles and guides (verified by the experience of work in the village) by which we must be directed, so that in relation to the middle peasant we shall *stand on the ground of a firm alliance,* and exclude the possibility of the recurring deviations and errors which have torn the middle peasant away from us, even when in fact we, as the directing Communist Party which had helped the Russian peasant for the first time finally to throw off his landlords and to establish for himself a genuine democracy—we might have completely reckoned on his full confidence." [13]

And later at the same congress:

"At the congress we must not only lay particular stress on our accommodating attitude towards the middle peasantry, but also think over a number of measures, as concrete as possible, which will directly give the middle peasantry something at least. This is insistently demanded both by interests of self-preservation and by the interests of the struggle against our enemies, who know that the middle peasant vacillates between us and them, and who are endeavouring to win him away from us."[14]

Middle peasants—and even poor peasants—had to be fought when they were lured into giving active assistance to anti-Soviet forces. But at no time were coercive measures to be applied against the middle peasants as small producers. Their support of socialist agriculture must be won by experiment and demonstration.

"We fully realise that such vast upheavals in the lives of tens of millions of people as the transition from small individual peasant production to the social cultivation of the land, affecting as they do the most profound roots of life and habits, can be accomplished only by prolonged effort, and can in general be accomplished only when necessity compels people to reshape their whole lives."[15]

Poverty in the countryside had been greatly increased by the war. Uncounted thousands of draught cattle and implements had been ruined without possibility of replacement. "The impoverishment bequeathed us by the war simply does not allow us to restore the old small-scale peasant form of production."[16]

The aim to develop collective farming had been embodied in a Soviet law of February, 1918. By the end of the following year nearly six thousand experiments in various kinds of collective farming were already under way, encouraged and assisted by the Soviet government in so far as means were at hand.[17]

Great estates which had been operated in a technically progressive manner as large-scale farms were held intact, to be operated by state-employed wage workers with the aid of agricultural specialists. This

Lenin set forth as a special challenge to the poorest peasants who were wage workers:

"By orders and decrees it was possible to overthrow landlords and capitalists, it is possible to curb the kulaks. But if the millions of agricultural workers do not have their own organisation and do not learn in this organisation, step by step, themselves to decide their own affairs, not only political but economic (and the economic are the most important of all); if they do not learn to administer the great estates, bringing them into better condition than other estates, and transform them from examples of exploitation, where formerly blood and sweat were squeezed from the workers, into examples of comradely agriculture—then this will be the fault of the toilers themselves." [18]

No mass campaign for collective operation of peasant farms would be attempted until considerable experience had been assembled from all parts of the country, and until the state could supply farm machinery and special training of machine operators. But even without this normal technical base for large-scale collective farming, peasants in collective farms were finding a practical advantage in pooling their scanty resources in livestock and implements.

"We have to give the peasant, who not only in our country but all over the world is a practical man and a realist, concrete examples to prove that the commune is the best possible thing. Of course, nothing will come of it if hasty individuals go flitting to the villages from the cities, come there, make a speech, stir up a number of intellectual and at times unintellectual brawls, and then shake the dust from their feet and go their way. That sometimes happens. Instead of arousing respect, they arouse ridicule, and deservedly so." [19]

"When we say, 'Encourage association,' we are giving instructions which must be tested many times before the final *form* in which to put them into effect is found. When it is stated that we must strive to gain their voluntary consent, it means that the peasants must be convinced, and convinced in practice. They will not allow themselves to be convinced by mere words, and they are perfectly right. It would be a bad thing if they allowed themselves to be convinced merely by decrees and agitational leaflets. If it were possible to reshape economic life in this way, such reshaping would not be worth a brass farthing. It must first be demonstrated that such association is better, people must be united in such a way that they are actually united and are not at odds with each other—it must be proved that association is advantageous. That is the way the peasant puts the question and that is the way our decrees put it. If we have not been able to achieve that so far, there is nothing to be ashamed of and we must admit it frankly." [20]

These outstanding points in Lenin's programme for the transition from small peasant production to socialist agriculture were included in the agrarian section of the programme adopted by the Russian Communist Party at its Eighth Congress (March, 1919).*

In Defence of Soviet Power

Carrying-out of this programme was enormously complicated by the capitalist forces which tried by every conceivable means to destroy the Soviet revolution. Almost immediately after November, 1917, the very existence of the Soviet power was threatened: by elements within Russia opposed to the Bolsheviks; by the advance of the German army, checked only at the price of the harsh treaty of Brest-Litovsk; by White Guard insurrections, usually with assistance from foreign powers; by open attacks of foreign forces; and by the disorganisation of all production and transportation. For a considerable time the most productive wheat regions and the richest mineral resources were held by the counter-revolutionists.

Throughout the years of civil war and intervention (1918-21), with increasing hunger and destitution, Lenin kept in the forefront of his thinking the increasingly complex problems of obtaining food for the

* For text of agrarian section, see Appendix B, p. 211. For special resolution on middle peasantry see *Selected Works,* VIII, pp. 184-87. Much of Lenin's contribution to the programme discussion at the Seventh Congress (1918) and the Eighth Congress (1919) will be found in Volume VIII of his *Selected Works.* Lenin died (January, 1924), before the road was open for a mass campaign for collectivisation of agriculture, but when the restoration of Soviet industry had given way to rapid expansion and reconstruction under the First Five-Year Plan, such a campaign was successfully carried through. See Chapter XI.

city workers and the Red Army; holding the support of the peasant masses; and preparing the way for collective farming.

Politically the poor and middle peasants learned again in the course of the struggle who were their most trustworthy friends. Two years after the November revolution Lenin summed up the waverings of the peasants "in the regions where the influence of the proletariat was least felt."

"At first they were for the Bolsheviks, when the latter gave them land and when the demobilised soldiers brought the news of peace. Then they went against the Bolsheviks, when the latter, in the interests of the international development of the revolution, and in order to preserve the hearth of revolution in Russia, accepted the Brest-Litovsk Peace, thereby 'offending' one of the most profound of petty-bourgeois sentiments, patriotism. The dictatorship of the proletariat was not to the liking of the peasants in regions with large surpluses of grain, when the Bolsheviks showed that they would be stern and unbending in demanding that these surpluses be surrendered to the state at fixed prices. The peasants of the Urals, Siberia, and the Ukraine thereupon turned towards Kolchak and Denikin.

"Next, the experience of the 'democracy' of Kolchak and Denikin, so trumpeted by every journalist in every White Guard paper in Kolchakia and Denikinland, proved to the peasants that the talk about democracy and the Constituent Assembly * was only a screen for the dictatorship of the landlords and capitalists.

* In the early months of the Provisional Government, Lenin had favoured the calling of a Constituent Assembly. But as the Soviets developed further and were representing broad masses of workers and peasants, Lenin saw that the time was ripe for this new form of democratic government.

Between the elections for a Constituent Assembly (carried out from the middle of October) and the meeting of the Constituent Assembly three months later, a decisive break had occurred within the Socialist-Revolutionary Party between the Lefts who supported the Bolsheviks and the Rights who opposed them. Also, the Soviets had displaced the Provisional Government, and the struggle between the Soviets and the bourgeoisie had moved far beyond the earlier period of discussion.

When the Constituent Assembly met, it refused to recognise the decrees of the Second Congress of Soviets on peace, land, and the transfer of power to the Soviets. A statement of principles presented to the Constituent Assembly by the All-Russian Executive Committee of the Soviet Government was categorically rejected without discussion. The

"A new swing-over to the Bolsheviks began: the peasant uprisings in the rear of Kolchak and Denikin multiplied. The Red troops were greeted by the peasants as liberators.

"In the long run it was these vacillations of the peasants, who constitute the greater part of the petty-bourgeois toiling masses, that decided the fate of the Soviet power and of the power of Kolchak and Denikin. But the 'long run' was preceded by a fairly long period of bitter struggle and painful experience, which even now, after the lapse of two years, has not ended in Russia, has not ended, that is, in Siberia and the Ukraine. And one cannot vouch that it will *finally* end within, say, another year or so." [21]

The central regions of European Russia, where industrial workers were most numerous, most politically developed, and most active in reaching the peasant masses, were the strongest base of the revolution. Here tens and hundreds of thousands of poor and middle peasants joined the new Red Army which fought valiantly against the White Guards and brought decisive victory to the Soviet power.

Obtaining food for the city workers and for the Red Army was one of the most urgent problems from the spring of 1918 throughout the years of civil war and intervention.

"We are now facing the most elementary task of human society—to vanquish famine, or at least to mitigate at once the direct famine, the painful famine which has afflicted both capitals and numerous districts of agricultural Russia. And we have to solve this problem in the midst of a civil war and the furious and desperate resistance of the exploiters of all ranks and colours and of all orientations." [22]

Kulak revolts had already cut off the supply from the richest grain regions of the Ukraine, the Kuban, and the Volga. And within the loyal revolutionary provinces the government grain trade monopoly

---

Bolsheviks and Left Socialist-Revolutionaries then withdrew from the Constituent Assembly and it was dispersed. When the Right Socialist-Revolutionaries, the Mensheviks, and the Constitutional Democrats (Cadets) tried to arouse popular protest against this action, they found very slight response among the masses. (See *History of the Communist Party of the Soviet Union*, p. 214. And for Lenin's own statements on the Constituent Assembly, see a series of articles in his *Selected Works*, VI, pp. 447-85.)

(instituted early in the World War and continued by the Soviet government) faced increasing difficulty in drawing the peasants' surpluses out of hiding. For the kulaks were carrying on an illegal private grain trade, with prices enormously higher than the fixed prices paid by the government. As time went on, the kulaks drew some of the middle peasants and even a few poor peasants into this illegal speculation, letting them have part of the kulak surplus grain at prices above the government price but less than the illegal trader could obtain from the hungry people in the city.

Lenin regarded the battle against illegal grain trading as a major political issue. He appealed repeatedly to the organised workers to support the government monopoly. For example, in May, 1918:

"Half-measures are of no avail. Complaining will lead us nowhere. Attempts to secure food and fuel 'in a retail fashion,' *i.e.*, every factory, every workshop for itself, will only increase the disorganisation and assist the avaricious, filthy, and dastardly work of the profiteers." [23]

The common struggle for bread was a primary revolutionary task.

"Proper distribution of food and fuel, their procurement in greater quantities and their strict registration and control *by the workers* on a national scale—that is the real and chief approach to socialism, that is not so much a revolutionary task in general as a *communist* task, one of the tasks on which the toilers and the poor must offer determined battle to capitalism." [24]

Lenin summoned the class-conscious workers of "Red Petrograd" to go forth and lead the struggle for bread, to arouse and organise the poor peasants. They must take the surplus grain from the kulaks by force, if necessary, as the hunger in cities and towns might literally undermine and destroy the revolution.

"That is why, comrades, workers of Petrograd, I have taken the liberty of addressing this letter to you. Petrograd is not Russia. The Petrograd workers are only a small part of the workers of Russia. But they are one of the best, most advanced, most class-conscious, most revolutionary, most steadfast detachments of the working class and the toilers of Russia, and the least liable to succumb to empty phrases, to weak-willed despair and to the intimidation of the bourgeoisie. And it has frequently happened at critical moments in the life of a nation that even small but advanced detachments of advanced classes have drawn the rest after them, have fired the masses with the spirit of revolutionary enthusiasm and have accomplished tremendous historic feats." [25]

Of course, the chief brunt of the day by day struggle against the kulaks was borne by the Committees of Poor Peasants, which were organised in this food campaign and to which we have already referred. Their work was stimulated by special privileges: In villages where grain requisitions were promptly carried through, textiles and implements were sold to the poor and middle peasants at much lower prices than the kulaks had to pay.[26]

As the months went by, normal trade with the villages was made impossible by a severe shortage of goods, for industry and transportation became more and more disorganised. Loss of coal and iron mines, lack of other raw materials, and the continuing life-and-death struggle of defence against counter-revolution were added to the serious difficulties of the workers' inexperience in management. Production declined disastrously, instead of rising to meet the needs and expectations of the peasants.

From a government grain trade monopoly, paying fixed prices in currency to peasants who delivered their surplus grain, the emergency required a shift to government requisitions of grain according to quotas set for every region and every village. No industrial products and no currency were available in exchange, but the peasants received promises of future payment in farm equipment and consumers' goods as soon as industry could be restored.

Under this "War Communism" increasing amounts of grain were delivered to the government, but illegal private trading in grain continued, and all of the once "revolutionary" parties except the Bolsheviks clamoured for revival of free trading.

"We are reproached for establishing the dictatorship of the proletariat. . . . But we are proud of this dictatorship, of this iron rule of the workers, which said: 'We have overthrown the capitalists and we will lay down our lives to prevent any attempt on their part to restore their rule.' No one during these two years starved so much as the workers of Petrograd, Moscow and Ivanovo-Vosnesensk. It has now been computed that during these two years they received not more than seven poods of bread a year, whereas the peasants of the grain-bearing provinces consumed not less than 17 poods.* The workers made great sacrifices, they suffered epidemics, and the mortality among them increased. But they will prove that the workers rose up against the capitalists not out of vengeance but with the inflexible determination to create a social system in which there will be no landlords and no capitalists.... Those who are so keen on calumniating the Bolsheviks should not forget that the dictatorship entailed above all sacrifice and above all starvation for the workers who were making it a reality." [27]

As the Soviet power regained control of Siberia and the southern wheat regions, supplies of grain within the nation became more abundant, but at the same time the struggle against kulaks was intensified and hunger in the cities remained a serious problem. Lenin put this before the Ninth Party Congress, in the spring of 1920, when the civil war was ended and the Polish invasion was still in the future:

"We are now faced with a very difficult task: having won on the bloody front, we must now win on the bloodless front. This war is a more difficult one. This front is the most arduous. We say this frankly to all class-conscious workers.... The fact is that the more we were victorious, the more we secured regions like Siberia, the Ukraine, the Kuban. In those regions there are rich peasants; there are no proletarians, and what proletariat there is has been corrupted with petty-bourgeois habits. We know that everybody who has a piece of land in those parts says: 'A fig for the government! I will skin the hungry as much as I want to. I don't give a hoot for the government!' The peasant profiteer who when left to the tender mercies of Denikin swung towards us will now be aided by the Entente. The war has changed its front and its forms. It is now taking the form of trade, of bag-trading, † which it has made international." [28]

* A pood equals 36 pounds.

† Smuggling or speculation. Peasants carrying on illegal trading took their stuff to the railroad station or nearest town in a rough bag slung over their shoulders.

But Lenin never lost confidence in the power of the masses to triumph over all difficulties.

"We have started a great war, a war which we shall not end soon. This is a bloodless war waged by the labour armies on starvation, cold, and typhus, a war for an enlightened, joyous, well-fed and healthy Russia. But we shall end this war with victory as decisive as the one with which we ended the struggle against the White Guards." [29]

Upbuilding Begins

Finally, as the long period of civil war and armed intervention in European Russia was ended with the Polish peace (October, 1920), and the smashing defeat of Wrangel in the Crimea (November, 1920), the way was open for more constructive measures in relation to the peasants. In spite of the poor harvest in 1920, there was more bread for the workers, there was more fuel for the factories. Transport was beginning to be restored, bringing again a little cotton from Turkestan to the textile mills, and a little iron and steel from the Ukraine. In November, 1920, Lenin told a party conference of the Moscow province:

"We are only just beginning to emerge from that situation in which we managed to keep going with the utmost difficulty by expending old stocks, and approach a situation in which Russia will set about restoring her shattered industry and be in a position, by taking grain from the rural districts, to give the peasants salt, kerosene and, even if only in small amounts, textiles. Without this there can be no talk of socialist construction.

"...In order to vanquish capitalism in general, we must, firstly, vanquish the exploiters and uphold the power of the exploited—that is the task of overthrowing the exploiters by revolutionary force; secondly, there is the constructive task—the task of building up new economic relations, setting an example in how it is to be done....

"We have convinced the peasants that the proletariat ensures them better conditions of life than the bourgeoisie; we have convinced them of that in practice. When the peasants, dissatisfied though they were with the Bolshevik regime, compared it in practice with the system of the advocates of the Constituent Assembly, Kolchak, and the rest, they arrived at the conclusion that the Bolsheviks had assured them a better life and military protection from attack by the imperialists of the whole world. However, under the bourgeoisie, half the peasantry lived on a bourgeois basis—and they could not live otherwise.

"The proletariat must now perform the second task, that of demonstrating to the peasants that it can, by example and practice, create economic relations that will prove to be of a higher order than those under which each peasant family conducted its own affairs in its own way. To this day the peasants believe only in this old order; to this day they regard it as normal. There is no doubt about that. It would be sheer nonsense to think that our propaganda could induce them to change their attitude on vital questions, on economic questions. They are watching and waiting; their attitude towards us has changed from hostile neutrality to benevolent neutrality....

"But that is not enough; we have not done the main thing, which is to show that the proletariat will restore large-scale industry and social economy in such a way as to lead the peasants to a higher economic system. Having proved that we are able, by means of revolutionary organisation, to repulse violence offered to the exploited, we must prove the same thing in another sphere, setting an example which will not so much try to persuade in words as to demonstrate by action to the vast mass of the peasants and the petty bourgeoisie, and to other countries as well, that the proletariat which has been victorious in war can create a communist system, a communist order." [30]

In presenting to the Eighth Congress of Soviets (December, 1920), a bill embodying "Measures for Consolidating and Developing Peasant Farming," Lenin brought forward the urgency of the situation and the problems involved in making these measures really effective among the peasant masses.

"Arrangements must at once be made to have this bill thoroughly discussed—in the light of local experience (it is based on local experience, and they are already beginning to realise this in the localities) —by the congress and also by the representatives of the local executive committees and the departments of the executive committees. Probably not a single comrade can now be met with who doubts the necessity for specific and very energetic measures of assistance—not only in the form of encouragement but also in the form of constraint—for improving our agricultural production.

"Our country has been and still is a small peasant country, and the transition to communism is far more difficult for us than it would have been under any other conditions. In order to accomplish this transition the peasants must themselves participate in it ten times more than they participated in the war.... The peasants are not Socialists. And to build our socialist plans on the assumption that they are Socialists would be to build on sand; it would mean that we do not understand our tasks and that we have not learned during these three years to adjust our programmes and carry out our new undertakings in accordance with the poverty and squalour by which we are surrounded. We must clearly realise the problems that face us.

"The first task is to unite the Communists working in the Land Departments; general conclusions must be drawn from their experience; we must grasp what has been done locally and embody it in the legislative acts which will be passed at the centre, by the government departments, and by the All-Russian Congress of Soviets. And we hope that with your help we shall be able to do it. But this is only the first step.

"The second step is to convince the non-party peasants, precisely the non-party peasants—because they constitute the mass and because what we are in a position to do can be done only by heightening in this mass, which in itself is active and full of initiative, the realisation that this task must be tackled. Peasant husbandry cannot continue in the old way....

"...We are now launching a new military campaign against the relics of inertia, unenlightenment, and mistrust that prevail among the peasant masses. We shall achieve nothing by the old methods; but we shall achieve victory by the methods of propaganda, agitation and organised influence which we have learned. And the result will be that not only will decrees be adopted, institutions created and documents written—it is not enough to send orders flying all over the country—but also that by the spring all the fields will be sown better than before, that a definite improvement will be achieved in the husbandry of the small peasant. Let it be even the most elementary improvement—the more cautious we are the better—but it must be achieved at all costs on a mass scale. . . . And unless we succeed, unless we achieve a practical improvement in the husbandry of the small peasant on a mass scale, there is no salvation for us. . . .

"We admit that we are in debt to the peasant. . . . We must repay that debt, and we shall repay it when we have restored our industry. But in order to restore it we need a surplus of agricultural products. And that is why our agrarian bill is important, not only because we must secure practical results, but also because around it, as around a focal point, are grouped hundreds of decisions and legislative measures of the Soviet government."[31]

Detailed measures embodied in the bill of December, 1920, followed lines indicated in the agrarian programme which had been adopted by the Eighth Party Congress a year and a half earlier.* They included plans for tractor-renting stations, implement repair shops, grain-cleaning stations, and livestock breeding centres. The bill also provided for a nationwide sowing plan to be drawn up by the People's Commissariat of Agriculture and to be allotted by regions and villages. According to it "all agriculturalists should fully sow their land in accordance with the assignment of the government [worked out locally by elected peasant committees.—*A.R.*] and should cultivate it properly in accordance with the example shown by the best and most assiduous husbandmen among the middle and poor peasants." Rewards in kind were to be granted to village communities, collective farms and individual peasants who properly fulfilled the plan and also improved their farms.[32]

Before the spring sowing began it had become clear that further measures were necessary.

* See Appendix B.

CHAPTER IX

Toward Socialism: The NEP Detour

WITH the ending of the Polish war and the final defeat of Wrangel, internal problems came to the fore. Industry was only starting on the upgrade in the winter of 1920-21 as it very slowly emerged from the extreme disintegration of the preceding years. The peasant masses, who had loyally supported the revolution against its enemies without and within, were chafing under the continued absence of trading which seemed to them unnecessary now that the war was over.

For the war emergency, peasants had accepted War Communism, with its requisition of all surplus grain. This treatment of the peasants had had temporarily a certain economic and political basis:

"The peasants received from the workers' state all the land, and protection against the landlords and the kulaks; the workers have been receiving from the peasants loans of food supplies until large-scale industry is restored." [1]

But this could not satisfy the peasants once the war emergency had passed. A way must be found to create a more normal basis for the indispensable alliance of workers with poor and middle peasants.

"Normal relations are those and only those under which the proletariat, controlling large-scale industry and its products, not only fully satisfies the needs of the peasantry but, in providing them with the means of subsistence, so alleviates their conditions that the difference compared with the capitalist system becomes obvious and palpable. This and this alone will create the basis for normal socialist society. At present, however, we are unable to do this—to such an extent are we crushed by ruin, want, impoverishment and despair. But to help to rid ourselves of this accursed heritage we are reacting in a definite way to the relations which were established during the period of desperately burdensome war."[2]

To hasten the revival of industry, foreign capitalists were offered "concessions" to operate certain mines and oil wells and a few factories, under stated terms and for definitely limited periods of time. This first step in Lenin's New Economic Policy was a temporary measure which provided quickly some desperately needed products and, when the concessions expired, gave the Soviet government a few more well-equipped establishments.

Why the Peasants Were Restless

But meantime, as the months went by in the winter of 1920-21, the peasants' restlessness was increasing. They did not quite grasp the tremendous difficulties involved in restoring industrial plants, obtaining fuel and raw materials, replacing skilled workers who had given their lives to the revolution, and drawing back into the apparatus of production some of the technical experts whose scientific or managerial skill could not be immediately replaced from the ranks of the working class and the Communist Party.

A very poor harvest in 1920 meant not only shorter rations for the cities, but lack of fodder and loss of cattle in the villages. This was followed by serious drought and a devastating crop failure in the important Volga and southeastern wheat regions in 1921, which brought severe famine and mass death among the peasants of those districts and less bread than ever in the cities.

Speaking in the spring of 1921, Lenin recognised clearly that under War Communism peasant agriculture had deteriorated.

"We could not act otherwise under the conditions which the imperialists and capitalists imposed upon us by their war. We had no other choice. But these circumstances brought us to the position that, after a war that had lasted so long, peasant farming had so deteriorated that the harvest failed—as a result of the diminution of the sown area, as a result of the deterioration of the means of production, as a result of the decline in the yield, as a result of the shortage of labour, etc. The failure of the harvest was enormous and the collection of the surplus food stocks, which after all turned out to be much better than we expected, was accompanied by such an intensification of the crisis as will, perhaps, give rise to even greater difficulties and suffering for us in the forthcoming months." [8]

White Guards and other émigrés in Paris and elsewhere were poised ready to utilise the peasants' difficulties against the Bolsheviks. At the end of February (1921) counter-revolutionary elements succeeded in provoking a brief armed insurrection among the soldiers and sailors at the Kronstadt fortress near Petrograd. This revolt and the peasant restlessness which it reflected were analysed by Lenin at the Tenth Party Congress which opened its sessions a few days later.

"The Paris newspapers reported a mutiny in Kronstadt two weeks before the events in Kronstadt took place. It is absolutely clear that this is the work of the Socialist-Revolutionaries and of the White Guards abroad; at the same time, the movement amounted to a petty-bourgeois counter-revolution, an outburst of the petty-bourgeois, anarchist element. This is something new.... This petty-bourgeois counter-revolution is undoubtedly more dangerous than Denikin, Yudenich, and Kolchak put together....

"We must understand that in the midst of the crisis of peasant economy we cannot exist unless we appeal to this peasant economy to help town and country. We must remember that the bourgeoisie is striving to rouse the peasantry against the workers, is striving to rouse the petty-bourgeois anarchist element against the workers by means of workers' slogans, that this will lead directly to the overthrow of the dictatorship of the proletariat, and consequently to the restoration of capitalism, to the restoration of the old landlord and capitalist rule. Here the political danger is evident....

"Then follow economic problems. What is the significance of the slogan of free trade which the petty-bourgeois element has brought to the front? It shows that in the relations between the proletariat and the small tillers of the soil there are difficult problems, difficult tasks that we have not yet solved. I refer to the relations between the victorious proletariat and the small proprietors at a time when the proletarian revolution is sweeping a country in which the proletariat is in the minority and the petty bourgeoisie is in the majority. The role of the proletariat in such a country is to guide these small proprietors towards socialised, collective, communal labour. There can be no doubt about this theoretically....

"... We could not demonstrate the superiority of large-scale production in practice, because this large-scale production has been destroyed, it is itself dragging out a miserable existence and can be restored only if sacrifices are imposed upon the small tillers of the soil.... In the midst of the crisis, of lack of fodder and the dying of cattle, the peasant must advance credits to the Soviet government for the sake of large-scale industry from which he is getting nothing as yet. This is the economic situation which creates enormous difficulties, this is the economic situation which compels us to ponder more deeply over the conditions of transition from war to peace.... The danger of this slogan [of free trading] does not lie in the fact that it conceals White Guard and Menshevik strivings, but in that it may become widespread, notwithstanding the hatred these very peasants entertain towards the White Guards. *It will become widespread because it answers to the economic conditions of existence of the small producer.*"[4] [My emphasis.—*A.R.*]

What NEP Could Accomplish

Under Lenin's New Economic Policy, the Soviet government drew back from its attempt to bring small producers and small traders directly and immediately into a socialist organisation of economy. It restored a certain freedom of trading and producing for the open market. It was made necessary by the serious crisis which followed the sufferings and deprivations of the civil war.

"This was the first and I hope the last time in the history of Soviet Russia that large masses of peasants were hostile towards us, not consciously, but instinctively. What gave rise to this peculiar, and for us, of course, very unpleasant, situation? The fact that we had advanced too far in our economic offensive, the fact that we had not created an adequate base, that the masses sensed what we ourselves were not yet able consciously to formulate, but what we, soon after, a few weeks later, admitted, namely: that the direct transition to purely socialist forms, to purely socialist distribution, was beyond our strength, and that if we were not able to retreat, to confine ourselves to easier tasks, we were doomed." [5]

Lenin showed that War Communism was "a temporary measure," which had been "thrust upon us by war and ruin." [6]

"In this connection we did much that was simply wrong, and it would be a great crime not to see and realise that we did not keep within proper limits, that we did not know how to keep within proper limits. Some of the things, however, we were compelled to do by necessity: up to now we have been living under such conditions of furious and incredibly severe war that we had no other alternative but to act in a wartime manner in the sphere of economics.... At the same time, it is an undoubted fact, and we must reveal it in our agitation and propaganda, that we went further than was necessary theoretically and politically. We can permit a fair amount of free local turnover without destroying, but on the contrary strengthening, the political power of the proletariat." [7]

In the village, the New Economic Policy was essentially a retreat from an unsuccessful attempt at storming the peasant stronghold of petty capitalism. In discussing the need for abandoning War Communism, Lenin repeatedly used such phrases as "frontal attack." For example:

"We tried to solve this problem in an onrush, by a frontal attack, as it were, but we suffered defeat. Such mistakes occur in every war, and they are not even regarded as mistakes. If a frontal attack fails, we shall try a flank attack, we shall operate by means of siege and sapping." [8]

But in speaking of frontal attack and retreat, Lenin never for one moment implied any abandonment of his revolutionary purpose. And the new economic methods of 1921 were in fact much closer to the principles which Marx, Engels, and Lenin had developed as the guide for socialist revolution in a peasant country—and much closer to the Russian party's original plans—than was the War Communism which had been imposed in the emergency and which the peasant masses had accepted until the fighting was ended.

In the New Economic Policy, Lenin sought—and found—the conditions for a fresh start, a correct transition, from the chaotic, self-centred, individual production of the middle peasant to successful socialist agriculture.

Requisitioning of the peasants' entire surplus grain must be stopped. On this the Tenth Congress of the Russian Communist Party (March, 1921) was unanimously agreed. The peasant should be required to give a much smaller, definitely stated amount of grain as a tax in kind, while he would be free to use the rest of his surplus pretty much as he might choose.*

For the peasants, the tax in kind had several immediate advantages over the food collections of War Communism. Not only was the total amount taken by the state reduced by nearly half, but the exact totals required were to be made known in advance of spring sowing. Tax gatherers were to put through their collections before a given date so that the peasant would realise exactly what remained for his own free disposal.

"The task that confronts the local workers is to collect the food tax in full, and to collect it in the shortest possible time.... The tax will not be paid voluntarily, we shall not be able to dispense with coercion, the collection of the tax will cause a number of hardships for peasant farming; if we drag out the process of collecting the tax longer than is necessary the peasant will be discontented and will say that he has not obtained the freedom to dispose of his surplus....

"This is one task. Another task is to enable the peasant to enjoy freedom to trade to the utmost limits and to raise small production;

* The full text of the resolution adopted by the Tenth Party Congress is given in Appendix C.

to give a certain amount of freedom to the capitalism that grows up on the basis of small production and petty trade." [9]

Since the tax rate was to be lowered for those who increased their sowings or followed certain practices, the peasants were given individual stimulus to increase production and improve their technique.

"As long as he remains small, the small farmer must have a stimulus, an impetus, something to rouse him, corresponding to his economic base, *i.e.,* small, individual farming. We cannot get away from local free turnover in this case." [10]

Freedom of local trading would revive small industries, which would be allowed to develop, subject only to some state supervision. At the same time, the Soviet government undertook to increase as rapidly as possible the products of big industry for which the peasant's free surplus might be exchanged. As these industrial products became more abundant, the tax in kind would be reduced and the government would obtain through normal exchange of products the grain required for city workers and the armed forces.

"The real and only basis upon which we could consolidate our resources for the erection of socialist society is large-scale industry.... It is, of course, absolutely ridiculous and absurd to assume that we could ever forget about this fundamental aim. The only question that arises here is: How could such doubts and perplexity arise in the minds of comrades; how could they think that this main, fundamental aim, without which the material production basis of socialism is impossible, has been relegated to second place? These comrades have simply misunderstood the relation between our state and small industry. Our main task is to restore large-scale industry; and in order to approach the task of restoring large-scale industry at all seriously and systematically we must restore small industry." [11]

Lenin squarely faced the fact that revival of local trade and local industries would mean the sharpening again of class differences among the peasants which had been greatly lessened since 1917.

"The peasantry has become much more of a middle peasantry than before; antagonisms have been smoothed out, the land has been distributed and tenure is much more equal; the kulaks have been struck at the roots and to a large extent expropriated—in Russia more than in the Ukraine, and less in Siberia. Taken as a whole, however, statistics quite incontrovertibly show that the countryside has been leveled, smoothed out, *i.e.*, the sharp extremes of kulak and landless peasant have been smoothed out." [12]

But now this trend would temporarily be reversed. "Free turnover means individual goods exchange, *i.e.*, it means encouraging the kulaks. . . . They will grow where they could not grow before." [13]

Small production and freedom of trading are the economic soil from which capitalism sprouts naturally and inevitably.

"Of course, free trade means the growth of capitalism; one cannot get away from it. And whoever thinks of getting away from it and brushing it aside is only consoling himself with words. If small economy exists, if free exchange exists, capitalism will appear." [14]

"Freedom of turnover and freedom to trade mean commodity exchange between individual, small proprietors. All of us who have learnt at least the A B C of Marxism know that this turnover and freedom to trade inevitably lead to the division of the commodity producers into owners of capital and owners of labour power, a division into capitalists and wage workers, *i.e.*, the restoration of capitalist wage slavery, which does not come like a bolt from the blue, but all over the world grows precisely out of commodity agriculture." [15]

Such revival of petty capitalism was obviously dangerous. "But can you point to a single path in revolution, to any stage and method which did not have its dangers?" [16] Lenin, as a great creative leader, weighing class forces and the hard realities of the moment, had pointed the way to the most fruitful and least perilous path.

"The postponement of the restoration of large-scale industry, the unbearableness of 'locked in' exchange between industry and agriculture were revealed; and that meant that all efforts had to be concentrated on what was more accessible—the restoration of small industry: helping things from that side, propping up that side of the structure that was half demolished by the war and blockade; doing everything possible to develop trade at all costs without being afraid of capitalism, because the limits we have put to it (in economics, the expropriation of the landlords and of the bourgeoisie; in politics, the workers' and peasants' government), are sufficiently narrow, sufficiently 'moderate.' This is the fundamental idea of the food tax; this is its economic significance." [17]

"Since the workers' state has taken possession of the factories, works, and railways, this capitalism has no terrors for us. It will help to improve the economic exchange of peasant produce for the manufactures of neighbouring handicraftsmen, who, although they will not cover the peasants' requirements of manufactured goods to a very large extent, will nevertheless cover them to some extent; peasant economy will improve compared to what it was before, and it desperately needs improvement. Let small industry expand to some extent, let state capitalism expand—the Soviet power need not fear that; it must look things straight in the face and call things by their proper names; but it must control this, determine its limits.

"Concessions need not frighten us; if we give concessionaires a few factories and retain most of them in our own hands, there is nothing terrible about it.... Growing capitalism will be under control, under supervision, while political power will remain in the hands of the working class and of the workers' state." [18]

State capitalism was in no sense the goal in Lenin's mind but only one of the transition steps toward socialism. And he drew a sharp distinction between state capitalism in the Soviet Union and state capitalism in a country dominated by private capital.

"Free trade means freedom for capitalism, but at the same time it means a new form of capitalism. It means that we are recreating capitalism to a certain extent. We are doing this quite openly. It is state capitalism. But state capitalism in a society in which power belongs to capital and state capitalism in a proletarian state are two different concepts. In a capitalist state, state capitalism is recognised by the state and is controlled by it for the benefit of the bourgeoisie, and in opposition to the interest of the proletariat. In the proletarian state, the same thing is done for the benefit of the working class for the purpose of withstanding the as yet strong bourgeoisie and of fighting it." [19]

Building Socialist Industry and Trade

In the spring of 1922 Lenin believed that the time had come for halting what he called the "retreat" in the economic field. No new concessions were to be given. No new "mixed companies" * were to be formed. And while the freedom of peasant trading would not be checked, much more vigorous and efficient effort must be put into the upbuilding of state-owned industrial production and distribution.

"The retreat is at an end; it is now a matter of regrouping our forces.... The capitalists are creating an economic link with the peasants in order to amass wealth; you must create a link with peasant economy in order to strengthen the economic power of our proletarian state. You have the advantage over the capitalists in that political power is in your hands, you have a number of economic implements at your command; the only thing is that you cannot make proper use of them. Look at things more soberly ... sit down simply to learn a simple matter. If you do that we shall beat the private capitalist. We possess political power; we possess huge economic resources. If we beat capitalism and create a link with peasant economy we shall become an absolutely invincible power. Then the building of socialism will not be the task of the drop in the ocean that is called the Communist Party, but that of the masses of the toilers. Then the rank-and-file peasant will see that we are helping him and will follow our lead, so that, even if the pace is a hundred times slower, it will be a million times more certain." [20]

One of the problems directly affecting the relation of workers and peasants was the lack of highly developed enterprises in the field of distribution and retail trade. Co-operatives gave the closest approach to

* Companies in which private capital and the state were both represented.

an integrated system. These had played and would play a considerable role (to which we return in the following chapter). But exchange with city industry had always been limited by the peasants' poverty and by the prevalence of village handicrafts. In planning for restoration and expansion to meet the peasants' needs and desires, the young Soviet state had no such wealth of statistical material at hand as capitalists in the western countries had developed for their own guidance.

At the Third All-Russian Food Conference (June, 1921), Lenin asked for close attention to the gathering of exact information, urgently needed to guide the development of trade between peasantry and large-scale industry. The apparatus which had been created under War Communism for bringing the food supply from the villages to the towns would continue to function for the new tax in kind. But it must become more flexible. It must learn a new kind of efficiency, so as not merely to collect a stated quantity of grain but also to study and report on the needs and desires of the peasants.

"You have fought the bag traders; you have combated illicit trade conducted in contravention of government orders. You will still have to fight them. But in order to engage in the exchange of commodities and avoid being beaten in the free market, being beaten by this free trade, you must know it thoroughly, compete with it and beat it at its own game, fight it with its own weapons—but to be able to do that you must know it thoroughly.

"We don't want the old bureaucratic methods, but knowledge of commercial conditions, precise knowledge, ability to react quickly to every change. For this purpose food products and articles for exchange must be rapidly transported from place to place over the vast territory of the R.S.F.S.R.* The difficulties ahead of us are enormous. But this will be the basis of the whole of our new economic policy for the period until we fully restore large-scale industry. And this period may last no less than ten years, during which we must create such relations between the working class and the peasantry—the only classes that can serve as a base on which to build up our economy—we must create such an alliance between them as will economically satisfy both sides,

* Russian Socialist Federated Soviet Republic, the largest unit in the Union of Soviet Socialist Republics.

an alliance in which the small peasant will be reckoned with as a small peasant, until we are able to provide him with all the products of large-scale industry.

"We must reckon with the small proprietor who sells his surplus products. We must also reckon with the fact that the conditions of the urban population, the workers, must be improved. Unless we do that, our further work of construction—that will make the transition to socialism so permanent that it will be impossible to turn back—will be unsuccessful. That is why commodity exchange is at present the most important part of our economic policy. This is the task you food supply workers, business managers, and co-operators will have to tackle." [21]

Socialist Industry and Small-Scale Farming

Building up of mutually satisfactory trade relations between the peasants and working-class industry would open the way for stable progress toward socialist agriculture. Throughout the transition years there would continue a conflict between petty capitalist anarchy, growing out of the free commodity exchange of the small producer, and the well-integrated production and distribution which the revolutionary working class was laboriously developing. This was an inner conflict between two forces which were dependent upon one another. The peasants could not expand without the aid of industry, and socialist industry could not develop independently of economic and political support from the peasants. But it was a genuine conflict (which continued throughout the 1920's) and the fate of the revolution depended upon its outcome.

"The task of our party is to spread the realisation of the fact that the enemy within our midst is anarchic capitalism and anarchic commodity exchange. We must clearly understand this essence of the struggle and strive to make the broadest masses of workers and peasants understand it—'Who will defeat whom?' 'Who will win?' . . .

"The outcome of the struggle depends upon whether we succeed in organising the small peasants on the basis of the development of their productive forces and proletarian state assistance for this development, or whether the capitalists succeed in subordinating them." [22]

For developing the productive forces of the small peasants, a new technical base adapted to large-scale operation was a prime necessity. Without a socialist industry capable of supplying great quantities of agricultural machinery, socialist agriculture would remain a visionary's dream. It was not surprising that many of the experiments in collective farming, started in the first year of the workers' revolution, had failed. They had given valuable experience, however, and they made it very clear that good intentions and enthusiasm could not transform the villages throughout the Soviet country until tractors and reapers swept in to convince the peasants that collective large-scale farming was easier, pleasanter, and more productive.

"If any Communist ever dreamt that it would be possible to transform the economic basis, the economic roots of the small farmer within three years, he was, of course, a visionary.... Of course, practice has shown what an enormous part all sorts of experiments and innovations can play in the sphere of collective agriculture. But practice has shown that these experiments, as such, also played a harmful part when people, filled with the best intentions and desires, went into the countryside to organise communes and collectives without the ability to organise, because they lacked collective experience.

"...I repeat that this is not surprising, because the transformation of the small farmer, the remoulding of his mentality and habits is a work of generations. Only a material base, technique, the employment of tractors and machinery in agriculture on a mass scale, electrification on a mass scale, can solve the problem of the small farmer, make his whole mentality sound, so to speak. This is what would radically, and with enormous rapidity, transform the small farmer." [23]

This remoulding and transformation must be an integral part of the development toward socialist agriculture.

"If peasant farming can develop still further, we must firmly assure the transition to the next stage; and the next stage will undoubtedly be the gradual amalgamation of the least profitable and most backward, small and disintegrated peasant farming into social, large-scale agriculture. This is how Socialists have always pictured it. This is exactly how our Communist Party looks upon it." [24]

Elsewhere, Lenin had spoken of the tremendous acceleration of progress which might confidently be expected once the masses of peasants were convinced that there was a better way.

Lenin's faith in the creative power of the workers and poorer peasants was more than justified by the quality and the speed of the changes which he did not live to witness. By 1927 industrial production had been restored to pre-war levels of tsarist Russia. Then the first Five-Year Plan, carried out with widest and most devoted enthusiasm and technical skill, included great new plants for the manufacture of farm machinery. With imported machines supplementing temporarily Soviet Russia's own tractors, reapers, and combines, the technical base was prepared for socialist agriculture. In less than a generation after the revolution, collective farms and state farms were producing over 98 per cent of the total agricultural output of the Soviet Union, the "peasant" had given place to the well-educated, socially conscious collective farmer, and the conflict between city and village had been liquidated.

CHAPTER X

The Role of Co-operatives

NO summary of Lenin's ideas and tactics in relation to agriculture can pass over the question of co-operatives. For Lenin drew a sharp distinction between the role of co-operatives in Russia before the Soviet revolution—or in any capitalist country—and the role of co-operatives as part of the socialist economy. This distinction, rooted in his class analysis of the pre-socialist world, is of great importance, theoretically and practically.

Take first the question of co-operative farming. We have seen that Lenin before the revolution vigorously opposed the Narodniks (Populists) and others who cherished the old village commune, with its semi-feudal remnants. He recognised, as most of them did not, the class differences which had grown up within the commune. He demonstrated that capitalism was already rooted in the village. The co-operative elements in the life of the commune were merely obscuring the fact that commercial grain was actually produced on a capitalist basis and sold in a capitalist market.

Co-operatives Ineffective Against Capitalism

To those Populists and others who admitted this breaking-down of the commune but wanted consciously and aggressively to restore the commune as a unit of collective, co-operative production, Lenin emphasised the futility of such units for solving the problems of the smaller peasants in a country dominated by private trading. He wrote of this repeatedly. For example, in his first long analysis of Russian populism in 1894, he said:

"They do not understand the antagonism within our relations of production (within the 'peasantry' as within the other estates), and instead of striving to bring this antagonism out into the open road, instead of frankly taking sides with those who are enslaved as a result of this antagonism and trying to help them to rise to the struggle, they dream of terminating the struggle by measures that would satisfy everybody, that would reconcile and unite....

"The same must be said of 'artels'* and 'communal tillage.' Mr. Yuzhakov [a Populist writer] calls the latter 'the socialisation of agriculture.' This is simply funny, of course, because socialisation necessitates the organisation of production on a wider scale than the limits of a single village, and because it necessitates the expropriation of the 'bloodsuckers' who have monopolised the means of production and who now rule Russian social economy.

"...and [such measures] do more harm by diverting the exploited from the struggle than the good that might accrue from possible improvements in the position of separate individuals, which cannot but be paltry and precarious on the general basis of capitalist relations." [1]

Nineteen years later, when the World War and the victorious revolution were still in the future, Lenin replied in similar vein to a Populist who had spoken for collective farming as the salvation of the smaller peasants:

"It is obvious that this Narodnik [Populist] prescription is simply childish. Landlords and kulaks drive from the land millions of peasants, ruining other millions. The whole of world capitalism, the whole force of international interchange, the whole might of billions of capital of the bourgeoisie of all countries, drags Russia after itself, nourishes and supports Russia's bourgeoisie, both in the city and in the *village*, including those within the commune. And then they tell us that communal cultivation by these ruined peasants of the scraps of their 'own land' is 'salvation'!! This is just as if one tried with a hand wheel-

* A form of group or co-operative production.

barrow to overtake a railroad train—in speed and quantity of transportation....

"Not backwards, from the train to the wheelbarrow, but forward: from the capitalist train to the united proletariat.

"The innocent dream of the Narodniks is not only childishly naïve—it is directly harmful because it diverts the thoughts of the poor from the class struggle. *Apart from* the class struggle of the proletariat against the bourgeoisie for the reshaping of the whole capitalist structure there is no salvation for the village poor. And all leagues, co-operatives, artels, etc., can be useful only in their conscious participation in this class struggle."[2]

Such conscious participation in class struggle by co-operative societies of any type in a non-socialist country is extremely difficult to achieve. Whether the co-operative unit in a capitalist environment is nourished "on the generosity of the philanthropic bourgeois"[3] or represents only the pooling of small individual resources, it tends to focus on the effort to defend its own property interest as a separate group functioning under the existing system, and to lose the perspective of the broader struggle through which alone a genuinely co-operative system can be created. So, in 1902, Lenin said that "by including in their minimum programme the support and development of co-operation, the Socialist-Revolutionaries abandon the ground of the revolutionary struggle and degrade their would-be socialism to the level of the most banal petty-bourgeois reformism."[4]

This inner contradiction within the co-operative movement was sensed by Lenin from the beginning. He opposed consistently the Populist emphasis on the old village commune. He opposed experiments in co-operative farming until these could be part of the broader building of a socialist economy. And he paid little attention to the marketing co-operatives of the kulaks, and the consumer co-operatives of rural and city petty bourgeoisie, so long as the educating and organising of industrial wage workers for revolutionary struggle was the one big challenging task of the moment.

Trading co-operatives had been dominated by the Mensheviks and the Socialist-Revolutionaries with whom, as we have seen, Lenin carried on continuous political discussion. His arguments with them were directed less against co-operatives as such than against the leaders' political thinking which had wandered from the path of proletarian revolution. These "Socialist" opponents of Lenin rejected the basic idea that only in the working class were the masses prepared by their experience under capitalism to push resolutely forward toward the building of socialism. They knew that workers would find many allies in other classes. But Mensheviks and Socialist-Revolutionaries never understood the leading role of the working class which had no property interests to defend.

Co-operatives Useful Under Socialism

After November, 1917, Lenin placed great emphasis on the dual nature of the Russian trading co-operatives. They had been concerned primarily with such property interests as markets, credit, and prices, and were essentially a form of *capitalist* organisation among the small producers and others of the petty bourgeoisie. As such, they were alien to the new socialist world which the revolution was trying to build. But at the same time, they represented collective action among the naturally individualistic and scattered non-proletarian masses.

In the economic backwardness of old rural Russia, the co-operatives provided in November, 1917, the most highly developed apparatus inherited from capitalism for the exchange of products. They must be utilised for carrying out in the field of distribution the "accounting and control" which Lenin regarded as an essential first step towards socialist economy. They must become an integral part of the socialist distributive apparatus.

Also, under a socialist government building socialist industry, village trading co-operatives could serve to prepare the way for co-operative peasant production. Under capitalism, such co-operative production had been merely the dream of visionaries, a futile panacea against peasant sufferings. But under socialism, some form of co-operative production had become the essential basis for socialism on the land.

Various measures were adopted between April, 1918, and the turn toward the New Economic Policy in the spring of 1921, in an effort to bring the trading co-operatives under government control without destroying local initiative or losing the administrative skill of those non-Communist executives who were not actively supporting counter-revolution. In discussing the problems involved in this, in the spring of 1918, Lenin illuminated the whole question of co-operatives.

"The co-operative is a store and no changes whatsoever, no improvements and reforms, can change the fact that it is a store. The capitalist period has accustomed Socialists to this view. And there is no doubt that these views were a correct expression of the nature of co-operatives so long as they remained a small appendage to the mechanism of the bourgeois order. But the point is that the situation of co-operatives is radically changed in principle with the conquest of state power by the proletariat, from the moment when the proletarian state power advances to the systematic creation of a socialist order. Then quantity passes over into quality. The co-operative, as a little island in capitalist society, is a store. The co-operative which embraces the whole of a society in which land is socialised, and factories and mills are nationalised, is socialism. The task of the Soviet power, after the bourgeoisie is expropriated politically and economically, clearly consists (chiefly) in this: to extend co-operative organisations to the whole of society, to include all citizens of a given country, without exception, as members of one nationwide or more truly statewide co-operative." [5]

And nearly a year later:

"It is no rare thing to meet a Soviet intellectual or worker, a Communist, who sniffs contemptuously at the mere mention of co-operative societies and proclaims with an air of profound importance—and with equally profound stupidity—that these are not Soviet hands, but bourgeois, shopkeepers, Mensheviks, that at such and such a place and time the co-operators had, by their financial manipulations, concealed aid given to White Guards, and that in our socialist republic the machinery of supply and distribution must be built up only by clean Soviet hands.

"Such arguments are typical for the fact that in them truth is so mingled with falsehood as to present a most dangerous distortion of the aims of communism, which is liable to do incalculable harm to our cause.

"Yes, the co-operatives are an apparatus of bourgeois society, an apparatus which grew up in a 'shopkeeping' atmosphere, which has trained its leaders in the spirit of bourgeois politics and in a bourgeois outlook, and has therefore produced a large proportion of White Guards or accomplices of the White Guards. That is undeniable. But it is a bad thing when from undeniable truths, by over-simplification and slap-dash application, absurd conclusions are drawn. We can only build communism from the materials created by capitalism.... That is the difficulty of building communist society, but it is also a guarantee that it can be built, and will be built. In fact, what distinguishes Marxism from the old, utopian socialism is that the latter wanted to build the new society not from the mass representatives of human material produced by bloodstained, sordid, rapacious, shopkeeping capitalism, but from especially virtuous men and women reared in special hothouses and nurseries. This absurd idea is now seen to be absurd by everybody, and has been abandoned by everybody, but not everybody is willing or able to ponder over the converse teaching of Marxism and to think out how communism can (and should) be built from the mass human material, which has been corrupted by hundreds and thousands of years of slavery, serfdom, capitalism, small individual enterprise, and the war of every man against his neighbour for a place in the market, for a higher price for his product or his labour.

"The co-operatives are a bourgeois apparatus. From this it follows that they do not deserve to be trusted *politically;* but it does not follow that we may turn our backs on the task of utilising them for purposes of administration and construction....

"Political distrust of the representatives of a bourgeois apparatus is legitimate and essential. But to refuse to utilise them in the work of administration and construction would be the height of folly, fraught with untold harm to communism." [6]

While many of the leaders in the Russian co-operatives were politically hostile, and the membership was united in pursuit of a small business advantage, Lenin recognised as an achievement the mere fact of such independent organisation among the petty bourgeoisie.

"Many of the co-operative societies consisted chiefly of petty-bourgeois elements, the middle peasantry, whose aims in the co-operative movement were determined by their petty-bourgeois interests. However, these co-operatives had the undoubted effect of developing the independent initiative of the masses, and that was greatly to their credit. ... Co-operation is an immense cultural heritage which must be treasured and utilised."[7]

Expansion and Development

Practically, there were two main points of conflict which developed between the Soviet government and the co-operatives, apart from the actual counter-revolutionary efforts of certain leaders in the co-operative movement. These issues reflected a clash between Lenin's conception of socialist economy, both in purposes and in structure, and the petty-bourgeois habits and attitudes of the co-operators.

After the revolution the co-operatives wished to maintain a completely separate and independent existence, outside of any state apparatus for distribution of products. Lenin understood their distrust of state control, but he emphasised repeatedly the difference between the capitalist state and the new proletarian government which would be primarily an administrative organ of genuinely socialist economy. So, for example, in the spring of 1918, he wrote:

"The state, which for centuries has been an organ of oppression and robbery of the people, has left us a heritage of mass hatred and suspicion of everything that is connected with the state. It is very difficult to overcome this, and only a Soviet government can do it. But even a Soviet government will require plenty of time and enormous perseverance. This 'heritage' particularly affects the question of accounting and control—the fundamental problem facing the socialist revolution on the morrow of the overthrow of the bourgeoisie. A certain amount of time will inevitably pass before the masses, who for the first time feel free after the overthrow of the landlords and the bourgeoisie, will understand—not from books, but from their own, *Soviet* experience—will understand and *feel* that without all-sided state accounting and control of production and distribution of goods, the power of the toilers, the freedom of the toilers, cannot be maintained, and that a return to the yoke of capitalism is *inevitable*.

"All the habits and traditions of the bourgeoisie, and of the petty bourgeoisie in particular, also run counter to *state* control, and support the inviolability of the 'sacred right of property,' of 'sacred' private enterprise.... The fight to instill into the minds of the masses the idea of *Soviet* state control and accounting, and to carry out this idea in practice; the fight to break with the cursed past, which taught the people to regard the gaining of bread and clothes as a 'private' matter, as buying and selling, as a transaction 'which concerns only myself'—is a great fight of world-historical significance, a fight between socialist consciousness and bourgeois-anarchist spontaneity.... In our agitation we do not sufficiently explain that lack of accounting in the production and distribution of goods means the death of the rudiments of socialism.... And until workers' control has become a fact, until the advanced workers have organised and carried out a victorious and ruthless crusade against the violators of this control, or against those who are careless in matters of control, it will be impossible to pass from the first step (from workers' control) to the second step, to socialism, *i.e.,* to pass on to workers' regulation of production.

"... Capitalism left us a heritage of mass organisations which can facilitate our transition to the mass accounting and control of the distribution of goods, viz., the consumers' co-operative societies."[8]

Later in the same year, Lenin addressed the Third Congress of Workers' Co-operative Societies and answered the grumbling of those who protested the relation that had been established between the trading co-operatives and the Administration of Food Supply.

"We know that the friction mentioned by the previous speaker in reference to Petersburg exists nearly everywhere. We know that such friction is absolutely inevitable, because we are at a point when two totally different apparatuses are meeting and amalgamating; nevertheless, we also know that this is inevitable and is a stage we have to go through. And you, too, must realise that the resistance which the workers' co-operatives have been putting up for so long was bound in the end to arouse distrust, and quite legitimate distrust, on the part of the Soviet government.

"You say you want independence. It stands to reason that anyone who makes such a demand risks arousing distrust. If you complain of friction and want to eliminate it, then you must first of all abandon the idea of independence, for anybody who holds that view at a time when everything is tending to closer and closer amalgamation is by that very fact an opponent of the Soviet system. As soon as the workers' co-operatives amalgamate quite openly, honestly, and frankly with the Soviet system, such friction will begin to disappear. I am perfectly well aware that when two groups amalgamate there is bound to be at first a certain amount of discordance in their work, but in the course of time, as the group incorporated wins the confidence of the one with which it is incorporated, all friction gradually disappears. On the other hand, if these two groups remain divided, constant interdepartmental friction is liable to arise. There is one thing I cannot understand: why this talk of independence? After all, we are all of the opinion that in the matter of both supply and distribution our society as a whole should represent one universal co-operative.... Such hopes of 'independence' can be cherished only by those who are still harbouring the hope of some sort of reversion to the past."[9]

Closely related to this question of organisational independence was the co-operatives' reluctance to broaden their basis of membership. Lenin defined the difference between bourgeois co-operation and the co-operation which could serve for communist supply and distribution.

Communist co-operation, he said, was not being developed "*if* this co-operation (1) gives profits (dividends on shares, etc.) to a group of special stockholders; (2) maintains its own special apparatus, not drawing into it the population in general, and primarily the proletariat and semi-proletariat; (3) in distribution of products does not give advantages to the proletarians over the middle peasants, to the middle peasants over the rich; (4) in obtaining products it does not 'clean up' the surpluses first from the rich, then from the middle peasants, and for this does not lean on the proletarians and the semi-proletarians. Etc., etc.

"The whole difficulty of the problem (and the whole *content* of the present problems standing immediately before us) consists in this: to work out a system of *practical* measures for the *transition* from the old co-operation (inevitably bourgeois in so far as there is set apart a stratum of *shareholders,* constituting a *minority* of the population, and also for other reasons) to a new and actual *commune,*—measures for transition from bourgeois-co-operative to proletarian-communist supply and distribution."[10]

Transition to the New Economic Policy in the spring of 1921, with its relative freedom of trading, involved giving a freer hand to the co-operatives. Even before that definite turn, Lenin had urged the importance of more active work by individual Communists within every co-operative organisation. "We need less fist-shaking," he had said in this connection at the Ninth Congress of the Russian Communist Party (1920).[11] Under NEP, the co-operatives assumed a new importance. They would develop again as a form of petty capitalism, but they would be less difficult to control than private traders. At this time (April, 1921) Lenin wrote in his pamphlet on the food tax:

"The co-operatives are also [like concessions] a form of state capitalism, but less simple; its outline is less distinct, it is more confused and therefore creates greater practical difficulties for our government. The small commodity producers' co-operative societies (and it is the latter, and not the workers' co-operatives that we are discussing as the predominant and typical form in a *small-peasant* country) inevitably give rise to petty-bourgeois capitalist relations. . . . Under the conditions prevailing in Russia at present, freedom and rights for the co-operative societies mean freedom and rights for capitalism. It would be stupid and criminal to close our eyes to this obvious truth.

"But, unlike private capitalism, 'co-operative' capitalism under the Soviet government is a variety of state capitalism, and as such it is advantageous and useful for us at the present time—in a certain measure, of course. Since the food tax means the free sale of surplus grain . . . we must exert every effort to direct *this* development of capitalism—for free sale, free trade *is* the development of capitalism—into the channels of co-operative capitalism. Co-operative capitalism is like state capitalism in that it facilitates accounting, control, supervision and the establishment of contractual relations between the state (in this case the Soviet state) and the capitalist. Co-operative trade... facilitates the amalgamation, the organisation, of millions of the population, and later the whole of the population; and this in its turn is an enormous gain from the point of view of the subsequent transition from state capitalism to socialism."[12]

Lenin urged constant study and detailed comparison of the efficiency of private capitalists, co-operatives, and state trade organs.

After two years of NEP, one of Lenin's latest writings stated even more clearly the key position of co-operatives, especially in relation to the peasants.

"I think that inadequate attention is being paid to the co-operative movement. Not everyone understands that now, since the October Revolution, and irrespective of the NEP (on the contrary, in this connection we must say, precisely because of the NEP), the co-operative movement acquires absolutely exceptional significance. Much of what was in the dreams of the old co-operators was fantastic. Sometimes they were ridiculously fantastic. But why were they fantastic? Because they did not understand the fundamental, root significance of the political struggle of the working class for the overthrow of the rule of the exploiters. We have accomplished this overthrow, and much that was fantastic, even romantic, and even banal, in the dreams of the old co-operators is now becoming the most unvarnished reality.

"...But not all comrades appreciate the enormous, boundless significance that the organisation of Russia in co-operative societies now acquires....As a matter of fact, the power of state over all large-scale means of production, the power of state in the hands of the proletariat, the alliance of this proletariat with the many millions of small and very small peasants, the assured leadership of the peasantry by the proletariat, etc., is not this all that is necessary in order from the co-operatives—from the co-operatives alone, which we formerly treated as huckstering, and which, from a certain aspect, we have the right to treat as such now, under the NEP—is not this all that is necessary in order to build complete socialist society? This is not yet the building of socialist society, but it is all that is necessary and sufficient for this building.

"... Our co-operatives are looked down upon with contempt, but those who do so fail to understand the exceptional significance of our co-operatives, first, from the aspect of principle (the means of production are owned by the state), and, second, from the aspect of the transition to the new order by means that will be *simplest, easiest, and most intelligible for the peasantry.*

"But this again is the most important thing. It is one thing to draw up fantastic plans for building socialism by means of all sorts of workers' associations; but it is quite another thing to learn to build it practically, in such a way that *every* small peasant may take part in the work of construction. This is the stage we have reached now."[18]

Some years later, with the expansion of industrial production under the First Five-Year Plan, more emphasis was placed on government trade. Free competition was encouraged between city consumers' co-operatives and the stores operated by the People's Commissariat of Trade. The technique of supply and distribution was improved and, as the government stores became more efficient, the city co-operatives were no longer considered necessary and were merged into the People's Commissariat of Supply. Co-operatives have continued to function, however, as an essential part of socialism in the villages.

CHAPTER XI

Soviet Agriculture After Lenin's Death

WHEN Lenin died in January, 1924, the foundations of socialist agriculture had not yet been laid. A few thousand collective farms were operating and their number was slowly increasing. State farms—larger than the collective farms—were already utilising some of the landlord estates. Here agricultural experts and peasant wage workers were demonstrating modern technique and the advantages of large-scale operation.* But these were only a small beginning, and until 1929 most of the farming was carried on by individual peasant families. In the spring of that year, state farms and collectives had only 5.4 per cent of the total sown area of the country.[1]

Contrasts within the village, formerly so extreme, still existed to some extent. The landlords were gone and the land was owned by the state. Poor and middle peasants had been given the use of more land and had the aid of production credits on generous terms. Poor peasants were exempt from taxation, but many of them still lacked draft animals and equipment. Kulaks—rich peasants—remained, although they had lost

* In this demonstration, nine American farmers under the leadership of Harold Ware (son of Ella Reeve Bloor) had made a singular contribution. Going to the Soviet Union in the winter of 1921-22, these farmers were sent to a very bad drought area in Perm, to see what their experience in North Dakota and their twenty carloads of American farm equipment could produce from the dry Russian plains with the aid of Russian peasants. It was a decisive demonstration of large-scale mechanised farming under very difficult conditions, and it was enthusiastically recognised by Lenin. (Letter, *Collected Works,* XXVII, Russian, p. 308.) Later, Ware organised one of the first state farms near Rostov. And, in 1929, he assisted in the establishment of *Verblud,* the second state grain farm to combine with large-scale mechanised operation the functions of a scientific experiment station and a school for complete agricultural training.

possession of much of the land they had formerly used. Their employment of wage labour was sharply restricted and they were subject to heavy taxation.

Where formerly the middle peasants were slipping down into destitution and swelling the ranks of poor peasants, now great numbers of those who had been poor peasants were able to maintain themselves independently on the land. Before the revolution it had been estimated that two-thirds of the peasants were poor—that is, unable to make a living on their allotments—and one in seven was a kulak. Eight years after the revolution (1925-26) only about one peasant in 27 was a kulak, and roughly one in five (instead of two out of three) was unable to maintain himself without finding other employment.[2]

Co-operative trading had been systematically encouraged among the poor and middle peasants, for Lenin had emphasised that this was a natural and necessary step leading (under the proletarian dictatorship) toward co-operative farm production. As time went on, small co-operative processing plants such as cheese factories, oil presses, and starch factories were also organised.[3] In 1926, Joseph Stalin could report that "the co-operative societies, which now have over ten million members, have begun to link up with socialist industry."[4]

As industrial production was restored and reached its pre-war level in 1926, the supply of textiles and other goods needed by the peasants for everyday use had been increased. In return for grain and other products sold to the government, the peasants could now obtain through their co-operatives most of the things they were accustomed to having. But prices for industrial products were still relatively higher than the government price of grain. This disparity—the famous "scissors" of the NEP period—was a source of some discontent among the peasants until the problem was taken up as a primary task early in 1927.

Five years of slowly improved conditions among the peasants had not, however, solved the city food problems. Production of grain in 1925 approached the pre-war volume and the following year it surpassed the 1913 output. But much more of the grain was being consumed by the peasants themselves, and the amount available for city consumption was only about half as much as had been marketed for the city and for export in 1913. Livestock of all kinds had been greatly reduced. Horses, cattle, and hogs were, until after 1930, fewer than they had been before the war. Rapidly increasing numbers of wage workers, drawn from agriculture into industry, needed more meat, more milk and butter, more fruit and vegetables. The low food standards of workers in tsarist Russia could not be accepted as adequate in a socialist country, but even these old standards could not be maintained without a higher level of production on the land.

The workers generally understood the difficulties involved and the reasons for the food shortages. But the problem of expanding the city food supply was very basic. Its solution could not be indefinitely postponed. Very similar, though somewhat less urgent, was the question of cotton and wool and leather for clothing and footwear. These problems of food and raw materials could be correctly solved, in a socialist manner, only by drawing the peasants toward much more widespread collective farming.

Within the villages, in the meantime, new class struggles had developed as the kulaks found new ways of exploiting the poor peasants and trying to alienate the middle peasants from the Communist Party and the Soviet power. Many kulaks had obtained a foothold in cooperatives and perverted them to their own profit, wherever the poorer peasants were too easy-going (or too backward) to prevent it. In some places where a collective farm had been started, the kulak succeeded in joining in order to disrupt the project. When the poorer peasants resisted such tactics, they would be violently attacked, or their buildings would be burned or livestock stolen or injured. Such criminal action by the kulaks was severely punished by the Soviet courts.

Kulaks also devised a way of obtaining additional land by working on shares the acreage of poor peasants who still had no equipment. This meant that the kulak allowed the poor peasant to use his team, for which gracious favour the kulak took part of the poor peasant's crop and also demanded labour by the poor peasant on the kulak's own land.[5]

These village capitalists had shown their determination to fight against collective farming and to do their utmost to undermine Soviet authority in the villages, because their own prosperity depended upon the poor peasants' being unable to exist without selling their labour power.

At the Fourteenth Party Conference in April, 1925, and at the Fourteenth Party Congress in December of the same year, it was recognised that the old struggle to win the middle peasant as a firm ally of the working class had not been decisively won. It would not be won until the material advantages of socialist agriculture with modern technical equipment could be demonstrated on a much wider scale. This mechanical equipment could not be provided in mass volume without a much greater development of Soviet industry.

Discussions within the party revealed wide differences of opinion as to the solution of this complicated problem. Some were for immediate intensification of the class struggle, suppressing the kulaks by force. Others went to the other extreme, refusing to recognise any danger in the situation. The majority agreed with Stalin that the situation was exceedingly serious and full of danger to the revolution, but that in 1925-26 the time was not yet ripe for forcible suppression of the kulaks as a class. The poor peasants must immediately be drawn into more active, more effective organisation, but their resistance to the kulaks must be guided into constructive work within co-operatives and collective farms.

Bureaucrats must be eliminated from the local Soviets by new elections, bringing into office those who were trusted by the poor and middle peasants. As Stalin said:

"We cannot carry on by simply ordering the peasants about. We must learn to explain patiently to the peasants the questions they do not understand. We must learn to convince the peasants, sparing neither time nor effort for this purpose....

"Further, in order to lead, nowadays, one must be a good manager, one must know and understand economic affairs.... The period of economic construction has begun, and only those who are well grounded in the economics of agriculture, who are capable of giving good and practical advice to the peasant in economic construction, only such as these are fit for leadership. To study farming, to link themselves closely with agricultural life, to acquire a better knowledge of all the detail work of economic construction—these are the duties of Communists in the rural districts today. Without this it is no use even dreaming of leadership." [6]

For the period which must still ensue before great masses of poor and middle peasants could be drawn into collective farming and the village would be ready for a frontal attack on the kulaks as a class, certain practices which had developed illegally in relation to leasing poor peasants' land and employing wage labour were recognised and made subject to regulation by the Soviets.[7]

Stalin also emphasised at the Fourteenth Party Congress that even though there could not yet be any rapid shifting of agriculture to a new technical base, some definite progress could be made within the existing set-up. "Even the simple raising of the cultural level of the peasants, literacy, even such a simple measure as the cleaning of seed, could increase by 10 per cent to 15 per cent the gross production of our agriculture." [8]

After this congress, work for the liquidation of rural illiteracy was much more broadly developed. A few machine and tractor stations were set up to assist some of the existing collective farms, and to provide centers for technical assistance and the encouragement of new collectives.[9]

From this period also dates the beginning of the contract system which was to play an increasingly important part. At first this linked farms raising technical crops (such as sugar beets, cotton, tobacco) to government-owned processing plants. Later, in the years of more definite preparation for widespread collective farming, the contract system was widely developed. Then the contract was made only with a collective farm or with a whole village of individual farmers as a group. It required of the peasants certain standards in the operation of their farms, and the buyer (whether a state agency or a co-operative) undertook to provide production assistance—expert advice, fertiliser, selected seeds, or even items of improved equipment.

Stalin cited this contract system as one important aspect of transition from the New Economic Policy to the socialist exchange of products.[10]

Looking Toward Mass Collectivisation

Meanwhile, a decisive turn towards expansion and reconstruction of Soviet industry was under way. Russian industry had been notoriously backward. It included a high percentage of very large concerns, but these had depended upon imported machinery. For the first workers' state in a hostile capitalist world, genuine economic independence was of primary importance, and this could not be achieved without a vast expansion of heavy industry. No less important were the problems of expanding production on the land and drawing the peasant masses into some form of socialist agriculture. For this a modern technical basis must be created. It was not enough to supply the peasants with matches and calico and kerosene. They must have tractors and reapers and innumerable items of farm machinery for large-scale farming.

By 1927 the drafting of the First Five-Year Plan had been completed. Under it the foundations of heavy industry were laid, the development of new industrial areas was begun, and new industrial plants began turning out for the peasants tractors, motor trucks, and agricultural machinery. Industrial development was carried forward at an increasing tempo, and all the world knows that it proved to be a decisive military factor when Nazi Germany invaded the Soviet Union in 1941, in the midst of the Third Five-Year Plan.

This rapid industrial development was no less decisive for the inner strength and stability of the workers' first socialist country. Carried into the former subject areas of Russian Central Asia, it opened new horizons to non-Russian peasant peoples who had been peculiarly oppressed, and created a strong economic basis for their new political equality with European Russia. It made possible throughout the Soviet Union the mass campaign for large-scale collective agriculture which drew the middle peasants toward socialism and brought the final struggle against capitalism in the village.

The 15,000 collective farms existing in 1927 were made up chiefly of poor peasants. They were usually small, with only ten to thirty peasant households operating together an average of 150 acres of crop land. Although poorly equipped, they were learning better methods of cultivation and better organisation of work. And as a rule the peasants' labour was more productive and the yield per acre was higher, even on these small collective farms, than among the neighbouring peasants.[11]

As first steps towards mass collectivisation, the Fifteenth Congress of the Russian Communist Party (December, 1927), recognised the importance of further developing the machine and tractor stations so that the less than 27,000 tractors then available in the Soviet Union (and imported chiefly from the United States) might be fully utilised to raise the level of existing collectives.* These machine and tractor stations were also given definite political tasks: to prepare the peasant masses for collective farming. New Soviet farms with most modern equipment were to be established. These would provide additional demonstration centres and sources of better livestock and better seeds. They would also rapidly increase the supply of marketable grain. The old emphasis on improving the work of trading co-operatives was restated, and a fresh campaign was undertaken to draw all the rural poor and the majority of the middle peasant households into co-operative activity.

All this was the signal for new disruptive efforts by the kulaks. They were still producing about one-fifth of the marketed grain. When they began withholding grain as a hostile measure, they were able to create a food crisis which became extremely acute at the very time when the workers were beginning to strain every effort and making new adjustments under the Five-Year Plan. And, of course, kulaks had never ceased to be a disturbing element in the village, intriguing among the middle peasants and stirring up discontent.

In the spring of 1928, Stalin delivered an important speech on the grain crisis, the political danger in the kulak element, and the underlying relationship between the working class and the masses of the peasantry. Of the kulaks he said:

"It must not be forgotten that in industry we can oppose to the small urban capitalist our large-scale socialist industry, which produces nine-

* Tractors numbered "about 27,000" in 1928. Through "perversions of the correct class policy" some 450 of these were on kulaks' farms. (*Razvitiye Sovietskoi Ekonomiki*, pp. 295-96.) Among the more than 400,000 tractors on farms of the Soviet Union ten years later, the great majority were manufactured within the country. The First Five-Year Plan (1927-32) had ended quantity importation of farm tractors.

tenths of the total output of manufactured goods, whereas in the sphere of production in the rural districts we can oppose to large-scale kulak farming only the still weak collective farms and state farms, which produce but one-eighth of the amount of grain produced by the kulak farms." This means that "the relative weight of the kulaks in the rural districts is a hundred-fold greater than that of the capitalists in urban industry." [12]

The whole future of socialism in the Soviet Union would depend upon successful struggle against these petty-capitalist rich farmers, and this in turn would depend upon drawing the masses of both poor and middle peasants into some form of collective farming. For the petty-capitalist viewpoint tended also to prevail among the middle peasants and made them easy dupes of kulak intrigue against the very measures which had already improved the position of the middle peasant. Only under the leadership of the working class could the peasant masses find the road to socialism. Conflict between the workers and the kulaks for leadership among the middle peasants was the underlying political issue in those years.

Lenin had repeatedly emphasised that the middle peasants could become loyal allies of the workers even though the peasantry was "the last capitalist class." And in 1928 when some Communists were still wavering between the two extremes of coddling *all* the peasants (including the kulaks) and of carrying out a mass offensive by the working class against all peasants, Stalin set forth again the principles which guided the struggle during the ensuing years.

It would be a primary task to give expert aid to small and middle peasants, drawing them into trading co-operatives and developing more collective and Soviet farms. Such measures would decrease the importance of the kulak farms as a source of supply and would make plainer the advantages and possibilities of socialist agriculture. They would draw the peasant masses closer to the working class. As Stalin put it:

"If, as a result of these and similar measures, the kulaks are curbed and gradually overcome—is it not clear that the contradictions between the working class and the peasantry within the alliance of workers and peasants will thereby be smoothed out more and more; that the need for emergency measures in the purchase of grain will disappear; that the large masses of the peasantry will turn more and more to collective forms of farming and that the fight to overcome the capitalist elements in the rural districts will assume an increasingly mass and organised character? Is it not clear that the cause of the alliance between the workers and the peasants can only benefit by these measures?" [13]

At the same time, Stalin reminded the Communist students whom he was addressing that the alliance of workers and peasants is a very special relationship.

"It is a special form of class alliance between the working-class and the labouring masses of the peasantry, which sets itself the object (*a*) of strengthening the position of the working class, (*b*) of ensuring the leading role of the working class within this alliance, and (*c*) of abolishing classes and class society." [14]

But if, as Lenin said, the peasantry is "the last capitalist class," does this not mean that all peasants are capitalists? This question Stalin answered as follows:

"It means, first, that the peasantry is a special class, which bases its economy on the private ownership of the implements and means of production and which, for that reason, differs from the class of proletarians, who base their economic life on the collective ownership of the implements and means of production. It means, secondly, that the peasantry is a class which throws up from its midst, engenders, and nourishes capitalists, kulaks, and all kinds of exploiters in general." [15]

And in building the alliance of workers and peasants, a sharp distinction must be made between the kulaks and the toiling peasantry.

"The alliance of the proletariat with the peasantry under the conditions of the dictatorship of the proletariat is not an alliance with the whole of the peasantry. The alliance of the proletariat with the peasantry is an alliance of the working class with the labouring masses of the peasantry. Such an alliance cannot be effected without a struggle against the capitalist elements of the peasantry, against the kulaks. Such an alliance cannot be a durable one unless the poor peasants are organised as the bulwark of the working class in the rural districts. That is why the alliance between the workers and the peasants under the present conditions of the dictatorship of the proletariat can be effected only in accordance with Lenin's well-known slogan: Rely on the poor peasant, establish a firm alliance with the middle peasant, and do not for a moment relax the fight against the kulak. For only by applying this slogan can the bulk of the peasantry be drawn into the channel of socialist construction." [16]

And later in the same year Stalin said:

"We do not need the close bond [between workers and peasants] for the purpose of maintaining and perpetuating classes. We need this bond in order to bring the peasant nearer to the working class, to re-educate the peasant, to transform his individualist psychology, to re-mould him in the spirit of collectivism, and thus prepare for the liquidation, the elimination of classes on the basis of socialist society." [17]

Throughout this period the Soviet government had the difficult task of stimulating and aiding collective farming and directing the trade in farm products through co-operative and government channels while it was also trying to raise the productive level on small individual farms. While total retail trade was increasing, the volume of private trade did show a very marked decline. Government stores and co-operatives had only 50 per cent of the total retail trade (all products, industrial and agricultural) in 1924. Five years later they had 86 per cent of a much larger total.[18]

Peasant production had increased enough to create a rural demand for manufactured goods which Soviet industry was still unable fully to satisfy. But production of grain for the market was not keeping pace with the increase in city population. When the kulaks withheld their grain and created an acute grain crisis in the spring of 1928, food rationing was resorted to. The standard of rationed supplies was higher than it had been during the emergency of the civil war years, but this system was maintained until 1934, when the success of the mass collectivisation campaign had provided an assured abundance.[19]

The city food crisis of 1928 reflected and also created fresh difficulties in the villages. Some local authorities had been too lax in enforcing grain collections. Others became too zealous and adopted arbitrary measures and even made unreasonable raids on middle peasant farms. These Stalin rebuked sharply as "violations of revolutionary law." The whole matter was thoroughly analysed at the meeting of the Central Committee of the Russian Communist Party in July, 1928. The rights of peasant trading bazaars were reaffirmed and new standards were set for regulating such trade. A higher scale of prices was fixed for grain bought by the government. The supply of goods to the grain-producing regions was to be expanded and more efficiently handled. And creation of a state grain reserve was to be unconditionally begun.[20]

In spite of local problems and errors in relation to the peasants revealed in the grain crisis of 1928, the sown area of peasant farms continued to increase and more and more peasants were setting up collective farms.

The Mass Campaign

By 1929 the party decided that for several reasons the time was ripe for a mass campaign for collective farming and for the liquidation of the kulaks as a class. Why such a campaign could then be attempted was shown at the plenary meeting of the party's central committee in April, 1929.

First of all, the serious grain difficulties had impressed upon the entire party membership the basic importance of collective farming. The more than a million Communists in the Soviet Union were now ready to throw their enthusiasm, their intelligence, and their organising ability into the campaign.

And quite as important, the peasant masses were now "convinced by experience of the advantage of collective farming over individual farming.... Now we have whole strata of the peasantry who regard the state farms and collective farms as a source of assistance to peasant farming in the way of seed, improved cattle, machines, and tractors." [21]

By 1929, the Soviet government had accumulated reserves from which they could make large appropriations for aid to collective and Soviet farms. This would have been absolutely impossible at any previous time, but such practical aid was essential to any rapid improvement.*

Now also for the first time an increasing supply of agricultural machinery was beginning to pour from Soviet factories.

Experience had also shown the best form of collective farm organisation. During the years since the revolution three different types of peasant collectives had appeared, each of them distinct from the Soviet farms operated by poor-peasant wage workers under the supervision of agricultural experts. In communes all the peasant possessions were turned over to the group as a whole and the product was equally divided. In associations for collective cultivation of the land, individual possession of all fields and tools was combined with more or less systematic co-operation in field work. In artels the peasants retained individual possession of their houses, with a small patch of land on which they could keep chickens, bees, and a limited amount of livestock primarily for their own family use. They held in common the fields and tools and livestock with which they produced for the market, and the market return was distributed among the members according to the amount of labour and the kind of labour they performed.

Most of the peasants were unprepared for the communal form of production. The associations for collective cultivation of land had proved to be lacking in stability and in incentive for genuinely collective development. As the movement for mass collectivisation gathered momentum, the artel form of organisation was encouraged, and this became the general type of peasant collective farm in the Soviet Union.

Emphasis on the artel form of collective farming contributed to the rapid success of the movement for collectivisation. It left the peasant households freedom to produce independently for home use—and even to sell individually a small surplus when this could be produced without interfering with their work in the collective. At the same time, the artel drew the member families into social labour with means of pro-

* Ample production credit to collective farms on genuinely easy terms, which include generous allowance for small crop returns in poor years, has remained a basic point in the government's agricultural policy.

duction collectively owned and gave them rich experience of the advantages of modern, large-scale agriculture carried on without exploitation of labour.

The land used by collective farms has remained the property of the state, but the collective farms have been granted use of it in perpetuity. The tractors and heavy machines used by the collective farms are also owned by the state, through the local machine and tractor station which takes responsibility for mechanical assistance and general technical advice to the collective.

The machine and tractor station is one of the most distinctive and important features of Soviet agriculture. Through it the collective farmers obtain the use of up-to-date mechanical equipment with routine servicing. During the winter every tractor and field implement is gone over, worn-out parts are replaced, and the farming season opens with machines ready in top-notch condition. Payment is made in kind, as a percentage of the total crop, and in case of severe crop loss the machine and tractor station aids the collective instead of receiving payment for its services. Mechanisation of Soviet agriculture was rapidly carried through without piling a hopeless burden of debt upon the farmers.*

In starting the mass campaign, the Communist leaders set as a goal for the first year (1929-30) the drawing into collectives of one-fourth of the peasant households. They wanted no coercion of poor and middle peasants. The campaign was to proceed in a great wave of education and demonstration with practical assistance for groups which genuinely desired to combine. But in many places the organisers' zeal outran discretion. The country as a whole overshot the mark so that 50 per cent instead of 25 per cent were brought into collectives within the

* By 1938, the number of stations had increased to 6,350, and they were providing about 400,000 tractors for collective farms. In addition, some 84,000 tractors were owned and used by state farms. (*The Land of Socialism Today and Tomorrow*, Moscow, 1939, pp. 25-26.) Total number of tractors in the Soviet Union is roughly one-third the number in the United States, but they are on the whole heavier machines and much more fully utilised. According to a writer in *Soviet Russia Today* (January, 1942) they have averaged four times as much work per tractor as those on American farms. More than half the total crops were combine-harvested in 1938. (*Moscow Daily News*, June 12, 1939.)

first year of the campaign.[22] This meant, of course, some losses and setbacks. And it called forth Stalin's classic essay, *Dizzy with Success,* in which he rebuked those who had resorted to coercion; or who had reported as collectives farms organised only "on paper"; or who thought that when the collective was launched the organiser's work was finished. Stalin emphasised again and again the importance of solid advance on a voluntary basis.

"The art of leadership is a serious matter. One must not lag behind the movement, because to do so is to become isolated from the masses. But neither must one rush ahead, for to rush ahead is to lose contact with the masses. He who wants to lead a movement, and at the same time keep in touch with the vast masses must wage a fight on two fronts—against those who lag behind and against those who rush on ahead." [23]

In spite of errors and difficulties, the movement had a broad and firm foundation among the masses of the peasants. And by 1936 over 90 per cent of the peasant farms were carrying on collective production.

Frontal attack on the economic basis of kulak class power was an integral part of the campaign for mass collectivisation. Up to this time the activities of the kulaks had been *restricted* by heavy taxation and by limitations on employment of hired labour and renting of land. But many of them had survived and grown richer in spite of these restrictions. For so long as poor peasants could not make a living from their own allotments of land they could not resist the kulak's offer to employ them as wage workers and to hire their land. Also, so long as total grain supplies were barely sufficient for the city workers' needs, the private trader and the kulak could evade the law and manipulate the kulaks' marketing surplus at great profit to themselves.

But when great masses of poor peasants (and middle peasants also) had been drawn into collectives and found themselves on the road to security and even prosperity, they and their land could be completely released from kulak exploitation. As grain production on Soviet farms and collective farms increased and city needs could be met through government and co-operative channels, it would no longer be necessary to tolerate the speculating traders and kulaks. In an historic resolution the Central Committee of the party decided on January 5, 1930, that the policy of *restricting* the kulaks, which was all that could be attempted in the earlier years of the revolution, should now give place to a determined policy of *eliminating* the kulaks as a class.[24] Practically, what did the party aim to accomplish?

"In order to squeeze out the kulaks as a class we must *break down* the resistance of this class in open battle and *deprive* it of the productive sources of its existence and development (the free use of land, means of production, the renting of land, the right to hire labour, etc.). This is the *turn* toward the policy of eliminating the kulaks as a class. Without this, all talk of squeezing out the kulaks as a class is idle chatter, pleasing and profitable only to the Right deviationists. Without this, serious collectivisation, let alone solid collectivisation of the rural districts, is inconceivable. This has been grasped quite well by the poor and middle peasants in our rural districts who are routing the kulaks and realising solid collectivisation."[25]

How this drive against the kulaks was carried out by the peasants themselves is vividly described by Anna Louise Strong, an American writer who has lived in the Soviet Union much of the time since the revolution and who had traveled widely through the countryside during the years of mass collectivisation. She wrote in 1934 about the removal of kulaks from European Russia and the Ukraine to the rich Siberian frontier land:

"The usual assumption outside the Soviet Union is that this exiling occurred through drastic action by a mystically omnipotent G.P.U. The actual process was quite different; it was done by village meetings of poor peasants and farmhands which listed those kulaks who 'impede the collective farm by force and violence' and asked the government to deport them. In the hot days of 1930 I attended several of these meetings. They were harsh, ruthless discussions, analysing one by one the 'best families,' which had grabbed the best lands, exploited labour by owning the tools of production, as 'best families' normally and historically do, and who were now fighting the rise of the collective farms by arson, cattle-killing and murder. Meetings of poor peasants and farmhands discussed them, questioned them, passed on them, allowing some to remain but listing others as 'dangerous to our peaceful development—should be deported from our village.'" Before these kulaks were sent away, "township and provincial commissions reviewed the lists of 'kulaks for exile' and greatly cut them down, guarding against local spites and excesses." [26]

Even those kulaks who had not committed criminal acts and were not even removed from their native regions were deprived of their tractors, harvesters, and other large-farm equipment. In all, agricultural machinery valued at some 400 million rubles was turned over from kulak farms to collectives.[27] Land that had been utilised by kulaks was incorporated in the collective farms. Some kulaks received a small individual allotment either in their place of exile or in the region where they had lived. Others found jobs in construction work or in industry. Later, kulaks who had shown by "three years of honest work and support of the measures of the Soviet government that they have reformed" were permitted to join a collective farm.[28] And under the Soviet Constitution of 1936, full electoral rights were extended to former kulaks and their families, except those individuals who had been convicted of crime and whose sentences had explicitly included "deprivation of electoral rights." [29]

The struggles and difficulties involved in transforming Soviet agriculture from small-scale individual farms to large-scale co-operative (collective) farming temporarily interfered with increased production. Another serious food crisis developed in 1932-33, affecting especially peasants in regions where crops were poor. Then a peaceful army of 25,000 experienced Communists volunteered for service in the countryside, to aid the collective farmers in organising their work. These included agricultural specialists, teachers, and others gifted in dealing with people, and some five thousand bookkeepers. With their aid, the new collectives rapidly straightened out their organisation tangles, and by 1934 production was once more on the upgrade. It increased more rapidly than ever before, and after 1934 the government was able to combine the building of great national grain reserves with the free, unrationed sale of bread throughout the Soviet Union.

Collective farms faced several difficulties of inner adjustment. One problem arose in the conflict of interest between the collective farmer's cultivation of his own patch of land and his work on the collective product. This difficulty had been carefully cultivated by the kulak enemies of collectivisation who would be reminding one and another member of the collective how he could make more from his little patch of land if he did not work so hard on the collective land. The problem was, of course, tied in with the matter of fair variations in payment for collective work. It also became less serious as the collectives themselves gained in experience and stability and greatly increased their total group income. Still, under the regulations adopted by each collective farm, all able-bodied members are expected to perform at least a stated minimum number of days of collective work. This varies from sixty days to one hundred days according to region.[30] Individual incomes from the collective farm are exempt from taxation while income derived from the member's separate enterprise is subject to a steeply graduated tax.[31]

Another basic and universal problem was the distribution of the collective income among the members. Like many other questions arising in the creative progress of the Soviet Union, this was solved only after much free experimentation. When the mass campaign for collectivisation was under way, experience was already being assembled and studied. In February, 1935, a model constitution for agricultural artels was drafted and adopted first by a Congress of Shock-Brigade Workers from Collective Farms and then by the Council of People's Commissars. Its principles are embodied in the regulations which are drafted by each local artel and which vary in detail according to the special needs of its region and its type of farming.

Under this model constitution, the work actually done day by day is the sole basis of payment to able-bodied members over sixteen years of age. The various broad types of work are to be classified according to the degree of skill required, and each member's actual accomplishment —reflecting classification of work, volume of work, speed, and efficiency —is taken account of. Members form brigades in which small groups work together throughout the farm year (or for a longer period on livestock farms) with full responsibility for a certain acreage, or certain animals, and carry on socialist competition with one another for regularity of work and quality and quantity of results. But each member of the brigade is paid according to his or her individual work.

Although they are paid according to work done, collective farmers are not wage workers. During the farm year each working member receives limited advances, related to work that he or she has done. At the end of the year, the members themselves decide on the disposal of the collective product. Under Soviet law, certain percentages of the total must be set aside for seed and fodder, and for the agricultural tax to the government; for agricultural improvements, for the collective's social insurance fund, and for cultural needs. The collective may, at its discretion, increase these appropriations, and it may carry also funds for other social purposes. But not less than 60 per cent and not more than 70 per cent of the collective money income must be apportioned among the individual members, male and female, according to the total work that each has contributed during the year. Children under 16 are supported by their parents. But the collective farm's social insurance fund which pays maternity benefits (before and after confinement) and provides for illness and old age, assumes responsibility for orphans and those whose parents are disabled.[32]

Products of collective farms are disposed of through several different channels. Under the nationwide agricultural plan, each collective is assigned a quota—the minimum which it is expected to produce and sell to the government at a fixed price. Separately from this, those collectives served by a machine and tractor station give this government agency part of their output in payment for its assistance. If the collective has signed a contract for sales, this product must be delivered. Then, having set aside a supply of seed and fodder for the following year and made distribution in kind among the members, the collective decides on how the rest of the product shall be sold. The possibilities include sale to a government trust; sale to a co-operative; or sale direct to consumers through a collective farm market, to a public dining room, or even to individual customers.

Absolutely forbidden are sales to private traders. Collective farms may not even employ a non-member as salesman in the market stall, since experience showed that this opens the door to speculation.*

Actually most of the product goes to government and co-operative bodies. Prices fixed by the government for its purchases prevail generally for the rest of the output. Speculation is eliminated.

The state and co-operative bodies for purchase and distribution of collective farm products have gone through several stages of experiment and development. In the future, when the problem of full abundance has been completely solved, there will doubtless be further basic changes.

Thus far, the Soviet Union has faced as its primary agricultural problem the increase of supply for current needs and for national food reserves. It has been drawing into planned social economy millions of peasants who had had no experience of large-scale production but had existed and survived solely through hard work and personal initiative. It has more and more successfully combined strict social handling of the minimum volume basically necessary under the nationwide economic planning, with a considerable measure of free initiative in increasing production beyond the minimum plan. Through the 4,000 state farms and the quarter of a million collective farms which include over 90 per cent of the twenty million peasant households, agriculture has become an inseparable part of the democratically planned socialist economy.

Within the framework of socialist planned economy, the collective farmers have complete freedom to manage their own affairs. The production assigned to each collective under the nationwide plan is related to the farmers' own estimate of what they can do. To guard against bureaucracy within the collective, the administrative committee is

* Employment of non-members is permitted under very strict limitations. A collective farm may employ "persons possessing special knowledge and training (agronomists, engineers, technicians, etc.)." Also: "The hiring of temporary workers shall be permitted in exceptional cases only, when urgent work cannot be carried out within the alloted period of time by the forces of the members of the artel while working at full capacity, and also for construction work." (*Moscow Daily News*, February 21, 1935.) Since 1930 there has been no industrial unemployment in the Soviet Union. Such seasonal wage labour as is still required in Soviet agriculture is fitted in with full employment in other occupations during the rest of the year.

directly responsible to the membership and may be dissolved and replaced by the general members' meeting at any time. Administrative decisions on such points as the plan of production, the finance plan, the building plan, the norms of work performance, the agreement with the machine and tractor station, and the organisation of work must be discussed and approved, and may be amended, by the membership meetings. This meeting determines the distribution of income and the general plan for disposal of the output. For several of the most important questions—including election or recall of the administrative committee and the admission or expulsion of members—at least two-thirds of the members must be present.[33]

Collective farmers have not only economic but direct social bonds with industrial workers. Every factory and every mine or other industrial production unit is responsible for at least one collective farm in its own region. At first this relationship was developed in order that the workers, more experienced in organisation, might give friendly assistance in the solving of the collective farmers' problems. It has become more and more a matter of personal contacts, with equal interchange of all sorts of cultural, technical, and athletic interests.

A Few of the Achievements

All the problems of social growth are of little importance in comparison with the broad basic facts already known and abundantly proved by the course of the Second World War. Under the guidance of Lenin's teachings and Stalin's leadership, the Soviet countryside has risen in less than a generation from the depths of ignorance and poverty, in which little islands of "progress" were supported by the crudest and most brutal exploitation, to the highest peak of agricultural development yet attained by any section of the human race. Before our very eyes the Soviet people have carried through in agriculture changes technically comparable with the industrial revolution, which began in England in the eighteenth century, and even more significant in the upsurge of a new creative consciousness among the tens of millions of the rural population.

Agricultural science in the Soviet Union has opened new horizons, with undreamed-of possibilities of new plants, new biological and chemical techniques, new utilisation of Arctic wastes, new sources of industrial materials.

Soviet farming moved in less than a generation from the home-made wooden plough—used by more than half the Russian peasants before the revolution—to tractor and combine and other machines which immeasurably increase the productivity of human labour. While much technology was taken over from the achievements of capitalist countries, the Soviet Union has developed it and given it a distinctive usefulness. Only there have machines been utilised to their utmost capacity, and only there have they been introduced without bringing benefit to a minority at the expense of greater impoverishment for the mass. Collective farms, serviced by the extraordinary network of machine and tractor stations, represent the most modern form of farming.

In the Soviet Union the once illiterate peasants and their sons and daughters follow the latest technical and scientific literature and achieve on a wide scale crop yields outstripping those on model laboratory farms in other countries.

Drought—the scourge of wide areas in almost every grain country—is being conquered, in part by forestation, in part by bold and vast offensives of construction, attacking in a unified plan the need for irrigation, the need for water power, and the possibilities of water transport. Where water supply is still scanty and uncertain, a new "vernalisation" of seed before planting shortens the period between sowing and harvest. Dry seasons that would formerly have brought crop failure and famine have seen the gathering of normal crops. The socialist economy has not only stimulated creative scientific work but has made possible the unrestricted application of scientific principles and methods.

Agriculture and industry have become equal partners in the whole social and economic enterprise. Collective farmers are now firmly, inseparably united with the working class. Experience and achievement under working-class leadership have transformed the once wavering individualists into confident, active members of the socialist whole. They work together for a genuine planned abundance which, before the Nazi attack, was raising the material standard of living of the masses both in city and country. Opportunity for every individual to work, to serve, to create without exploiting others, without driving others into destitution; had become the basic reality of Soviet life.

In their onslaught against the Soviet Union in 1941, the Nazis looked in vain for Fifth Columnists among the peasants, even in the Ukraine and Byelo-Russia. Instead, peasant guerrillas—including older men who had lived and worked as individual farmers—showed devoted heroism and accomplished amazing feats against the invaders. And when the Nazis tried to break up collective farms in occupied territory, they were met by stubborn passive resistance combined with persistent sabotage.

Lenin's original thesis of unity between worker and toiling peasant has been completely realised in the Soviet Union.

CHAPTER XII

Underlying Principles of Lenin's Analysis and Programme

TO Lenin, as to Marx before him, economic understanding was important primarily as the basis for correct and fruitful revolutionary action. Only with the guidance of a party having a clear view of economic trends and class relationships could the depressed masses achieve creative activity and obtain their rightful share of the material abundance and the intellectual and social riches which humanity is now equipped to produce and enjoy.

Marx had stated that the purpose of *Capital* was "to lay bare the economic law of motion of modern society."[1] Lenin carried this forward with special detail in relation to agriculture. Lenin shared also the Marxist standpoint that "the evolution of the economic formation of society is viewed as a process of natural history."[2] In his earliest arguments with the Russian Populists, Lenin set forth the relation between the "economic formation of society" and the role of the individual.

"Just as Darwin ... was the first to put biology on an absolutely scientific basis by establishing the mutability and succession of species, so Marx put an end to the view that society is a mechanical aggregation of individuals, which will tolerate any kind of modification at the will of the powers that be (or, what amounts to the same thing, at the will of society and the government) and which arises and changes in a fortuitous way. He was the first to put sociology on a scientific footing by establishing the concept of the economic formation of society as the sum total of the given relations of production and by establishing the fact that the development of these formations is a process of natural history.

"... The real question that arises in judging the social activity of an individual is: What conditions ensure the success of this activity, what guarantee is there that this activity will not remain an isolated act lost in a welter of contrary acts? This also involves a question which is answered differently by Social-Democrats and by the other Russian Socialists, namely, in what way must activity which aims at bringing about the socialist system enlist the masses in order to secure real results? Obviously, the answer to this question depends directly and immediately on the conception of the grouping of social forces in Russia, of the class struggle out of which the actualities of Russian life arise."[3]

And again, in *The Economic Content of Narodism* [*Populism*]:

"The existence of 'business at the expense of others,' the existence of exploitation, will always engender ideals antithetical to this system among the exploited themselves and among certain representatives of the 'intelligentsia.'

"These ideals are extremely valuable to the Marxist; he argues with Narodism only on the basis of these ideals; he argues exclusively about the construction of these ideals and their realisation.

"The Narodnik [Populist] thinks it enough to note the fact that gives rise to such ideals, then to refer to the legitimacy of the ideal from the standpoint of 'modern science and modern moral ideas' (and he does not realise that these 'modern ideas' are only concessions made by West European 'social opinion' to the new force that is arising), and then to cry to 'society' and the 'state': Ensure it, protect it, organise it!

"The Marxist proceeds from the same ideal; but he compares it not with 'modern science and modern moral ideas,' but with *the existing class contradictions,* and therefore formulates it not as a demand of 'science,' but as a demand of such and such a class, provoked by such and such social relations (which must be objectively investigated), and achievable only in such and such a way in consequence of such and such properties of these relations. If ideals are not based on facts *in this way,* they will remain but pious wishes with no chance of being accepted by the masses and, hence, of being realised."[4]

Capitalism in Agriculture

Differences between the Marxists and reformist Socialists in Russia included very different interpretations of peasant life and the trend of agricultural development. These differences among Russian revolutionists reflected in part an old controversy among western European Socialists. For non-Marxists generally—and some who considered themselves Marxists—did not and do not yet recognise the essentially capitalist nature of small-scale agriculture producing for the market. They have dreamed of restoring and perpetuating small farming, oblivious to the economic forces which operate to undermine it and which make possible and necessary the struggle for a more productive, more civilised form of agriculture. In Russia, more than elsewhere, the underlying capitalist trends in life on the land were obscured by the form of the Russian village community, with its supposedly equal allotments of land to the peasants, and by the strong semi-feudal survivals of peasant exploitation by the landowners.

Lenin cut through this non-Marxist confusion with sharp historical-economic analysis. He showed that the "Great Reform" of 1861—emancipating the serfs—had marked a turning point in Russian agricultural development. In allowing the peasants to retain part of the land which they had used from time immemorial, the decree had required from them redemption payments in money. Markets, prices, and money were forcibly injected into peasant life as a primary factor in their poverty or well-being. Even while many must continue to give "labour rent" to the landowner in payment for the use of essential pastures, watering places, and forest patches that had been "cut off" from their lands, the peasants could meet their redemption payments only by selling for money either part of their product or part of their labour power.

"To the oppression of the landlords, which was preserved thanks to the magnanimity of the officials who introduced and carried out the reform, was added the oppression of capital. The power of money, which crushed even the French peasant—who was emancipated from the power of the feudal landlords, not by miserable half-hearted reforms, but by a mighty popular revolution—this power of money bore down with all its weight upon our semi-serf muzhik. The peasant had to obtain money at all costs in order to pay the taxes which had increased as a result of the beneficent reform, in order to rent land, to buy the few miserable articles of manufactured goods—which began to squeeze out the home manufactures of the peasant—to buy corn, etc. The power of money not only crushed the peasantry, but split it up. An enormous number of peasants were steadily ruined and converted into proletarians. From the minority arose a small group of shrewd and greedy kulaks, who began to lay their avaricious hands upon the lands and farms of the peasants, and who represented the first cadres of the rising rural bourgeoisie."[5]

Balance of Russian peasant production shifted more and more from natural economy (home production for home use) to the production of commodities for the market. By the end of the nineteenth century, many rural handicraft shops employing wage labour were already outside of the peasant household. Peasants and artisans had advanced towards social division of labour with dependence upon trade within the village, and between the village and the town. Poor peasant wage workers and well-to-do kulaks had become clearly distinct from the traditional middle peasant household which had little to sell and lived by its own labour on its own land.

Lenin showed that such trends inevitably result among producers dependent upon money and the market. As commodity production displaces natural economy, the small producer becomes subject to the owner of money. Even among those who still own their tools and employ no wage labour, the seeds of capitalist development have been planted.

"In fact, what is this bondage [of the small producer]? It is the dependence of the proprietor (who owns his means of production and is compelled to work for the market) on the power of money, a dependence which however variously it may be expressed (in the form of usurer's capital or of buyer's capital which monopolises the sale) always leads to this—that a tremendous part of the product of labour falls not to the producer but to the owner of money. Consequently, its essence is purely capitalistic.... [Note by Lenin:] Here are present all the signs: commodity production, as the basis; monopolising of the product of social labour in the form of money, as a result; and the transformation of this money into capital. I do not in the least forget that these primary forms of *capital* are met with in certain instances even of pre-capitalist orders. But the point is precisely this: that they appear in contemporary Russian peasant economy not as single instances, but as the rule, as the dominating system of relationships. They are already tied in (by commodity exchange, by banks) with large-scale factory machine capitalism and thereby have shown their trend;—they have shown that the representatives of this 'bondage' are only the fighting soldiers of the one and indivisible army of the bourgeoisie."[6]

Elsewhere in the same work against the Populists, Lenin inserts a note defining briefly the basis of the capitalist order:

"To avoid misunderstanding I explain that by the 'basis' of capitalism I mean the social relationship which, under various forms, rules in a capitalist society and which Marx expressed in the formula: money—commodity—money with an increment.

"The Narodnik measures *do not touch upon* this relationship, since they do not disturb either commodity production (which gives into the hands of private persons money, the product of social labour) or the division of 'the people' into those possessing money and the destitute.

"The Marxist turns to this relationship in its most developed form, which reveals the quintessence of all the other forms, and shows the producer his task and goal: to destroy this relationship, to replace it with another."[7]

Just how commodity production and dependence upon money become the basis for capitalist development had been concisely stated by Lenin in a paper read before the Marxist circle in St. Petersburg during his first winter in that city (1893).

"By commodity production is meant the organisation of social economy in such a way that products are made by separate, individual producers, with each one specialising in the production of some one thing, so that the buying and selling of products (which thereby become commodities) on the market is essential for the satisfying of social needs. By capitalism is meant that stage of development of commodity production when not only the products of human labour have become a commodity but also human labour power itself.

"Thus in the historical development of capitalism two periods are important: (1) the transformation of natural economy of the producers themselves into trade [economy], and (2) the transformation of trade economy into capitalist [economy]. The first transformation is accomplished as a result of the appearance of social division of labour—specialisation of individual separate producers occupied with only one branch of industry. (N.B.: this is the invariable condition of trade economy.) The second transformation is accomplished as a result of this: that the separate producers, each one by himself producing commodities for the market, come into a relation of competition, each one tries to sell dearer and buy cheaper, and the inevitable result is the strengthening of the strong and the decline of the weak, the enriching of a minority and the ruin of the mass, leading to the transformation of independent producers into hired workers, and many small establishments into a few very large."[8]

In comparison with feudal exploitation and stagnant peasant existence in the self-sufficing village of natural economy, dependence upon the market and money enters as a historically progressive force. It stimulates technical progress and increases the productivity of human labour. It breaks down the personal dependence of the peasant upon the kindness or cruelty of his individual landowner and throws him into direct relation with the larger world. And at the same time it introduces new tensions and conflicts which open the way to further progress from capitalism to socialism.

"The progressive feature of capitalism consists precisely in the fact that it destroyed the old, cramped conditions of human life, which dulled the mind and prevented the producers from taking their destinies into their own hands. The tremendous development of trade relations and world exchange and the constant migrations of vast masses of the population shattered the immemorial fetters of the tribe, family and territorial community and created that variegation of development, that 'variegation of talents and wealth of social relations,' * which plays so great a role in the modern history of the West. In Russia this process was fully manifested in the post-Reform era, when the ancient forms of labour very rapidly collapsed and prime place was assumed by the purchase and sale of labour power, which tore the peasant from the patriarchal, semi-feudal family, from the stupefying conditions of village life, and which replaced the semi-feudal forms of appropriation of surplus value by purely capitalist forms.... And, furthermore, it was capitalism that freed the individual from all feudal ties, that placed him in independent relation to the market, that made him a commodity owner (and as such the equal of all other commodity owners), and that heightened the sense of individuality."[9]

Increasing productivity of human labour, which provides the material basis for a higher standard of living among the masses of the population, appeared first as a direct result of market competition and capitalist development. Referring to the old "labour rent system and patriarchal peasant economy," Lenin said:

"Within the internal structure of this economic regime there is nothing to stimulate the change of technique; on the contrary, the exclusiveness and isolation of this system of economy, the poverty and degradation of the dependent peasant excludes the possibility of introducing improvements.... And the facts do indeed show that [in Russia—*A.R.*] the wide movement for the reform of agricultural technique commenced only in the post-Reform period of the development of commodity production and capitalism. Competition, which was created by capitalism, and the fact that the farmer is dependent on the world market, made the reform of technique necessary and the drop in grain prices caused this necessity to become very urgent."[10]

Landlord estates, producing grain for the world market, began to substitute machinery operated by wage workers for the semi-feudal

* Karl Marx, *The Eighteenth Brumaire of Louis Bonaparte.*

service of peasants using their own old-fashioned implements. The more fortunate peasants followed suit, usually with borrowed capital, and expanded production for the market with the aid of improved implements and wage workers drawn from the ranks of the formerly self-sustaining peasants.

In the class differences among peasants that had developed to a marked degree by the 1890's, the ruin of the rural masses was characterised by Lenin as "complete catastrophe."[11] Technical progress under capitalism—in agriculture as in industry—creates the material possibilities of abundance for all, but it gradually separates the producing masses from ownership of their tools and plunges them into insecurity. The masses are able to produce much more, but most of the increased product is taken from the producers by the owners of capital.

This capitalist exploitation assumes its most highly developed form in the employment of wage labour. But small producers toiling for the market themselves, with good equipment which they regard as their own property, are usually paying toll to some capitalist in the form of interest on borrowed money and rent for the use of the land. At the foot of the scale among small producers are the poorest, most backward farms, operated with terrific overwork and a most wretched standard of living.

"Indeed, the fundamental and main trend of capitalism is the elimination of small production by large-scale production both in industry and in agriculture. But this process must not be taken *only* in the sense of immediate expropriation. This elimination process also includes a process of ruination, of deterioration of the conditions of farming of the small farmers, which may extend over years and decades. This deterioration manifests itself in overwork or underfeeding of the small farmer; in an increased burden of debt; in the deterioration of cattle fodder and the condition of the cattle in general; in the deterioration of the methods of cultivating and manuring the land; in the stagnation of technical progress, etc."[12]

Lenin shows that subjection to the market, with all its new cruelties, is from another aspect also a genuinely progressive historic force. The social division of labour advances under capitalism. Increasingly specialised production penetrates agriculture as well as industry and makes every capitalist, every landowner, every farmer, every worker a part of the complex total economy. A social structure is created by which, through the exchange of products, human beings become mutually dependent, and their activities are integrated, one with another.

"The socialisation of labour by capitalist production does not consist in the fact that people work under one roof (that is only a small part of the process), but in the fact that concentration of capital is accompanied by specialisation of social labour,... in the fact that many divided processes of production are merged into one social process of production."[18]

This socialisation of labour goes forward more slowly in agriculture than in industry, since the farmers' production of food for home use continues until commercial (capitalist) agriculture reaches its very last stage of corporation farming. But the commercial farm output and the farms, both large and small, from which it comes are an integral part of the capitalist whole. And production for the market by small "independent" producers represents in itself the process of socialising agricultural labor.

"Indeed, the fact that agriculture has been transformed from a privileged occupation of the higher estates and a burden for the lower estate into an ordinary commercial and industrial occupation; the fact that the product of the labour of the tiller of the soil has become subject to social accounting on the market; the fact that monotonous, routine agriculture is being converted into technically transformed commercial agriculture with a variety of forms; the fact that local isolation and the separation among small tillers of the soil is being broken down; the fact that the various forms of bondage and personal dependence are being squeezed out by impersonal transactions in the purchase and sale of labour power—all these are links in the single process, which is socialising agricultural labour. They are more and more intensifying the contradictions between the anarchy of market fluctuations, the individual character of separate agricultural enterprises, and the collective character of large-scale capitalist agriculture.

"Thus (we repeat once more), in emphasising the progressive historicale role of capitalism in Russian agriculture, we do not for a moment forget the historical transitional character of this regime, or the profound social contradictions which are peculiar to it."[14]

The socialising of labour is carried out by the owners of money with a ruthless disregard for human suffering. And the integration of the capitalist market is so crude and works so badly that ever since the early nineteenth century economic crises have been a normal periodic occurrence. Long before the twentieth century, when capitalism had brought chronic unemployment in the cities and "over-population" on the land, the grain producers of Europe and England had faced a long-drawn out agrarian crisis due primarily to the increasing flood of imported wheat, first from the United States, then from Canada, Argentina and Australia. Even before the first World War the seeds of a similar profound agrarian crisis had been planted in the United States.*

Crises, in turn, speed up the technical developments in agriculture, increase the commercial farmers' dependence not merely upon the market but upon money capital in its more developed forms, and create new millions of rural poor who must sell their labour power. As Lenin wrote in 1903:

"Money has everywhere become the ruling power. All the goods produced by the labour of man can be exchanged for money. Money can even buy men, that is to say, it can force a man who owns nothing to work for another who has money. In former times, under serfdom, land used to be the ruling power; whoever possessed land possessed power and authority. Now it is money, capital, that has become the ruling power. Money will buy all the land you like. Unless you have money land is of little use to you: for you want money to buy a plough or other implements, to buy livestock, to buy clothes and other goods in the towns, not to speak of paying taxes....

"For the sake of money everyone today is waging a fierce war against everyone else. Each tries to buy cheap and to sell dear, each tries to outdo the other, to sell as much of his wares as he can, to underbid the other, to conceal from him a profitable market or a profitable

* For certain aspects of the present agrarian crisis in the United States, see Chap. XIII.

order. In this general scramble for money it is the small man, the small artisan, or the small peasant, who fares worst: he is always beaten by the big merchant or the rich peasant. The small man never has any reserves; he lives from hand to mouth; the first difficulty, the first accident, compels him to pawn his last belongings or to sell his livestock dirt cheap. Having fallen into the hands of a kulak or of a money lender, he very rarely succeeds in extricating himself from his clutches: in most cases he is utterly ruined. Every year tens and hundreds of thousands of small peasants and artisans lock up their cottages, surrender their holdings to the community, and become wage labourers, farmhands, unskilled workers, proletarians. Meanwhile, in this scramble for money, the rich grow rich and richer. They pile up millions and hundreds of millions of rubles in the banks; and besides their own money, the money deposited in the banks by others also helps them to become rich....

"This being the case, the Social-Democratic workers say that the only way to put an end to the poverty of the people is to change the existing order from top to bottom and to introduce a *socialist order.*"[15]

Landed Property

As commodity production displaced natural economy, and money became the ruling power instead of land, the relations between peasants and landowners living by peasants' labour were profoundly altered. But nowhere in the western world was private ownership of land abolished.

"Capitalism creates for itself its own suitable forms of agrarian relationships out of the old forms, out of feudal landed property, small peasants' commune property, clan property, etc."[16]

In the wide diversity of historical development, three chief types of relation to the land under capitalism were noted by Lenin. Under each of them the land is held as private property and is in itself a source of income to its owner.

Landowners might develop into large-scale capitalist farmers, utilising former peasants as wage workers. This was the predominant form in East Prussia.

Landowners might be content with receiving toll from their tenants, while these tenants developed into capitalist farmers and wage workers. This was the predominant form in England.

The land itself might be taken up by small owners: as among the French peasants in the Revolution of 1789-93, or among the colonial settlers in large sections of the United States.*

In all capitalist countries, landed property continued to exact a share of the surplus value produced by the labour of wage workers, toiling farmers and artisans. And Lenin made plain that this toll taken by landowners has amounted to monopoly exploitation, bearing down upon all classes of labourers, both on the land and in industry. It has definitely retarded technical development in agriculture. And the problems involved in landed property have tended to obscure the other problems of farm poverty under capitalism.

Absolute rent is exacted by private ownership from those who use even the least productive, least accessible, least desirable land. It thereby also increases the rent demanded by landowners from the better, more productive lands. Absolute rent raises the cost of farm production and under "normal" market conditions it has been reflected in the prices of all farm products and the wage workers' cost of living.

In a situation where farmers themselves own their land clear of mortgage and are selling their products in a freely competitive market with a rough balance between supply and demand, absolute rent is pocketed by farmers at the expense of the non-farm population. But actually this combination of circumstances has rarely been realised. For as capitalism develops, rent tends to increase and capital required for farm equipment and farm operation also increases. Owner farmers become burdened with debt. Great numbers slip into the status of tenants. (In most of the older countries, tenant farmers have always outnumbered those who owned their land.) Either way, the rent drawn

* In the northern colonies, absentee owners of great unsettled tracts could not exact high prices from settlers. Distribution of public lands to small owners (after nominal payments to the government) dated only from the Homestead Act of 1862, and did not exclude distribution of public lands to railroad companies and others who received large tracts which they sold to settlers.

from private ownership of land is taken out of the farmers' pockets by absentee owners and capitalists (large or small) who "invest" in farm mortgages.

Rents and landlords in the older countries showed what Engels called a "wonderful vitality,"[17] which was threatened and gradually impaired as new countries with unsettled lands and undeveloped rent were brought into competition with Old World agriculture. Of the agrarian crisis in Europe during the last third of the nineteenth century, Lenin wrote:

"Agriculture in Europe has lost the opportunity of shifting to the masses of consumers the burdens which the private ownership of land and capitalist commodity production impose upon agriculture.... The burden of these rents falls upon the farmers and the landowners themselves and ruins them. Thus, the agrarian crisis has upset, and continues to upset, the prosperity which capitalist landed property and capitalist agriculture formerly enjoyed. Up to now capitalist landed property has exacted ever increasing tribute from social development; and it fixed the level of this tribute in the price of land."[18]

Nowhere except in the Soviet Union has private ownership of land, with its heavy social burden of rent, been abolished.

Private property in land has served, on the whole, as a barrier to rapid and rational development of agriculture. This is one of the contradictions inherent in capitalist economy. For competition, and an economic crisis (which for farmers is intensified by rent), stimulate technical advance. But at the same time the toll exacted from agriculture as payment for land has drawn off part of the surplus product which could otherwise have been retained by farmers and utilised as capital for technical improvement.

"Ground rent is that part of surplus value which remains after the average rate of profit on invested capital is deducted. The monopoly of landed property enables the landowner to appropriate this surplus, and the price of land (= capitalised rent) *keeps* rent at the level once reached. Clearly, rent 'hinders' the complete rationalisation of agriculture: under the tenant farmer system the stimulus to improvements, etc., becomes weaker, and under the mortgage system the major part of the capital has to be invested not in production, but in the purchase of land.... Stimuli to progress in capitalist agriculture are: growth of the population, growth of competition, and growth of industry; rent, however, is a tribute exacted by the landowner from social development, from the growth of technique.... Theoretically, it is quite possible for capitalist production to exist without the existence of private property in land.... This would not weaken the stimulus to agronomic progress; on the contrary, it would increase it to an enormous extent."[19]

And last, but not least, the problems of rent and mortgage debt which complicate the farmers' relation to the land tend to obscure the essential nature of agrarian crisis as a part of the maladjustment and injustice of the capitalist economy. The Russian Populists and Socialist-Revolutionaries—both of them groups dreaming of socialism—thought that if peasants had free access to the land their problems would be solved. They were against capitalism, but they recognised as capitalism only large-scale industry and banking. They could not see that peasant production for the market and peasant handicraft shops were the soil in which Russian capitalism was most deeply rooted. They even denied that small-scale private employment of wage-labour marked a definite stage in capitalist development. In their minds:

"If the workers have no land—there is capitalism; if the workers have land—there is no capitalism. And they confine themselves to this soothing philosophy, losing sight of the whole social organisation of production and forgetting the generally-known fact that ownership of land does not in the least remove the beastly poverty of these landowners, who are subjected to the most shameless robbery on the part of other similar landowners—'peasants.' "[20]

And elsewhere, Lenin after summarising a Populist description of the *facts* of Russian village life wrote:

"The originality of their theories consists only in this that they do not wish to call these facts by their actual names, they do not wish to see that they mean the *domination of capital in agriculture*. They forget that the primary form of *capital* always and everywhere was merchant capital, money capital; that capital always takes the technical process of production as it finds it, and only afterwards subjects it to technical transformation. They do not see because 'defending' (in words, of course, and nothing more) the present agricultural order from 'coming' (?!) capitalism, they are defending only the *mediaeval* forms of capital from pressure by its newest, purely bourgeois forms.

"In this way it is impossible to deny the capitalist character of the overpopulation in Russia, as it is impossible to deny the domination of capital in agriculture. But it is completely ridiculous, of course, to ignore the *degree of development of capital*... it dominates but in a very relatively undeveloped form; to its full development, to full separation of the producer from the means of production there are still many intermediate steps."[21]

Struggle for Socialism

From the beginning of his work, Lenin stressed the transitional character of this capitalist development in agriculture. He recognised it as essentially progressive by comparison with feudalism. And therefore he wanted his party to lead the peasants, first of all, in the struggle for complete, revolutionary release from the hindering remnants of serfdom and feudalism. These were the aspects of their oppression which the peasants themselves were feeling most deeply and which the Bolshevik revolution of 1917 dealt with immediately after the taking of power.

But to Lenin this struggle was merely preliminary to the next stage of revolution: the struggle to pass beyond capitalist agriculture to socialism. As he wrote even in 1901:

"To attempt to save the peasantry by protecting their small farms and their small properties from the advance of capitalism would mean uselessly retarding social development and deceiving the peasantry with illusions about the possibility of achieving prosperity under capitalism."[22]

Thirteen years later, in Lenin's essay on *Karl Marx,* the hopeless situation of the small producer under capitalism was summarised as follows:

"The small holding system, which is the normal form of small-scale production, deteriorates, collapses, perishes under capitalism.

" 'Small peasants' property excludes by its very nature the development of the social powers of production of labour, the social forms of labour, the social concentration of capitals, cattle raising on a large scale, and a progressive application of science.

" 'Usury and a system of taxation must impoverish it everywhere. The expenditure of capital in the price of the land withdraws this capital from cultivation. An infinite dissipation of means of production and an isolation of the producers themselves go with it. [Co-operative societies, *i.e.,* associations of small peasants, while playing an extremely progressive bourgeois role, only weaken this tendency without eliminating it; nor must it be forgotten that these co-operative societies do much for the well-to-do peasants, and very little, almost nothing, for the mass of poor peasants; and then the associations themselves become exploiters of wage-labour.] Also an enormous waste of human energy. A progressive deterioration of the conditions of production and a raising of the price of means of production is a necessary law of small peasants' property.'

"In agriculture, as in industry, capitalism transforms the process of production only at the price of the 'martyrdom of the producers.'

" 'The dispersion of the rural labourers over larger areas breaks their power of resistance while concentration increases that of the town operatives. In modern agriculture, as in the urban industries, the increased productiveness and quantity of the labour set in motion are bought at the cost of laying waste and consuming by disease labour power itself.' "[28]

What socialism would mean to those who toil on the land was summed up by Lenin in this same essay.

"Capitalism finally snaps the bond between agriculture and industry; but at the same time, in its highest development it prepares new elements of this bond, of a union between industry and agriculture based on the conscious application of science and the integration of collective labour....

"Finally, as regards the attitude of Marxian socialism towards the small peasantry, which will continue to exist in the period of the expropriation of the expropriators, we must refer to a declaration made by Engels which expresses Marx's views.

" 'When we take possession of the state power, we shall not even think of forcibly expropriating the small peasants (with or without compensation), as we shall have to do in relation to the large landowners. Our task as regards the small peasants will first of all be to lead their private enterprise and private property into co-operative lines, not forcibly, but by example and by granting public aid for this purpose. And then, of course, we shall have ample means of showing the small peasant all the advantages connected with such a transformation, advantages which even now should be explained to him.' "[24]

Economic understanding and struggle for socialism were inseparably connected in Lenin's thinking. Capitalism is progressive not merely because it increases the productive forces but because it creates the class basis for advance to socialism.

"...Marx deduces the inevitability of the transformation of capitalist society into socialist society wholly and exclusively from the economic law of motion of contemporary society. The socialisation of labour, which is advancing ever more rapidly in thousands of forms...is the chief material foundation for the inevitable coming of socialism. The intellectual and moral driving force and the physical executant of this transformation is the proletariat, which is trained by capitalism itself."[25]

"We recognise the class struggle as the central fact in the domain of agrarian relations in Russia. We base the whole of our agrarian policy (and, consequently, our agrarian programme) on an unswerving recognition of this fact along with all the consequences resulting from it. But the principal immediate object is to clear the road for the free development of the class struggle in the countryside, of the class struggle of the proletariat, directed towards the achievement of the final aim of international Social-Democracy, the conquest of political power by the proletariat and the laying of the foundations of a socialist society."[26]

Class leadership in the struggle for socialism must be assumed by the wage workers as the only class which capitalism tears completely loose from property interest in the means of production. Masses of small producers still living on the land are ruined by the development of capitalism, but their experience does not prepare them for clean-cut revolutionary action against it.

"How will our toiling peasant alter this relationship when he himself stands with one foot on this very foundation which it is necessary to change? How can he understand the disadvantage of isolation and commodity economy when he is himself isolated and produces at his own risk and fear, produces for the market? When these conditions of life create in him 'thoughts and feelings' peculiar to one who works by himself for the market? When he is crushed by those very material conditions, by the scope and essence of his economy, and when because of this his situation opposed to capital is still so undeveloped that he cannot understand that this is precisely *capital,* and not only 'swindlers' and shrewd people?"[27]

"The small producer (and his ideologue) are able to rail at capitalism, scold and curse capitalism, but are not able to renounce the very basis of this capitalism,* reliance upon its servants, and rosy dreaming that 'it would be better without struggle.' "[28]

Elsewhere, Lenin summed up the reasoning by which the Russian Marxists had arrived at the conclusion that revolutionary leadership must be taken by the industrial proletariat.

"It was precisely with a criticism of the subjective methods of the earlier Socialists that they [the Russian Marxists] began. Not satisfied with merely establishing the fact of exploitation and condemning it, they desired to 'explain' it. Realising that the whole post-Reform history of Russia consisted in the impoverishment of the masses and the enrichment of a minority, observing that the colossal expropriation of

* For Lenin's note at this point see quotation, "To avoid misunderstanding, etc.," given above on page 176.

the small producers proceeded side by side with universal technical progress, noting that these polar tendencies developed and became accentuated wherever, and to the extent that, commodity production developed and became accentuated, they could not but conclude that they were confronted with a bourgeois (capitalist) organisation of social economy, which 'necessarily' gave rise to the expropriation and oppression of the masses.

"Their practical programme was now directly determined by this conviction: this programme was—to join up with the struggle of the proletariat against the bourgeoisie; the struggle of the propertyless classes against the propertied classes, which constitutes the principal content of economic reality in Russia, from the most out-of-the-way village to the most up-to-date and perfected factory.

"How were they to join up? The answer was again suggested by real life. Capitalism had advanced the principal branches of industry to the stage of large-scale machine industry; by thus socialising production it had created the material conditions for a new system and had at the same time created a new social force—the workers of the mills and factories, the urban proletariat. Subjected to bourgeois exploitation—the same in its economic essence as the exploitation of the whole toiling population of Russia—this class, however, has been placed, as far as its emancipation is concerned, in rather favourable circumstances: it has no longer any connection with the old society, which was wholly based on exploitation; the very conditions of its labour and circumstances of its life organise it, compel it to think, and enable it to step into the arena of the political struggle."[29]

In binding together in common daily experience great masses of workers, large-scale industry creates the basis for successful revolutionary class action. Rural wage workers will be their most dependable allies, but only the leadership of the industrial proletariat can transform "into an organised class struggle for the emancipation of all the toiling folk"[30] the discontent and helplessness of the widely scattered wage workers on the land.

The extent to which wage labour is employed in agriculture becomes, however, an important factor in the speed with which the socialist revolution can be carried through in the countryside. Lenin stressed the importance of drawing "independent" small producers into the revolutionary movement of the proletariat. But he never expected to win large numbers of these small producers for socialist agriculture until the proletarian state power could demonstrate the advantages of collective production as part of the socialist economy. More than three years after the Russian workers had taken power, Lenin generalised as follows from the experience of those years:

"There is no doubt that it is possible to carry out the socialist revolution in a country in which the small farmer producers constitute the overwhelming majority of the population only by means of a number of special transitional measures which would be totally unnecessary in countries with developed capitalism, countries in which wage workers constitute the overwhelming majority in industry and agriculture. In the lands of developed capitalism there is a class of agricultural wage workers which grew up in the course of decades. Only such a class can socially, economically and politically serve as a support for the direct transition to socialism. Only in countries where this class is sufficiently developed is the direct transition from capitalism to socialism possible without special transitional nationwide measures."[81]

Lenin's New Economic Policy adopted when the civil war in European Russia was ended was such a "special, transitional" measure. This prepared the way for the socialist revolution in agriculture which was carried through in the Soviet Union under Stalin's leadership after Lenin died.

CHAPTER XIII

A Postscript on American Agriculture

TO Lenin, the Russian problems with which he was primarily concerned were always part of a world situation. He never saw the development of capitalist agriculture in Russia and the preparation for socialist revolution in the Russian village as something isolated and unique. For his thinking was essentially international. And his understanding of Russian problems was enriched by constant study of the economic scene and class relationships in countries which had reached a later stage of capitalist development.

He saw clearly the basic principles of capitalist growth and decay which underlie the tangled differences in historical background, in productive forces, and in political structure. He laid bare the underlying kinship between the backward capitalism of the semi-feudal Russian village and the capitalism which grew without let or hindrance among the squatters and homesteaders of our upper Mississippi Valley and the Great Plains.

Of course, principles common to a most backward and a most progressive country are intertwined with differences that become an inseparable part of each economic and social situation. Any attempt at easy mechanical application of Lenin's Russian programme to our problems in the United States would not only be absurd but would grossly distort the essence of his thinking. But the underlying kinship is real. And we in the United States have much to learn from Lenin's analysis of the capitalist process in agriculture and the principles guiding the socialist revolution in the Russian village.

This postscript does three things: first, it compares briefly the class differences in the old Russian village and the class differences among American farmers; second, it shows that the trends revealed by Lenin's study in 1914-15 of American farm census data have been confirmed and immensely sharpened in the later decades; third, it indicates how these trends within agriculture are an integral part of the development of American capitalism.

Russian Peasants and American Farmers

Colonial settlement in our country began after world trade was already well developed, and even in the midst of pioneer hardships colonial economy included some production of commodities for the market. The early stages of capitalist development were deeply rooted here before the American Revolution. Further free development was assured by the success of the revolution, which ousted British rule. Of this revolution, Lenin said:

> "The history of modern civilised America opens with one of those great, really liberating, really revolutionary wars of which there have been so few among the large numbers of wars of conquest.... It was a war of the American people against English robbers who subjected America and held it in colonial slavery." [1]

In the South, however, free capitalist development was retarded, since southern production of cotton, tobacco, and rice for export was still based on slavery, and the poorer white population, unable to compete on their less fertile inland farms, remained more dependent on subsistence farming than any group in the North. This slave economy was weakened by the advance of capitalism, and our Civil War marked the decisive victory of capitalism over slavery. Remnants of the slave economy survive in the South, and restrictions on Negro freedom taint life in the North as well. But the North and West, expanding on a capitalist basis with an abundance of unsettled land, developed a material standard of living, a degree of economic freedom, and a pioneering in democratic political structure completely unknown in tsarist Russia.

Even on the slave plantations of the old South, production for the world market was more important than it was on the serf properties of Russian landlords. When Russian serfs and American slaves were emancipated in the early 1860's, survivals of the old bondage remained: in Russia, semi-serf dependence upon and obligations to the landowners; in the American South, Jim-Crow, with restricted suffrage and plantation sharecropping under close supervision and extreme exploitation. But before emancipation, capitalism was already far more advanced in the United States than in Russia.

At the end of the nineteenth century, Russia was still bound down under semi-feudal ties, interwoven with and retarding its capitalist development. The United States was approaching the peak of its capitalist expansion. Lenin showed explicitly that the semi-serf bondage of Russian peasants was one chief factor in the backwardness of Russian agriculture and the narrow development of Russian industry. It was not by chance that American industry had achieved independence from British bankers and investors, while the industrial resources of Russia were still dominated by the finance capital of Germany and France. Nor was it by chance that in the American South, with its semi-slave sharecropping and its Negro masses living under special civil and economic restrictions, industry and finance were less developed than in the northern and western states.

Russian agriculture before the revolution had moved haltingly, painfully, away from feudalism and natural economy (family production for home use) on the road of commercial production which leads directly to capitalism. Four groups stood out distinctly in the agrarian population of European old Russia. What relation is there between these Russian groups and the classes and strata in American agriculture today?

1. At the top, with the largest farming enterprises, were members of the Russian landowning nobility.

A few of these had introduced modern agricultural machinery operated by large numbers of wage workers. These are roughly comparable with the much more numerous very large farming concerns—individual and corporate—in the United States.

But most of the Russian landowners were still using the semi-serf labour of so-called "middle" peasants. These backward Russian estates might be roughly compared with sharecropper plantations in the

American South. Both were engaged in commercial production, on the basis of individual labour with backward technique. Each involved a relationship marking definite advance over the bondage which preceded it, yet stopping short of personal freedom for the toiler. But southern plantations have always been more completely commercial concerns, bound up in the capitalist economy, than were those Russian estates which still depended primarily upon semi-serf peasant labour.

2. Next below the old Russian landowner estates were the kulaks—the large peasant producers. In actual scale of operation some rich peasants approached the smallest of the landowner farms, but differences in civil and political status set up an impassable barrier between them.

In the United States, the gradations among individual farmers are less clearly defined. But we all recognise that the absentee "farmer" who is also a bank official or grain trader or corporation director or cannery owner belongs with the top group of highly developed capitalist concerns, roughly comparable with those Russian landowners who employed wage labour and utilised modern farm equipment. This wealthy large-scale "farmer" cannot be confused with the well-set-up "dirt" farmer who is also an employer but actually puts in full time on the farm himself.

It is not far-fetched to compare the more prosperous of the "dirt" farmers in the United States with the kulaks of old Russia. In education and material standard of living, the kulak was way below the American well-to-do farmer. But he was also an employer and a sizeable commercial producer, and often he operated a well-equipped farm. As a local business man, the kulak was more active than most of these prosperous "dirt" farmers in the United States. For in Russia banking and trade were far less developed than here, and the kulak combined various capitalist functions (including trade and money-lending) which in this country have become more specialised.

3. In the next poorer group, comparison between old Russia and the United States breaks down. For the "middle" peasants of the old Russian village represented a survival of genuine subsistence farming and handicraft, and their independent commercial output was extremely small. They had to sell some grain or handicraft products to meet their

taxes and land redemption payments. In good years they might also have a little surplus for themselves. But they were poorer and far less commercially developed than the group of lower medium-sized farms in the United States. European Russia had nothing that even roughly corresponds with our poorer commercial producers who employ almost no wage labour and operate with second-rate equipment but still depend chiefly on a money income from the farm without selling their labour power.

The "middle" peasant of tsarist Russia was also involved in obligations to the landlord * suggesting—but with many differences—the position of the sharecropper on a plantation in the American South. But here again the differences are important. For unlike the middle peasant, the sharecropper puts his full time on a commercial crop from which he receives one-half of the total cash return, the other half being retained by the landlord as rent. Even if the sharecropper's half of the money return from his crop has been swallowed up by debts at the plantation store, so that he actually handles no cash, the sharecropper exists chiefly on purchased goods reckoned against the market price of the crop that he has laboured to produce.

Also, the "middle" peasant owned the tools and livestock with which he worked for the landlord, but he used his equipment primarily for subsistence farming on his own allotment. The cropper owns nothing. As "tenant" he works full time with the landlord's mule and equipment and under the landlord's supervision he produces the commercial crop which is sold by the landlord. He lives by selling his labour power to the landlord under a yearly contract disguised as tenancy.

And one more difference: The old Russian peasant was tied to his allotment of land. He might lease it, but until after 1905 he could not legally leave the village to seek employment elsewhere without an official permit issued with the approval of the landowner. American sharecroppers are legally free to leave the plantation at the end of the year, and the plantation owner is free to refuse them as tenants. Actually, they shift about from one plantation to another and from tenancy to wage labour or back to tenancy. For Negroes, however, opportunities for employment have been seriously restricted by racial discrimination.

* See Chapter I, p. 12*f*.

All these differences reflect the fact that in development of commodity production and capitalism the "newer" United States was more advanced than tsarist Russia.

4. At the foot of the agricultural scale in both countries were those who live by doing wage labour on other men's farms. But here again, the United States has represented a stage of capitalist growth that tsarist Russia had never reached.

Under the old Russian regime, it was difficult for the poor peasant in the European provinces to break away from his allotment of land. Wage workers employed by landowners and by rich peasants were chiefly their poor peasant neighbours. Thousands and thousands of poor peasants did leave the villages, in spite of restrictions, and sought industrial jobs. But the poor peasants living on the land and doing wage labour in their own villages, or migrating for seasonal work and returning to the home village, formed a numerous and fairly compact rural proletariat.

In the United States, except among the Negroes, the poorest farmer families have played a much smaller role in supplying wage labour for the richer farms. So long as industrial employment continued its rapid expansion, the extent to which poverty was overwhelming small American farmers was more or less concealed by their drift into industry. Those families who remained on farms and also worked for their more prosperous farm neighbours were only a fraction of the total number who had "failed" in farming. They were also a minority among all the farm wage workers in the country.

Traditionally in the North and West the "hired man" was a farmer's son who would climb the "farm ladder" and become in his turn an employer or at least an independent farmer. The extra "hands" at harvest time were mostly footloose workers who were timber-cutters or casual city workers in the winter and followed the crops in the summer. As large-scale capitalist farming developed and specialised farms required longer seasons of unskilled labour, the migrant, landless foreign-born family—of European peasant stock—became an important factor. In California, farm wage labour was drawn first from those stranded by the collapse of the gold rush, then from Oriental peasants, and Mexicans. Footloose "casual" workers from the East also played some part.

After the First World War, chronic unemployment in the United States became a serious problem in industrial towns, and an increasing number of rural poor remained stagnant and almost destitute in villages and on wretched, low-income farms. At the same time, these stationary rural poor must still compete for jobs as farm wage workers with a great stream of migrants—from the cities and from abandoned farms—who flood the farming areas at every season of heavy employment on the land. Those actually living on small farms are still a secondary source of farm wage labour in the United States. In 1939, for example, half a million farmers did some work on other men's farms. But more than 3,210,000 hired workers were employed on farms at some time during that year. Also, the poorer farm operators do more work in non-farm jobs than wage-labour on other men's farms.*

In old Russia, the peasants suffered from the retarded development of capitalism, both in industry and in agriculture. In our United States, farmers face the problems of a capitalism which has outgrown its periods of rapid expansion and has fallen into a serious crisis of decline.

For tsarist Russia, Lenin demanded release from semi-feudal survivals and a freer growth of capitalism. This would raise the technique of production and prepare the material basis for socialism. But again and again he emphasised that such a free growth of capitalism could bring only temporary relief to those who suffered from semi-feudal exploitation. For as capitalism develops, it creates new problems which it is totally unable to solve. Already in the 1890's, commodity production had led to sharp contrasts in Russia between large producers and small producers, between kulaks and poor peasants. It was separating masses of peasants and craftsmen from their means of production and compelling them to live by the sale of their labour power. In Russia such capitalist developments were cut short by the revolutionary upsurge of 1917, and the way to socialist revolution was opened while in

* The census of 1940 showed that 501,229 farm operators worked an average of 61 days on other men's farms, while 1,317,766 farm operators worked an average of 159 days in some non-farm occupation. These included 71,802 who did some work on other farms and also some non-farm work.

technique and productivity Russian industry and agriculture still lagged far behind the industry and agriculture of our United States.

Our white farmers, unlike the Russian peasants, have a long history of political freedom and still hold considerable power in Congress. Their dominating position in colonial times has left a vigorous tradition that farming and farm families are the one great national reservoir of physical and moral well-being. But now it is coming to be recognised that this reservoir is poisoned by extreme and widespread poverty. In 1937, for example, Secretary of Agriculture Henry A. Wallace (now Vice-President of the United States) told a congressional committee that one-third of our farmers were enduring a poverty worse than any he had ever seen among the poorest of European peasants.[2] Poverty on the land has increased along with unemployment, hunger, malnutrition, and preventable disease in the cities. And this poverty has overwhelmed masses of people in the very midst of the greatest national abundance that has ever yet been produced.

Our economic history and our own farm traditions still color the prevailing approach to the problem of mass poverty on the land. They make it peculiarly difficult for Americans to abandon the dream that by regulating some abuse, eliminating some obvious injustice, providing some federal aid, we can restore the "good old days" of our forefathers' farms. We hate to admit that the increasing poverty among farmers (like the mass unemployment among wage workers) has been rooted in the very freedom of capitalist development which characterised our country in its youth. But, in truth, by the inherent laws of capitalism, that economic freedom and that relatively widespread well-being on the land were the soil from which has grown the newer capitalism of monopoly in industry and trade, and of sharp contrasts between rich farmers and poor.

Lenin showed these trends within American agriculture when he made a detailed study of American farm census data for 1900 and 1910.* The following brief summary makes a similar approach to the subject. It shows from current data six aspects of the increasing contrasts among American farmers and then sketches the forces within

* Published in 1914-15 as "New Data on the Laws of Development of Capitalism in Agriculture," and included in Lenin's *Selected Works*, Vol. XII.

American capitalism with which these sharpening contrasts are interrelated.

Contrasts Among American Farmers

In emphasising the special problems of the present in this country, we do not idealise the past. Even in colonial days, pioneers were sorted into prosperous and poor, those who toiled and sweated for others and those who grew rich on the fruits of other men's labour. But the barriers between poor and rich were far less rigid than those of the present time. Many hired hands became independent farmers. And many who left the land actually could, and often did, attain "success" and wealth in industry.

As agriculture and industry grew side by side within the capitalist economy, the investment required for successful commercial farming increased. It remains lower, on the whole, than that required for a manufacturing concern. But it is high enough to destroy the possibility of any general climbing up from wage labour to farm operation. Wage earners have long since emerged as a separate and distinct class. And these trends which have closed the doors of opportunity to the wage workers have immensely sharpened the differences and the economic conflicts between the small "independent" producers and the large farms. More and more of the small farmers were unable to maintain themselves on the land. And at the same time, opportunities for industrial employment had declined. Our farm problem is inseparably bound up with the basic trends in industry.

Since the census began in 1900 and 1910 showing differences (other than acreage) in the scale of farm operation, certain farm trends have become even more unmistakably clear. These trends may possibly be checked by the "prosperity" of war emergency, but such easing of the farm situation can be only temporary. The underlying, long-range trends are inherent in our capitalist economy.

1. The numbers of farms employing wage labour have declined.

Between 1909 and 1939, more than 630,000 farms dropped out of the employing class. The percentage employing hired labour declined from 46 per cent of all to 37 per cent of all.

2. The total volume of wage labour on farms has increased. More of it is concentrated on very large farms, and the large farms have been growing larger.

Most notable is the fact that in the crisis of the 1930's, when the number of employing farms declined most sharply (from 2,631,600 to 2,260,000), the total volume of farm wage labour rose by roughly 20 per cent.*

3. Expansion of large farms has included a marked increase in large-scale operation with two or more tractors on the same farm.

Between 1929 and 1939 the number of tractors increased considerably more than the number of tractor farms. At the beginning of this decade, tractors outnumbered tractor farms by 8 per cent; at the end of the decade, by 11 per cent.† The census fails to tell us how many farms used two or more tractors, but obviously the operations of multiple tractor farms had increased.

4. In acreage, also, the large farms have grown larger and hold an increasing share of the total farm land in the country.

This trend was sharpened in the 1930's, when the number of farms having at least 1,000 acres increased from 80,620 (with 276,000,000 acres) to 100,531 (with 364,000,000 acres). At the beginning of this century, such farms were only eight in a thousand and had less than one-fourth of the total farm land. In 1940, they were sixteen in a thousand and had more than one-third of the farm land.

5. Large farms have produced an expanding share of the total farming output. At the same time, the numbers of very small farms have increased.

Even during the crisis decade of the 1930's, when farm prices remained lower than they had been in the "prosperity" years, the farms having over $20,000 worth of gross product pushed up their share from 8 per cent to 10 per cent of the total. There were fewer farms in this top group in 1939 than there had been ten years earlier, but in spite

* Measured by total farm wages paid, with correction for changes in farm wage rate index of the U. S. Bureau of Agricultural Economics.

† In 1929, there were 920,021 tractors on 851,457 farms; in 1939, there were 1,567,430 on 1,409,697 farms.

of lower prices their average output per farm had risen from $35,000 in 1929 to $45,000 in 1939.*

A long-range comparison is even more striking. For 1899 the Census of Agriculture showed no subdivision of the gross farm income groups above $2,500. Allowing for variations in prices received by farmers, this represents a scale of operation roughly equivalent to $6,000 and over in 1929, and $4,000 and over in 1939. Taking these groups for comparison what do we find? Such farms produced one-fifth of the total in 1899, one-fourth of the total in 1929, and more than one-third of the total in 1939. At the same time the numbers of farms in these groups had increased only from 2.7 per cent to 5.3 per cent of all farms in the country. †

Large farms won their increased share in farm production chiefly at the expense of the lower medium-sized farms. In 1899 these were 52 per cent of all farms and produced over 41 per cent of the output. In 1939, they were 44 per cent of the farms and produced only 27 per cent of the output.

More and more farms dropped into the lowest income groups, and even while very poor farms increased in number their small share in the total farm output grew even smaller. This trend was most marked during the 1930's when mass unemployment had blocked the road of escape into industry. By 1939, nearly two million (1,966,621) of the six million farms had less than $400 of gross annual output as against 1,681,667 with less than $600 in 1929. Even more serious is the fact that more than half (over 1,100,000) of these poor farmers in 1939 had under $250 as against less than 400,000 having this very low income ten years before.

In 1939, one-third of the farms in the country had less than $400 of gross income and produced about one-twentieth of the total farm out-

* In this comparison, the 1929 figures are based throughout upon the estimated distribution of farm production (National Resources Committee) on the basis of the distribution of farms according to value of product shown in the 1930 Census of Agriculture. (See National Resources Committee, Supplementary Report of Land Planning Committee, Part I, 1936, p. 5.) For 1899 and 1939 such distribution of farm production is given by the census.

† See Appendix D.

put. By contrast, one-twentieth of the farms had gross income of $4,000 and over, and produced more than one-third of the total output.

6. Fewer farmers were working away from their farms in 1939 than in 1929, but the number was still very large—more than one farmer in four. And those having regular employment (over 150 days) were more numerous by 40 per cent than they had been ten years earlier.

Summing up, on this question of economic groups: The farm crisis of the 1930's, and the government's attempt to solve it by reducing output to match the decline in markets, brought a definite sharpening of the contrasts between rich farmers—large operators—and those who could not live by their farming. Large-scale farms grew still larger and produced a greater share of the total output. More farms dropped into the group of the very poor, and in spite of this increase in the very poor group they produced a smaller share of the total than either ten years or forty years earlier.

Markets and Monopoly Capitalism

Lenin showed that such trends among farmers are directly due to the dictatorship of the market and the development of capitalism. The rich become richer and the poor become poorer among producers depending for their existence upon owners of money who will buy their products. In times of market crisis this sorting-out process is speeded up. For even while the rich producers complain of hard times, they are able to take measures which cut their costs and assure them of market outlets. If the crisis is severe, they may suffer temporary losses, but their relative position is strengthened and new thousands of their poorer competitors are completely ruined.

The acute market problems which greatly increased the poverty of small American farmers after the first World War—and especially in the crisis of the 1930's—have several aspects, each of which reflects in its own way the characteristics of capitalism in its period of ripe imperialism and general crisis.*

* We are speaking of the most basic trends affecting the country as a whole. These have been complicated by regional crises and problems peculiar to various specialised producers which cannot be included in a brief analysis.

Productivity of human labour in American agriculture had been enormously increased through technical progress (mechanical, chemical, biological), without a corresponding increase in the market demand for our farm products. Farmers' productive capacity rose while demand for their products was actually declining. Prices were depressed and this undermined the economic existence of backward producers who lacked the increased capital required for improvements.

In part, the slackening of the market demand for American farm products was due to competition from new sources of supply. Just as American grain in the nineteenth century created a crisis for European peasants and landowners, so American farmers in their turn were hard hit in the twentieth century by competitive exports from newer countries and from backward countries with more severely exploited masses.

In part, the farmers' markets were reduced by changes here at home. Increased dependence upon tractors, motor trucks, and automobiles had cut under the demand for draft animals and feed grains. Labour on the land was displaced by labour in factories and oil refineries. But the demand for industrial workers did not keep pace with the development of "surplus" farmers on the land. Then during the financial and industrial crisis of 1929-33, the farmers' markets were further reduced as cotton consumption dropped sharply, and the families of unemployed workers ate less meat, fruits, and vegetables, and their children drank less milk.

At the farm, the primary index of marketing conditions is the price the farmer receives for his products in relation to the prices he must pay. And here the effects of a market surplus were disastrously intertwined with control of prices by monopoly forces which operate against the farmers' interest. With processors and traders on the one side, and those who supply farm machinery, building materials, and fertiliser on the other side, the farmers have been consistently squeezed and exploited.

When farm prices drop much more suddenly and sharply than other prices (as they always do in time of economic crisis), the farmer as a little business man depending largely on credit of one kind or another is caught in a hopeless situation. Landlords evict tenants who cannot pay their rent. Mortgage lenders foreclose if the payments of the "owner" are too long overdue. Between 1925 and 1935, forced sales brought a change of ownership of 30 per cent of all farms in the United States.[3]

The situation was eased by emergency federal credit measures enacted in 1933, but the problems of farm debt and security on the land have not been solved. Widespread ownership of family farms clear of debt, which prevailed among the pioneers in the North and West, has developed into subjection to landlords and mortgage lenders. The then Secretary of Agriculture, Henry A. Wallace, pointed out in 1938 that taking all the farmers in the United States as a single group, they were paying toll (in mortgage interest and rental payments) on 38 per cent of the total value of all farm real estate in 1880 and on 61 per cent of the much greater total value in 1935.[4] Barely 30 per cent of the farmers own clear of mortgage all the land they operate. And their land and buildings represent less than 23 per cent of the total farm real estate.

This increasing toll exacted by landowners and mortgage lenders has been one of the basic forms under which farmers are exploited. And as farm ownership is more and more concentrated in the hands of large private estates, insurance companies, and other financial concerns, the "independent" farmer is subject to more systematic supervision and becomes more aware of this exploitation. The monopoly aspect of landholding registers deeply in his consciousness.

It is not so easy for the farmer to realise how the technical development of agriculture has been retarded by private ownership of land.* But the past hundred years of American farming have shown the deep inner contradictions which such ownership involves.

Hundreds of thousands of farms were cleared and operated by squatters and homesteaders who paid nominal fees for their title. But this "free" land was soon traded and mortgaged and rented. It acquired a price which rose rapidly as the last of the good homestead tracts were occupied. And the high cost of buying land greatly reduced the amount that the farmer who was also an owner could invest in improved equipment and working capital. If a farmer pays rent or mortgage interest (which is also a form of rent), this also cuts into his yearly

* See Chapter XII, p. 184*f*.

savings for improvements and expansion. His possession of the land he uses becomes much more insecure.

And yet, as the capital required for successful commercial farming increased, many thousands of the more prosperous farmers found it better business to pay yearly charges of mortgage interest or rent than to hold a clear title of ownership. They put all possible capital into the actual process of farming. And throughout the North and West it has come about that, on the whole, the unmortgaged owner-operators have had the less valuable farms.* The development of agriculture within American capitalism has brought the heirs and successors of free homestead settlers under subjection to mortgage lenders and absentee landowners.

Farmers resent the power of big banks and insurance companies and wealthy investors. They are keenly aware of their exploitation by monopoly processors and traders. They see how their exports have been cut by products from areas developed after the settlement of our land was completed. They know that home markets have been restricted by the extreme poverty of unemployed masses. But most of them do not yet see that these problems grow out of the broad essential trends of capitalism. Monopoly, finance capital, and imperialism are terms expressing three phases, three profoundly interrelated aspects of the present stage of capitalist development.

American farm products have been displaced by products of colonial and semi-colonial areas newly developed by the capitalists of rival empires. American business men seeking larger profits abroad have done their share in stimulating the foreign production that has flooded export markets formerly held by American farmers. Within the United States, the capitalists' pressure for speed-up and cost-cutting in industry to increase their own profits destroyed the balanced circulation of products on which economic health depends. Destitute unemployed workers lacked the very products which idle industrial equipment

* In the South this trend has not been so clear because cotton culture remained technically backward (capital required for its cultivation has been small), and much of the southern tenancy has involved a definitely inferior status. Farm value averages for different tenure groups are shown by regions in *Why Farmers are Poor,* by Anna Rochester, pp. 286-87.

could have produced. And the rich complained that they could not find profitable investment for all their capital!

Such contradictions prevailing throughout the capitalist world were analysed by Lenin in 1916:

"It goes without saying that if capitalism could develop agriculture, which today lags far behind industry everywhere, if it could raise the standard of living of the masses, who are everywhere still poverty-stricken and underfed, in spite of the amazing advance in technical knowledge, there could be no talk of a superfluity of capital. This 'argument' the petty-bourgeois critics of capitalism advance on every occasion. But if capitalism did these things it would not be capitalism; for uneven development and wretched conditions of the masses are the fundamental and inevitable conditions and premises of this mode of production. As long as capitalism remains what it is, surplus capital will never be utilised for the purpose of raising the standard of living of the masses in a given country, for this would mean a decline in profits for the capitalists; it will be used for the purpose of increasing those profits by exporting capital abroad to the backward countries. In these backward countries, profits usually are high, for capital is scarce, the price of land is relatively low, wages are low, raw materials are cheap.... The necessity of exporting capital arises from the fact that in a few countries capitalism has become 'over-ripe' and (owing to the backward state of agriculture and the impoverished state of the masses) capital cannot find 'profitable' investment."[5]

As industry and finance forged ahead of agriculture in the decades after the Civil War, the farmers began to realise that much of this new non-farm wealth was being piled up at their expense. Strong farm movements from the 1870's to the 1890's were directed chiefly against the railroads and the bankers. They won government regulation of interstate railroads, and ultimately certain other demands, such as a federal income tax, were realised. But the movements were weakened by lack of unity, including regional conflict over the Jim-Crow policy in the South. The last important flare-up of activity by these early movements was the Populists' endorsement of the Democratic "free silver" candidate, William J. Bryan, in the 1896 Presidential campaign.

Although these early movements disintegrated or lost their militancy, antagonism toward the forces of monopoly and finance has remained clear in the minds of all groups of working farmers. It turned to new forms of organisation, and it burst into actual struggle in the Farm Holiday movement against mortgage foreclosures in the 1930's.

After the First World War, the farmers' situation was more difficult than ever before. In spite of co-operatives and federal credit, agriculture never really recovered from the collapse of the war boom. New trusts closed in on the outlets for the farmers' products. The great milk combines, for example, became immensely more powerful after the First World War. A technical revolution on the land cut production costs for those who could raise the capital for new equipment, and at the same time it cut the ground out from under the poor farmer as a commercial producer. Even before the unstable basis of post-war "prosperity" toppled the whole capitalist mechanism into the profound crisis of 1929-33, the "farm problem" had been thrust into the forefront of national thinking. The larger "dirt" farmers clamoured for federal aid, and the poorer farmers were deeply discouraged.

Farmers and Workers

The years 1929-33 were a turning point in our whole economic life. Ever since then the basic crisis of capitalism has directly pressed upon broad sections of the American people. In the slow recovery from the lowest point in 1933, millions remained dependent upon relief. Mass unemployment continued even while industrial production was restored to pre-crisis volume. Small business was more and more excluded from possibilities of profit, and powerful units of big business and finance increased their share in production and trade.

Large farm units gained more rapidly than ever at the expense of the small farmers. These could no longer make a decent living on the land and very few of them could find steady well-paid employment in industry. The very small farmers have largely lost the hope of better days ahead which used to be more or less general among them. For the serious plight of the small farm and the gradual impoverishment of great numbers of medium-sized farms were only half realised, so long as the rural youth and the discouraged farmers themselves had a reasonable chance of a decent living in the city. Now they have begun to see that the system in which they live has nothing for most of them except destitution and very meagre relief.

Not so, the medium-sized farms which still survive as commercial producers. They never forget that they are squeezed and exploited. But these farmers themselves are essentially business men, with small properties which are a source of independent livelihood. Many of those in the upper middle farm-income groups are also small employers. They find it difficult to get the workers' viewpoint. This fact has been utilised by the Associated Farmers and other reactionary groups in the capitalist class who carry on systematic propaganda to alienate the farmers from the workers.

Actually, the workers and the commercial farmers have a very strong common interest in prices, railroad rates, taxation, rent, and other questions on which both groups feel the pressure of finance capital. But their problems are not identical and cannot be solved without separate and distinct organisation of wage workers and working farmers. The Congress of Industrial Organisation is on record as "for" the farmers. Only as labor unions and farm organisations co-operate more actively on vital common issues will the middle-income farm groups come into a friendly understanding with the working class.

Achievement of an understanding between the organised wage workers and the two mass groups of working farmers—the middle-income commercial producers and the very poor—is of paramount importance. Without this the United States cannot achieve the national unity which is essential for victory over fascism. And as the war effort develops into a genuine people's war in defense of democratic rights it will bring new changes, both social and political, which may even affect basic economic relationships.

In a very real sense, the course of development both during the war and afterwards will be largely determined by the role of the working farmers and their relation to the wage-earning class. Only together can they bring victory over fascism. Only together can they establish conditions of peace that will make a resurgence of fascism forever impossible and allow the masses of people in every country freely to determine their own future.

APPENDIX A

Draft of Agrarian Programme, April, 1906

PROPOSED BY LENIN AND THE AGRARIAN COMMISSION OF THE R.S.-D.L.P. AT THE FOURTH "UNITY" CONGRESS

For the purpose of removing remnants of the serf order, which lay a heavy burden directly upon the peasants, and in the interest of free development of the class struggle in the village, the party demands:

1. Confiscation of all church, monastery, appanage, state, imperial and landlord lands;
2. Setting-up of peasant committees for the immediate destruction of all traces of landlord power and landlord privilege and for the actual disposal of confiscated lands from now until the establishment of new land arrangements by the comprehensive Constituent Assembly;
3. Abolition of all taxes and obligations falling at the present time upon the peasantry as the tax-paying estate;
4. Abolition of all laws limiting the peasantry in disposal of its lands;
5. Giving to elected people's courts the right to lower unreasonably high rental payments and to declare void agreements having the character of bondage.

If a decisive victory of the present revolution in Russia fully assures sovereignty of the people, that is, creates a republic and a completely democratic state order, the party will strive for the abolition of private property in land and the transfer of all lands to social property of the whole people. [Note by Lenin.] Alternative wording: ... the party will support the efforts of the revolutionary peasantry for abolition of private property in land and will strive for the transference of all lands into property of the state. [End of note.]

Furthermore, the Russian Social-Democratic Labour Party, in all circumstances and whatever the state of the democratic agrarian reforms may be, strives continuously to secure the independent class organisation of the rural proletariat, and to explain to the latter the irreconcilable antagonism of its interests and those of the peasant bourgeoisie, to warn it against being deluded by the system of small-scale economy, which under the commodity system of production is never able to abolish the proverty of the masses and, finally, to point to the need for a complete socialist revolution, as the only means of abolishing all poverty and all exploitation.

Lenin, *Collected Works,* IX, Russian, pp. 75-76. (Closing paragraph is also in *Selected Works,* III, p. 564.)

APPENDIX B

Sections of Economic Programme Adopted by Eighth Congress of Russian Communist Party, 1919

ON HANDICRAFT INDUSTRY

4. In relation to small and handicraft industry it is essential to make general use of it through the granting of government orders to the craftsmen; the inclusion of handicraft and small industry in the general plan of supplying raw materials and fuel and also financial support, with the proviso that separate kustars [artisans], kustar artels, producing co-operatives and small establishments unite into much larger producing and industrial units; encouragement of such mergings through allowing them economic advantages, directed, along with other measures, toward paralysing the tendency of kustars to take on the form of small shops and toward creating a painless transition of these backward forms of production to much higher large-scale mechanised industry.

ON AGRICULTURE AND THE PEASANTS

10. The Soviet power, having effected complete abolition of private property in land, has passed on already to the enacting of a whole series of measures directed toward the organisation of large-scale socialist agriculture. The most important of these measures are: (1) organisation of Soviet farms, that is, large-scale socialist enterprises; (2) support of associations

and also of co-operatives for social cultivation of the land; (3) organisation of state sowing of all unsown lands, whomever they may belong to; (4) state mobilisation of all agronomic forces for vigorous measures to raise the level of agriculture; (5) support of agricultural communes, as completely voluntary associations of tillers of the soil for carrying on large-scale collective agriculture.

Considering all these measures as the only path toward the absolutely necessary increase of productivity of agricultural labor, the Russian Communist Party strives for the very fullest possible realisation of these measures, for their extension to the more backward districts of the country, and for further steps in this direction.

In particular, the Russian Communist Party insists upon: (1) complete government support of agricultural co-operatives, engaged in the processing of agricultural products; (2) a broadly carried out system of soil improvement; (3) broad and systematic providing of equipment for poor and middle peasants through renting stations.

Considering that small peasant agriculture will still continue to exist for a long time, the Russian Communist Party strives to carry through a number of measures directed toward raising the productivity of peasant agriculture. Such measures are: (1) setting in order peasant utilisation of land (doing away with strip farming, scattered holdings, etc.); (2) supplying of peasants with better seeds and artificial fertilisers; (3) improvement of the breed of peasants' livestock; (4) the spreading of agronomic information; (5) agronomic aid to peasants; (6) repair in Soviet repair shops of peasants' agricultural equipment; (7) setting up of places for renting equipment, experimental stations, demonstration fields, etc.; (8) improvement of peasant lands.

11. Considering that the contradictions between town and village are one of the most basic foundations of the economic and cultural backwardness of the village and, at a period of such profound crisis as the present, place both city and village before the immediate danger of degeneration and ruin, the Russian Communist Party sees in the abolition of these contradictions one of the basic tasks of communist construction, and along with general measures considers essential a broad and systematic summoning of industrial workers to communist construction in agriculture, and development of activity of the general government "Workers' Committee of Action" already created by the Soviet power for this purpose, etc.

12. In all its work in the village the Russian Communist Party depends as before on the proletarian and semi-proletarian forces of the village,

organises them, first of all, as an independent force, creating party nuclei in the village, organisations of poor peasants, labour unions of a special type of the proletarians and semi-proletarians of the village, etc., bringing them in every way nearer to the city proletariat and tearing them away from the influence of the village bourgeoisie and petty bourgeois interests.

In relation to the kulaks, to the village bourgeoisie, the policy of the Russian Communist Party consists in decisive struggle against their exploiting tendencies, in suppression of their opposition to Soviet policy.

In relation to the middle peasantry the policy of the Russian Communist Party consists in gradually and systematically drawing them into the work of socialist construction. The party sets itself the task of separating it [the middle peasantry] from the kulaks, drawing it to the side of the working class by attentive regard for its needs, struggling against its backwardness by measures of ideological influence, never by measures of suppression, striving for practical agreements with it in all cases where its vital interests are affected, making concessions to it in determining means to further socialist transformation.

IN THE FIELD OF DISTRIBUTION

13. In the field of distribution the task of the Soviet power at the present time consists in unswervingly continuing the replacement of trade by a planned distribution of products organised on a national government scale. The goal is an organisation of the whole population in a single network of consumers' communes, able with the greatest possible speed, system, and economy and with the least possible expenditure of labor to distribute all the essential products, strictly centralising the whole distributive apparatus.

As the foundation of consumers' communes and their unification, the existing general and workers' co-operatives must be utilised since these are the largest organisations of consumers and the apparatus of mass distribution most well prepared by the history of capitalism.

Since the Russian Communist Party considers correct, in principle, only the further communist development of the co-operative apparatus and not its rejection, the party must systematically continue its policy: require all members of the party to work in co-operatives, guide them with the aid also of the labour unions in a communist spirit; develop the initiative and the discipline of the toiling population, united into co-operatives; endeavour to have the whole population included in them and to have these merge into a single co-operative embracing the whole Soviet republic; finally, and chiefly, that the dominant influence of the proletariat over the other strata of toilers shall be constantly assured and for this purpose various measures should be tried out practically, facilitating and furthering the transition from petty bourgeois co-operatives of the old, capitalist type to consumers' communes, led by proletarians and semi-proletarians.

Lenin, *Collected Works,* XXIV, Russian, Appendix, pp. 700, 702-04.

APPENDIX C

The Tax in Kind, 1921

RESOLUTION OF TENTH CONGRESS OF RUSSIAN COMMUNIST PARTY

1. To guarantee sound and peaceful conduct of agriculture on the basis of freer disposition of their economic resources by the tillers of the soil, to strengthen peasant agriculture and raise its productivity, and also in order to fix exactly the obligations to the government that fall upon the tillers of the soil, quotas are to be replaced by a tax in kind as the method by which the government procures provisions, raw materials, and fodder.

2. This tax must be less than the assessment levied hitherto by means of quotas. The total of the tax must be so computed as to cover the minimum essential requirements of the army, the city workers, and the non-agricultural population. The total amount of the tax must be steadily reduced as the restoration of transport and industry enables the Soviet government to receive the products of agriculture in the normal way, *i.e.,* in exchange for manufactured and handicraft goods.

3. The tax is to be levied as a deduction of a percentage or share of the produce of a farm, based on the amount of the harvest, the number of consumers in the household, and the livestock it actually has.

4. The tax must have a progressive character: the percentage of deduction must be lowered for those who have small and medium-sized farms, for the farms of city workers, etc.

Households of the poorest peasants can be exempt from some, and in some exceptional cases even from all, forms of the tax in kind.

Efficient peasant-farmers, increasing the sown areas on their farms or increasing the productivity of the farm as a whole, are to be entitled to privileges upon the payment of the tax in kind, either in the form of a reduction in the tax rate or in the form of partial exemption from the tax.

5. The tax law must be drawn up in such a manner and promulgated within such time that the tillers of the soil would be as accurately informed as possible, before the beginning of the spring field work, on the extent of the obligations falling on them.

6. Surrender to the government of products due under the tax is to be completed on definite dates, fixed exactly by the law.

7. The amount of products due for surrender under the tax is to be computed by agricultural units (communities). Within the agricultural unit the tax is to be allotted among the farm households according to their decision in conformity with the general rates provided for in paragraph 3.

To control application of the rates of the tax and its collection, elective organisations of local peasants are to be formed for the groups paying different tax rates.

8. All stocks of provisions, raw materials, and fodder left over to the tillers of the soil after their payment of the tax are to be at their absolute disposal and can be used by them for improvement and strengthening of their farms, for raising their personal consumption and for exchange for the products of manufacturing and handicraft industry and of agriculture.

Exchange is to be allowed within the limits of local agricultural trade.

9. For the purpose of supplying the poorest population and providing exchange for the surplus provisions, forage, and raw materials voluntarily delivered by the population to the state after payment of the tax due from them, there is created a special fund of articles of agricultural equipment and of products for mass consumption. This fund is to be created from the output of domestic production and from those articles from abroad, for the obtaining of which there is to be allotted a part of the state gold stock and a part of the stock of raw materials.

The Congress, approving in principle the regulations introduced by the Central Committee on the replacement of quotas by a tax in kind, instructs the Central Committee of the party to adjust these regulations in a most speedy manner, to work out in detail the procedure for carrying out the tax, and to carry through an appropriate law in the All-Russian Central Executive Committee and the Council of People's Commissars.

Lenin, *Collected Works,* XXVI, Russian, pp. 590-91.

APPENDIX D

On Farm Gross Income Groups in the United States *

The group of farms with "$2,500 and over" of gross output in 1899 corresponds in volume of production with farms of $5,730 and over in 1929 and $3,575 and over in 1939. Since these figures do not appear in census classifications, we take for 1929 the group of "$6,000 and over" and for 1939 the group of "$4,000 and over." Obviously these groups make a basis of comparison which definitely understates the increasing importance of the upper groups of farms. In the same way, we compare farms "Under $250" in 1899 with those "Under $600" in 1929 and "Under $400" in 1939. For intermediate groups we take as the dividing line between lower medium-sized and upper medium-sized farms the gross income levels of $1,000 in 1899, $2,500 in 1929, and $1,500 in 1939. On this basis we have the following distribution of farms and of farm production:

	FARMS		
	1939	*1929*	*1899*
Very small	33.0	28.0	30.9
Lower medium-sized	44.1	52.8	52.0
Upper medium-sized	17.7	15.4	14.5
Large	5.3	3.9	2.7
	100.0	100.0	100.0
	FARM PRODUCTION		
Very small	5.4	5.7	6.6
Lower medium-sized	27.0	37.5	41.4
Upper medium-sized	31.7	31.3	32.1
Large	35.9	25.5	19.9
	100.0	100.0	100.0

Based on census data. Distribution of farm output in 1929 was estimated by National Resources Committee, Supplementary Report of Land Planning Committee, Part I, 1936, p. 5.

* To supplement Chapter XIII.

A NOTE ON SOURCES

The chief sources for any study of Lenin's ideas and programmes are the many volumes of his own writings. A considerable number of these are available in English, with full historical notes.

Publication of the English translation of the twelve volumes of *Selected Works* was completed by International Publishers, of New York, in 1938. The same publishers have issued in English six of the thirty volumes which make up the third Russian edition of Lenin's *Collected Works*. These translations include Volume IV covering the years 1900 to 1902; Volume XIII, a study (in 1908) of the philosophical tenets of Marxism; and Volumes XVIII to XXI covering the period from the beginning of the Imperialist War in 1914 to the Socialist Revolution of November 7, 1917. Where articles used in this study are available both in *Selected Works* and in an English volume of *Collected Works*, reference is made to the former.

In preparing this study, the writer used also the other volumes of the *Collected Works* (third Russian edition) which have not yet appeared in English. The writer had the privilege, however, of checking certain translations with available manuscript translations of a few additional volumes. One short excerpt in Chapter XII is translated from an essay appearing for the first time in Volume I of the new, *fourth* Russian edition of Lenin's *Collected Works*.

The writings of Stalin, referred to in Chapter XI, are also published by International Publishers. Reference is made to volumes issued in 1934 (with one exception), but the quotations given in the text are based on revised translations for a new edition now in preparation.

In the references which follow, the title of each work actually quoted or referred to in the present study is given once in full. These works include, of course, additional sources besides the writings of Lenin and Stalin.

REFERENCE NOTES

CHAPTER I: Pages 11 to 22

1. V. I. Lenin, "Imperialism, the Highest Stage of Capitalism," 1916, *Selected Works,* V, p. 46.
2. Lenin, "The Agrarian Question in Russia at the End of the Nineteenth Century," 1908, *Selected Works,* I, pp. 146-47.
3. A. V. Shestakov, *A Short History of the U.S.S.R.* (Moscow: Co-operative Publishing Society of Foreign Workers in the U.S.S.R., 1938), p. 118.
4. *History of the Communist Party of the Soviet Union* (New York: International Publishers, 1939), p. 3.
5. Lenin, *Selected Works,* I, p. 147.
6. Lenin, "The Workers' Party and the Peasantry," 1901, *Selected Works,* II, p. 235.
7. Shestakov, *op. cit.,* p. 115.
8. Lenin, "To the Rural Poor," 1903, *Selected Works,* II, p. 268.
9. Lenin, *Selected Works,* VI, editorial note, p. 604.
10. Lenin, *Selected Works,* I, pp. 142-43. Original figures are in dessiatinas, translated to acres: one dessiatina equals 2.7 acres.
11. *Ibid.,* pp. 144-45.
12. Lenin, *Selected Works,* II, p. 260.
13. Lenin, "Development of Capitalism in Russia," 1899, *Collected Works,* III, Russian, pp. 93, 96.
14. Lenin, "What the 'Friends of the People' Are and How They Fight the Social-Democrats," 1894, *Selected Works,* XI, p. 565.
15. Lenin, *Selected Works,* II, p. 248.
16. Shestakov, *op. cit.,* p. 121.
17. Lenin, *Selected Works,* II, p. 279.
18. *Ibid.,* p. 280.
19. Lenin, "The Agrarian Programme of Russian Social-Democracy," 1902, *Collected Works,* V, Russian, p. 88.
20. Lenin, "Development of Capitalism in Russia," excerpts in *Selected Works,* I, pp. 380-81.
21. Lenin, *Selected Works,* XI, p. 574.
22. Lenin, *Selected Works,* I, pp. 383-84.
23. *Ibid.,* pp. 384, 385.
24. Lenin, *Selected Works,* XI, p. 565.

CHAPTER II: Pages 23 to 33

1. Lenin, quoted in editorial note, *Selected Works,* III, p. 564.
2. Lenin's first draft, December, 1895, is in *Selected Works,* I, pp. 467-71. Draft under discussion, January, 1902, is in *Selected Works,* II, pp. 224-30. Program as published, June, 1902, and program as adopted in 1903, are in Lenin, *Collected Works,* V, Russian, Appendix, pp. 380-88. Peasant section, as adopted, is in editorial note, *Selected Works,* II, pp. 528-29.
3. Programme adopted 1903, Lenin, *Collected Works,* V, Russian, Appendix, p. 385.
4. *Ibid.*
5. Summary by Lenin, *Selected Works,* II, p. 285.
6. Lenin, *Collected Works,* V, Russian, pp. 90-91.
7. Lenin, quoted in editorial note, *Selected Works,* II, p. 527.
8. Lenin, *Selected Works,* II, p. 302.
9. Lenin, *Selected Works,* II, editorial note, p. 528.
10. *Ibid.,* pp. 528-29.
11. Lenin, "Correction in Agrarian Section of the Programme," 1902, *Collected Works,* V, Russian, p. 50.
12. Lenin, *Collected Works,* V, Russian, p. 103.
13. *Ibid.,* pp. 105-06.
14. Lenin, *Selected Works,* II, p. 257.
15. *Ibid.,* editorial note, p. 529.
16. *Ibid.,* p. 521.
17. *Ibid.,* pp. 521-22.
18. Lenin, *Selected Works,* II, pp. 290-91.
19. Lenin, *Collected Works,* V, Russian, p. 97.
20. Lenin, *Selected Works,* II, p. 305.
21. *Ibid.,* p. 306.

22. *Ibid.*, pp. 308-09.
23. Lenin, *Collected Works*, V, Russian, p. 121.
24. *Ibid.*, p. 104.
25. *Ibid.*, p. 388.
26. *Ibid.*, p. 97.

CHAPTER III: Pages 34 to 44

1. Lenin, "One Step Forward, Two Steps Back," 1904, *Collected Works*, VI, Russian, p. 184.
2. Lenin, "Criticism of Plekhanov's Second Draft," 1902, *Selected Works*, II, p. 232.
3. Lenin, *Collected Works*, V, Russian, p. 100.
4. Lenin, *Selected Works*, II, p. 300.
5. Lenin, "The Agrarian Programme of Russian Social-Democracy," 1902, excerpt in *Selected Works*, II, p. 312.
6. *Ibid.*, pp. 313-14.
7. Lenin, *Collected Works*, V, Russian, p. 101.
8. Lenin, *Selected Works*, II, pp. 298-99.
9. *Ibid.*, p. 314.
10. *Ibid.*, pp. 314-15.
11. *Ibid.*, p. 270.
12. *Ibid.*, pp. 272-73.
13. *Ibid.*, p. 270.
14. *Ibid.*, p. 271.
15. *Ibid.*, pp. 276-77.
16. *Ibid.*, p. 293.

CHAPTER IV: Pages 45 to 54

1. *History of the Communist Party of the Soviet Union*, p. 27.
2. *Ibid.*, p. 56; also Lenin, "Lecture on the 1905 Revolution," Jan., 1917, *Selected Works*, III, pp. 1-2.
3. *History of the Communist Party of the Soviet Union*, pp. 57-58.
4. See Lenin, "The Army and the Revolution," Nov., 1905, *Selected Works*, III.
5. Lenin, *Selected Works*, IV, editorial note, p. 415.
6. Lenin, *Selected Works*, III, editorial notes, pp. 527-29.
7. Lenin, *Selected Works*, III, p. 13.
8. Lenin, "Socialism and Anarchism," 1905, *Selected Works*, III, p. 343, and editorial notes, pp. 529, 531, 586.
9. Lenin, *Selected Works*, III, p. 14.
10. Lenin, 1906, *Collected Works*, IX, Russian, p. 153.
11. Lenin, *Selected Works*, III, pp. 3-4.
12. *Ibid.*, p. 8.
13. *Ibid.*, editorial note, p. 566.
14. Lenin, "Agrarian Programme of the Liberals," 1905, *Collected Works*, VII, Russian, p. 217.
15. Lenin, "Proletariat and Peasantry," 1905, *Collected Works*, VIII, Russian, p. 383.
16. On failure of 1905 Revolution, see *History of the Communist Party of the Soviet Union*, pp. 93-94; and Lenin, *Selected Works*, III, p. 11.
17. Lenin, "The Dissolution of the Duma and the Tasks of the Proletariat," July, 1906, *Collected Works*, X, Russian, p. 8.
18. Lenin, *Selected Works*, III, p. 16.
19. Lenin, "The Agrarian Programme of Social-Democracy in the First Russian Revolution, 1905-1907," 1907, *Selected Works*, III, p. 230.
20. Lenin, *Selected Works*, III, p. 6.
21. Lenin, "On to the High Road," 1909, *Selected Works*, IV, pp. 7-8.

CHAPTER V: Pages 55 to 71

1. Lenin, *Collected Works*, VII, Russian, p. 213.
2. Lenin, "On Our Agrarian Programme, a Letter to the Third Congress," 1905, *Collected Works*, VII, Russian, pp. 170-73.
3. Lenin, *Collected Works*, VII, Appendix, Russian, p. 434.
4. Lenin, "Revision of the Agrarian Programme of the Workers' Party," 1906, *Collected Works*, IX, Russian, p. 59.

5. *Ibid.*, p. 61.
6. See Lenin, "The Agrarian Programme of Social-Democracy in the First Russian Revolution, 1905-1907," especially Chapter 3, in *Selected Works*, XII, and Chapter 4, in *Selected Works*, III.
7. *History of the Communist Party of the Soviet Union*, pp. 85-86, 90.
8. Lenin, *Selected Works*, III, pp. 180-81.
9. *Ibid.*, pp. 184-85.
10. Lenin, *Selected Works*, II, p. 319.
11. Lenin, "Attitude of Social-Democracy Toward the Peasant Movement," 1905, *Selected Works*, III, p. 144.
12. Lenin, *Collected Works*, IX, Russian, pp. 62-64.
13. *Ibid.*, p. 75.
14. Lenin, *Selected Works*, III, p. 222.
15. *Ibid.*, p. 165.
16. See, *e.g.*, Lenin, *Selected Works*, XI, p. 587.
17. Lenin, at the "Unity" Congress, 1906, *Collected Works*, IX, Russian, p. 152.
18. Lenin, *Selected Works*, XII, p. 325.
19. *Ibid.*, pp. 307-10.

CHAPTER VI: Pages 72 to 83

1. Lenin, "On the Evaluation of the Present Situation," Nov., 1908, *Collected Works*, XII, Russian, p. 376.
2. *Ibid.*, p. 381.
3. Lenin, "On Some Peculiarities of the Historic Development of Marxism," January, 1911, *Collected Works*, XV, Russian, pp. 73-74.
4. Lenin, "Agrarian Debates in the Third Duma," Dec., 1908, *Collected Works*, XII, Russian, p. 405.
5. Lenin, *Collected Works*, XII, Russian, p. 375.
6. *Ibid.*, p. 377.
7. Lenin, *Selected Works*, III, p. 218.
8. Lenin, "The Question of the (General) Agrarian Policy of the Present Government," 1913, *Selected Works*, IV, pp. 234-35.
9. *Ibid.*, pp. 231-33; also, "The Significance of the Resettlement Business," 1913, *Collected Works*, XVI, Russian, pp. 373-77.
10. Lenin, *Selected Works*, IV, p. 233.
11. Lenin, "The New Agrarian Policy," 1908, *Collected Works*, XII, Russian, pp. 136-37.
12. Quoted by Lenin, *Collected Works*, XII, Russian, p. 408.
13. Lenin, "The Famine and the Black Duma," Jan., 1912, *Collected Works*, XV, Russian, p. 369.
14. Quoted by Lenin, *Collected Works*, XV, Russian, p. 369.
15. Lenin, *Selected Works*, IV, pp. 235-36.
16. Quoted by Lenin, May, 1914, *Collected Works*, XVII, Russian, p. 396.
17. *Ibid.*
18. Lenin, "Serf Agriculture in the Village," May, 1914, *Collected Works*, XVII, Russian, p. 338.
19. See, *e.g.*, Lenin, "Letter to I. I. Skvortsov-Stepanov," 1909, *Selected Works*, IV, pp. 219 *ff*.
20. *Ibid.*, p. 223.
21. Lenin, "Two Utopias," 1912, *Collected Works*, XVI, Russian, p. 165.
22. Karl Marx, *Poverty of Philosophy* (New York: International Publishers), p. 11.
23. Lenin, *Collected Works*, XVI, Russian, p. 165.
24. See, *e.g.*, "The Two Lines of the Revolution," 1915, *Selected Works*, V, pp. 158-63.

CHAPTER VII: Pages 84 to 104

1. Lenin, *Selected Works*, V, editorial note, p. 341.
2. *History of the Communist Party of the Soviet Union*, p. 172.
3. *Ibid.*, p. 173.
4. *Ibid.*, p. 177.

5. Lenin, *Selected Works,* VI, p. 34.
6. Lenin, "Letters on Tactics," April, 1917, *Selected Works,* VI, pp. 34-36.
7. Lenin, "The Tasks of the Proletariat in Our Revolution," April, 1917, *Selected Works,* VI, pp. 45-46.
8. Lenin, "Speech on the War," *Selected Works,* VI, p. 151.
9. Lenin, April, 1917, *Collected Works,* XX, Bk. 1, pp. 202-03.
10. Lenin, "The Tasks of the Proletariat in the Present Revolution," commonly known as the April Theses, *Selected Works,* VI, p. 21.
11. Lenin, "Letters from Afar," I, March, 1917, *Selected Works,* VI, p. 11.
12. *Ibid.*
13. Lenin, at Petrograd City Party Conference, April, 1917, *Collected Works,* XX, Bk. 1, p. 202.
14. Lenin, "Firm Revolutionary Power," May, 1917, *Collected Works,* XX, Bk. 2, pp. 47-48.
15. Lenin, May, 1917, *Selected Works,* VI, p. 346.
16. Lenin, "A Dual Power," April, 1917, *Selected Works,* VI, p. 29. See also, same volume, pp. 36-38.
17. See, *e.g.,* "The Threatening Catastrophe and How to Fight It," September, 1917, *Collected Works,* XXI, Bk. 1, especially pp. 210-12.
18. Lenin, at All-Russian Party Conference, May, 1917, *Collected Works,* XX, Bk. 1, p. 284.
19. Lenin, "From a Publicist's Diary," September, 1917, *Collected Works,* XXI, Bk. 1, p. 149.
20. Lenin, "Letters from Afar," III, March, 1917, *Collected Works,* XX, Bk. 1, note, p. 49.
21. Lenin, "The Elections to the Constituent Assembly and the Dictatorship of the Proletariat," 1919, *Selected Works,* VI, p. 475.
22. The April Theses are published under the title, "The Tasks of the Proletariat in the Present Revolution" (*Selected Works,* VI, pp. 21-24). A longer and less famous statement on party programme was published a few days later, under the title, "The Tasks of the Proletariat in Our Revolution" (*Selected Works,* VI, pp. 45-76).
23. Lenin, *Selected Works,* VI, p. 59.
24. *Ibid.,* p. 60.
25. Lenin, *Collected Works,* XX, Bk. 1, p. 220.
26. Lenin, *Selected Works,* VI, p. 60.
27. *Ibid.,* pp. 60-61.
28. *Ibid.,* p. 61.
29. Lenin, "Draft Resolution on Measures to Overcome Economic Chaos," *Collected Works,* XX, Bk. 2, p. 136.
30. Lenin, "On the Unauthorised Seizure of Land," June, 1917, *Collected Works,* XX, Bk. 2, pp. 103-04.
31. *Ibid.,* p. 105.
32. *Ibid.,* p. 106.
33. Lenin, "Open Letter to the Delegates of the All-Russian Soviet of Peasant Deputies," May, 1917, *Collected Works,* XX, Bk. 2, p. 57.
34. Lenin, "Three Crises," July, 1917, *Collected Works,* XXI, Bk. 1, pp. 31-32.
35. Lenin, "Lessons of the Revolution," August, 1917, *Collected Works,* XXI, Bk. 1, pp. 81-82.
36. Resolution at Sixth Party Congress, August, 1917, Lenin, *Collected Works,* XXI, Bk. 2, Appendix, p. 304.
37. Lenin, *Selected Works,* VI, editorial note, p. 618.
38. Lenin, "Report on the Land Question," *Selected Works,* VI, pp. 405-06.
39. *Ibid.,* pp. 406-08.
40. *Ibid.,* p. 409.

CHAPTER VIII: Pages 105 to 123

1. Lenin, at Moscow Soviet, March, 1918, *Collected Works,* XXII, Russian, p. 381.
2. Lenin, "The Anniversary of the Revolution," 1918, *Selected Works,* VI, pp. 490-91.

3. See Lenin, *Collected Works,* XXII, editorial note 112, Russian, p. 583.
4. See Lenin's speech to the agitators, *Collected Works,* XXII, Russian, pp. 248-51.
5. Lenin, "The Proletarian Revolution and the Renegade Kautsky," Nov., 1918, *Selected Works,* VII, p. 195.
6. Lenin, "The State and Revolution," 1917, *Selected Works,* VII, pp. 25-26.
7. Lenin, *Selected Works,* VI, p. 476.
8. *Ibid.,* p. 479.
9. Lenin, at Eighth Party Congress, 1919, *Selected Works,* VIII, p. 354.
10. Lenin, *Collected Works,* XXIV, Appendix, Russian, p. 696.
11. Lenin, *Selected Works,* VIII, p. 38.
12. Lenin, "Valuable Admissions by Pitirim Sorokin," Nov., 1918, *Selected Works,* VIII, p. 150.
13. Lenin, *Collected Works,* XXIV, Russian, p. 114.
14. Lenin, *Selected Works,* VIII, pp. 346-47.
15. Lenin, at Congress of Land Departments, etc., December, 1918, *Selected Works,* VIII, p. 158.
16. *Ibid.,* p. 159.
17. Lenin, at First Congress of Agricultural Communes and Agricultural Artels, *Selected Works,* VIII, p. 203.
18. Lenin, at Congress of Agricultural Workers, March, 1919, *Collected Works,* XXIV, Russian, p. 40.
19. Lenin, *Selected Works,* VIII, p. 179.
20. *Ibid.,* pp. 180-81.
21. Lenin, *Selected Works,* VI, pp. 477-78.
22. Lenin, "On Combating the Famine," June, 1918, *Selected Works,* VIII, p. 109.
23. Lenin, "The Famine: A Letter to the Workers of Petrograd," *Selected Works,* VIII, p. 18.
24. *Ibid.,* p. 19.
25. *Ibid.,* p. 18.
26. See Lenin, at Fifth All-Russian Congress of Soviets, July, 1918, *Collected Works,* XXIII, Russian, p. 128, and Appendix, p. 533.
27. Lenin, at Mine Workers' Congress, April, 1920, *Collected Works,* XXV, Russian, p. 134.
28. Lenin, *Collected Works,* XXV, Russian, pp. 107-08.
29. Lenin, at Non-Party Conference of Workers and Red Army Men, January, 1920, *Collected Works,* XXV, Russian, p. 16.
30. Lenin, at Moscow Province Party Conference, November, 1920, *Collected Works,* XXV, Russian, pp. 488-90.
31. Lenin, *Selected Works,* VIII, pp. 263-66.
32. Summarised in editorial note, Lenin, *Selected Works,* VIII, p. 439.

CHAPTER IX: Pages 124 to 137

1. Lenin, June, 1921, *Collected Works,* XXVI, Russian, p. 430.
2. Lenin, at Tenth Party Congress, March, 1921, *Collected Works,* XXVI, Russian, pp. 277-78.
3. Lenin, at Tenth Party Congress, *Selected Works,* IX, p. 90.
4. *Ibid.,* pp. 98-101.
5. Lenin, "Five Years of the Russian Revolution," 1922, *Selected Works,* X, p. 323.
6. Lenin, pamphlet, "The Food Tax," April, 1921, *Selected Works,* IX, p. 178.
7. Lenin, *Selected Works,* IX, p. 113.
8. Lenin, at Congress of Political Education Departments, October, 1921, *Selected Works,* IX, p. 265. See also speech of same period at Moscow Province Party Conference, *Selected Works,* IX, p. 290.
9. Lenin, at All-Russian Party Conference, May, 1921, *Selected Works,* IX, p. 218.
10. Lenin, *Selected Works,* IX, p. 112.
11. *Ibid.,* pp. 211-12.
12. *Ibid.,* p. 109.
13. *Ibid.,* p. 118.

14. Lenin, at Moscow Province Party Meeting, April, 1921, *Selected Works*, IX, p. 160.
15. Lenin, *Selected Works*, IX, p. 111.
16. Lenin, "The New Economic Policy," *Selected Works*, IX, p. 292.
17. Lenin, *Selected Works*, IX, pp. 188-89.
18. *Ibid.*, p. 162.
19. Lenin, at Third Congress of Communist International, 1921, *Selected Works*, IX, pp. 237-38.
20. Lenin, at Eleventh Party Congress, 1922, *Selected Works*, IX, pp. 345-46.
21. Lenin, at Third All-Russian Food Conference, June, 1921, *Collected Works*, XXVI, Russian, pp. 420-21.
22. Lenin, "The New Economic Policy and the Tasks of the Political Education Departments," October, 1921, *Selected Works*, IX, pp. 263, 264.
23. Lenin, *Selected Works*, IX, p. 110.
24. Lenin, Speech on the Food Tax, April, 1921, *Selected Works*, IX, p. 151.

CHAPTER X: Pages 138 to 149

1. Lenin, *Selected Works*, XI, pp. 514-15.
2. Lenin, "Land Reconstruction and Village Poverty," 1913, *Collected Works*, XVI, Russian, pp. 619-20.
3. Lenin, *Selected Works*, XI, p. 515.
4. Lenin, "Relentless War on the Socialist-Revolutionaries," *Selected Works*, II, p. 195.
5. Lenin, "Rough Draft of 'Immediate Tasks of Soviet Power,'" *Collected Works*, XXII, Russian, pp. 422-23.
6. Lenin, "A Little Picture in Illustration of Big Problems," *Collected Works*, XXIII, Russian, pp. 457-58.
7. Lenin, at delegates' meeting of Moscow Central Workers' Co-operative, 1918, *Collected Works*, XXIII, Russian, pp. 298, 301.
8. Lenin, "Immediate Tasks of the Soviet Government," *Selected Works*, VII, pp. 327-29.
9. Lenin, *Collected Works*, XXIII, Russian, pp. 416-17.
10. Lenin, memorandum to four comrades, February, 1919, *Collected Works*, XXX, Russian, p. 395.
11. Lenin, *Selected Works*, VIII, pp. 226-30.
12. Lenin, *Selected Works*, IX, pp. 183-84.
13. Lenin, "On Co-operation," January, 1923, *Selected Works*, IX, pp. 402-03.

CHAPTER XI: Pages 150 to 171

1. *Razvitiye Sovietskoi Ekonomiki* [*The Development of Soviet Economy*] (Moscow: Institute of Economics in the Academy of Sciences, 1939), p. 308.
2. *Ibid.*, p. 216.
3. *Ibid.*, p. 300.
4. Joseph Stalin, *Leninism*, I, p. 316.
5. *Razvitiye Sovietskoi Ekonomiki*, p. 217.
6. Stalin, *Leninism*, I, pp. 175-76.
7. *Razvitiye Sovietskoi Ekonomiki*, p. 218.
8. Stalin, *Leninism*, I (1932 ed.), p. 395.
9. *Razvitiye Sovietskoi Ekonomiki*, p. 295.
10. Stalin, *Leninism*, II, p. 135.
11. *Razvitiye Sovietskoi Ekonomiki*, p. 298.
12. Stalin, *Leninism*, II, p. 16.
13. *Ibid.*, pp. 20-21.
14. *Ibid.*, p. 21.
15. *Ibid.*
16. *Ibid.*, p. 22.
17. Stalin, *Leninism*, II, p. 50.
18. *Razvitiye Sovietskoi Ekonomiki*, p. 321.
19. *Ibid.*, p. 327.
20. Stalin, *Leninism*, II, p. 49.
21. *Ibid.*, pp. 141, 143.
22. *Ibid.*, p. 215.
23. *Ibid.*, pp. 220-21.

24. *History of the Communist Party of the Soviet Union*, pp. 304-06.
25. Stalin, *Leninism*, II, p. 210.
26. Anna Louise Strong, *Democracy and Dictatorship in the Soviet Union* (New York: International Pamphlets, No. 40, 1934), pp. 4-5.
27. Stalin, *Leninism*, II, p. 283.
28. *Moscow Daily News*, February 21, 1935.
29. *Constitution of the Union of Soviet Socialist Republics* (Moscow: State Publishing House of Political Literature, 1938), pp. 116-17.
30. *Moscow Daily News*, June 12, 1939.
31. *Soviet Russia Today* (New York), July, 1940.
32. Full text, *Moscow Daily News*, February 21, 1935; amendments in 1939 summarised, *Moscow Daily News*, June 12, 1939.
33. L. F. Boross, "The Basic Law of Socialist Agriculture," *International Press Correspondence*, April 27, 1935.

CHAPTER XII: Pages 172 to 191

1. Karl Marx, Preface to *Capital*, I (New York: International Publishers, 1939), p. xix.
2. *Ibid.*
3. Lenin, *Selected Works*, XI, pp. 421-22, 439
4. *Ibid.*, pp. 630-31.
5. Lenin, *Selected Works*, II, pp. 235-36.
6. Lenin, "Economic Content of Narodism," 1894, *Collective Works*, I, Russian, p. 344.
7. *Ibid.*, note, p. 259.
8. Lenin, "In Relation to This So-called Question of Markets," 1893, *Collected Works*, I, 4th Russian edition, p. 77.
9. Lenin, *Selected Works*, XI, pp. 628-29.
10. Lenin, *Selected Works*, I, p. 272.
11. Lenin, *Collected Works*, I, Russian, p. 351.
12. Lenin, New Data on the Laws of Development of Capitalism in Agriculture," 1914-15, *Selected Works*, XII, p. 248.
13. Lenin, *Selected Works*, XI, p. 454.
14. Lenin, *Selected Works*, I, p. 302.
15. Lenin, *Selected Works*, II, pp. 253-54
16. Lenin, *Selected Works*, III, p. 217.
17. Marx, *Capital* (Kerr ed.), III, note by Engels, p. 841.
18. Lenin, "Capitalism in Agriculture," 1899, *Selected Works*, XII, pp. 49-50.
19. *Ibid.*, pp. 38-39.
20. Lenin, *Selected Works*, XI, p. 485.
21. Lenin, *Collected Works*, I, Russian, pp. 329-30.
22. Lenin, *Selected Works*, II, pp. 236-37.
23. Lenin, "Karl Marx," 1914, *Selected Works*, XI, pp. 32-33, with quotations from Marx, *Capital* (Kerr ed.), III, pp. 938-39, and I, p. 555.
24. Lenin, *Selected Works*, XI, pp. 34, 36.
25. *Ibid.*, pp. 33-34.
26. Lenin, quoted in editorial note, *Selected Works*, II, p. 520.
27. Lenin, *Collected Works*, I, p. 253.
28. *Ibid.*, p. 259.
29. Lenin, *Selected Works*, XI, p. 469.
30. *Ibid.*, p. 512.
31. Lenin, "The Tax in Kind," 1921, *Selected Works*, IX, pp. 107-08.

CHAPTER XIII: Pages 192 to 209

1. Lenin, *A Letter to American Workers*, 1918 (New York: International Publishers, 1934), Little Lenin Library, Vol. 17, p. 9.
2. U. S. Congress, 75:I, Senate Committee on Appropriations, *Hearings* on Emergency Relief Appropriation, House Joint Resolution 361, June 9, 1937, p. 265.
3. U. S. Department of Agriculture, *Circulars* (new series), 209, 261, 417.
4. U. S. Secretary of Agriculture, *Annual Report*, 1938, p. 7.
5. Lenin, *Selected Works*, V., pp. 56-57.